INTRODUCTION
TO PUSHTU

INTRODUCTION TO PUSHTU

An Official Language of Afghanistan

Romanized

(formerly published as *The Modern Pushtu Instructor*)

Qazi Rahimullah Khan

Edited by H. L. Ogden

HIPPOCRENE BOOKS
New York

Hippocrene Books paperback edition, 2002.

First published as *The Modern Pushtu Instructor:* Peshawar, 1938.

ISBN 0-7818-0939-8

For information, address:
HIPPOCRENE BOOKS, INC.
171 Madison Avenue
New York, NY 10016

Printed in the United States of America.

CONTENTS.

Part I.

GRAMMAR.

Part II.

PROSE COMPOSITION.

PART I.

Pushtu Alphabet.

1. The Pushtu Alphabet consists of forty letters :—

Form	Power.	Name.
ا	A	*Alif*
ب	B	*Bé*
پ	P	*Pé*
ت	T (Soft)	*Thé*
ټ	T (Hard)	*Té*
ث	S	*Sé*
ج	J	*Jim*
ح	H (Arabic)	*Hé*
خ	Kh	*Khé*
څ	Ch	*Ché*
ځ	S or Z	*Sim* or *Zim*
د	D (Soft)	*Dal*
ډ	D (Hard)	*Dăl*
ذ	Z	*Zăl*
ر	R (Soft)	*Ré*
ړ	R (Hard)	*Ré*
ز	Z	*Zé*
ژ	Jh	*Jhé*
ږ	G	*Gé*

Form	Power.	Name.
س	S	*Sin*
ش	Sh	*Shin*
ڼ	Kh	*Khin*
ص	S	*Swād*
ض	Z	*Zwād*
ط	T	*Twé*
ظ	Z	*Zwé*
ع	A or I	*Ain*
غ	Gh	*Ghain*
ف	F	*Fé*
ق	Q	*Qaf*
ک	K	*Kaf*
ګ	G	*Gāf*
ل	L	*Lām*
م	M	*Mim*
ن	N	*Nūn*
و	O, W, U	*Wao*
٥	H (Round)	*Hé*
ه	H (Butterfly)	*Hé*
ء	Á	*Hamza*

Used generally in conjunction with ی = Y. broadening the sound.
ئ = ai
for example جنۍ =
= *Jinai*
= Girl.

ي =   E, I, or Y.

2. The following seven letter-forms are purely Pushtu viz:—

ټ	T (Hard)	*Té*
ځ	S or Z	*Sim* or *Zim*
ډ	D (Hard)	*Dal*
ړ	R (Hard)	*Ré*
ږ	G	*Gay*
ښ	Kh	*Khin*
ګ	G	*Gaf*

The following eight letter-forms are Arabic viz:—

ث	S	*Sé*
ح	H	*Hé*
ص	S	*Swad*
ض	Z	*Zwad*
ط	T	*Twé*
ظ	Z	*Zwé*
ع	A	*Ain*
ق	Q	*Qaf*

The following three letter-forms are common to Pushtu. Hindustani and Persian, but not found in Arabic viz:—

پ	P	*Pé*
چ	Ch	*Ché*
ژ	Jh	*Jhé*

The remaining letter forms are common to Pushtu, Arabic, Persian, and Hindustani.

3. Pushtu Script is written from right to left.

4. When writing a word, all except the following letters are joined together from the right hand side and not from the left :—

ا	A	*Alif*
د	D	*Dal*
ډ	D	*Dal*
ذ	Z	*Zal*
ر	R	*Ré*
ړ	R	*Ré*
ز	Z	*Zé*
ژ	Jh	*Jhé*
ږ	G	*Gé*
و	O, W	*Wao*
ه	H (Round)	*Hé*

See the shape of above letters in the middle of a word :—

ـا	A		ـو	O, W
ـد	D		ـه	H
ـر	R			

NOTE :—When writing a word in which any of the above letters occurs, a space is left between this letter and the next. See the position of the letter in the middle of the following words :—

خيال	*Khyal*
عدالت	*Adalat*
صدر	*Sadar*
سرَى	*Saray*
خراپ	*Kharap*
خوار	*Khwar*

5. The following are initial, medial and final forms of the letters :—

NAME	FINAL	MEDIAL	INITIAL
Alif	...ا	...ا...	ا
Bé	...ب	...ب...	ب...
Pé	...پ	...پ...	پ...
Thé	...ت	...ت...	ت...
Té	...ٹ	...ٹ...	ٹ..
Sé	...ث	...ث...	ث...
Jim	...ج	...ج...	ج...
Hé	...ح	...ح...	ح...
Khé	...خ	..خ...	خ...
Ché	...چ	...چ...	چ...
Sim or *Zim*	...ژ	...ژ...	ژ...
Dal	...د	د...	د

NAME	FINAL	MEDIAL	INITIAL
Dal	د...	د...	د
Zal	ذ...	ذ...	ذ
Ré	ر...	ر...	ر
Ré	ړ...	ړ...	ړ
Zé	ز...	ز...	ز
Jhé	ژ...	ژ...	ژ
Gé	ږ....	ږ....	ږ
Sin	س...	...س...	...س
Shin	ش...	...ش...	ش..
Khin	ښ...	...ښ...	...ښ
Swād	ص...	...ص...	...ص
Zwād	ض...	...ض...	ض..
Twé	ط...	...ط...	...ط
Zwé	ظ...	...ظ...	ظ..
Ain	ع...	...ع...	ع..
Ghain	غ...	...غ...	...غ
Fé	ف...	...ف..	...ف
Qaf	ق...	...ق.	...ق
Kaf	ک...	...ک...	...ک
Gaf	ګ...	...ګ...	...ګ
Lām	ل...	...ل...	ل
Mim	م...	...م...	م..
Nūn	ن...	...ن...	...ن
Wao	و...	....و...	...و
Hé	ه...	.. ه ..	...ه
Yé	ی...	...ی ..	..ی

6. Vowels :—

SHORT.		LONG.	
Zabar	= a, u	١ - ح - ع - ه - ٰ .	
Zer	= é,	‍ی = é ‍ي = ee, i, ‍ﻴ = ai	
Pésh	= o	‍و = ō, w. ‍ؤ = ū, oo	

EXAMPLES.

بُت	But	جَل	Jal
بيټ	Bét	جل	Jél
بُټ	Bot	جَل	Jol
كَل	Kal	دَر	Dar
كِل	Kél	دِر	Dér
كُل	Kol	دُر	Dor

‍ی	ay		i. e.	‍سَری	Saray	A man
‍ی	é (like 'a' in English)		i. e.	‍ونی	Wané	Trees
‍ي	ee, i		i. e.	‍مالي	Mali	Gardener
‍ﻴ	ai		i. e.	‍جني	Jinai	Girl
‍ه	a (H. soft)		i. e.	‍وَنه	Wana	Tree
‍ه	uh (H. hard)		i. e.	‍نيكه	Nikuh	Grand father.

NOTE—The short vowels are not written ex-
plicitly, but they are understood
and consequently pronounced.

(a) words ending in "ah" are prono ed as "a" = ة = h (Soft) i. e. تبة = *Taba* = Fever.

(b) o, or *u* (short) at the beginning or a word = أ = o or *u* i. e. أستاذ = *Ostāz* = Teacher.

(c) 'E' (short) or 'I' at the beginning of a word] = *é*, *i* i. e., إقرار = *Iqrār* = Agreement, promise.

7, In addition to the above vowels, there are certain signs used with consonants, to modify their sound ; they are :—

(i) · *mad*, only used on the top of] = *alif* to lengthen the sound, thus = آمين = *āmin* = so be it.

(ii) ـ *tashdid* ; an Arabic sign causing the consonant over which it is placed to sound double ; thus = اتّفاق = *Ittefāq* = a chance, union.

(iii) · *two zabars* on the top of alif sounds "*an*" as فوراً *fauran*   At once.
تخميناً *takhminan* Nearly.

Section 2.

(READING AND WRITING EXERCISES).

(I)

كور ـ مور ـ خور ـ جو پر . كار ـ مار ـ لار ـ سَر ـ ور ـ پَر ـ نَر ـ لم
ر مك ـ نَر ـ لور ـ سور ـ سور ـ پُل ـ چپ ـ سَل ـ ميخ ـ زيرو
وينس ـ زنى ـ بَر ـ حَق ـ پير ـ چَل ـ جال ـ مال ـ كال ـ ميل
كز ـ تذى ـ لبر ـ واك ـ خر ـ سيند ـ بازار ـ قول ـ مَد ـ اوښى
آس ـ اسپه ـ كبه ـ اوز ـ چرك ـ خوار . ـ سردار ـ إقرار ـ آخنر
أستاذ ـ اوده

Kōr. Mōr. Khōr. Jōr. Kār. Mār. Lār. Sar.
War. Par. Nar. Lām. Rag. Ghar. Lōr.
Sōr. Sūr. Pul. Chup. Sal. Maikh. Raig.
Wikh. Rang. Bar. Haq. Pir. Chal. Jal.
Māl. Kāl. Mil. Gaẓ. Tang. Lag. Wak
Khar. Sind. Bazār. Ṭōl. Mad. Ukh. Áss
Áspa. Kat. Aor. Cḥarg. Khwār. Sardar.
Iqrār. Ákhtar. Ostāz. Óbuh.

(II)

دَفتَر ـ چَرته ـ دوست ـ خَراپ ـ دَلته ـ پلار ـ ورور ـ غِيب ـ كوهاتٍ
لاهور ـ جلال آباد ـ كابل ـ نوكر ـ كتاب ـ ماخام ـ وَروكَى
پيښور ـ چترَل ـ مردان ـ رونَد ـ چرګه ـ زور ـ مَيز ـ كُرسِي
ناوخته ـ ټوكرَي ـ جواب ـ جنګ ـ واخهٔ ـ كلَى ـ سپَى ـ سرَى
ماليان ـ هلته ـ راشه ـ كينه ـ فارسي ـ پښتو ـ پښتون ـ هندوستاني
انګرېزى ـ بادشاه ـ

Daftar. Charta. Dōst. Kharāp. Dalta. Plār.
Vrōr. Gharib. Kohāt. Lāhōr. Jalālabād.
Kabal. Nōkar. Kitāb. Mā̦khām. Warūkay
Pékhawar. Chatrāl. Mardān. Rūnd. Charga.
Zōr. Maiz. Kursai. Nāwākhta. Tōkrai.
Jawāb. Jang. Wākhuh. Kalay. Spay.
Saray. Malian. Halta. Rasha. Kaina.
Fārsi. Pukhtō. Pukhtūn. Hindustāni. Angrézi.
Bādshāh.

(III)

زۀ دَ صاحب نوكريم ۔ دا هلك ځما ورور دیَ ۔ ځما كور پۀ كوهاټ كښې دیَ ۔ دا لار چرته تلی بَه ۔ ځما سپی ناجوړ دیَ ۔ دننه راشه۔ ستا پلار دلته راغلیَ نۀ دی پ.ته دَ هغۀ څۀ كیږی ؟ اوس ناوخته دیَ بیا راشه ۔ داخوک دیَ ۔ دَ هغۀ كور چرته دیَ ۔ دَ هغی مور چرته وَه سری باهر وَه ۔ ځما سلام وَركړه ورته ووايه چه دلته راشی ۔ زۀ به ډاكټر وبلم ۔ مردان خراپ ځای نۀ دیَ ۔ دا لار ښهر ته تلی بَه ۔ ډیره ښه ده

*Zuh da Sāhib naukar yam.   Dā halak zamā
vrōr day.   Zmā kōr puh Kohāt ké day.   Dā lār
charta talé dah.   Zamā spay nājōr day.
Danana rāsha.   Stā plār dalta rāghalay nuh
day.   Tuh da haghuh suh kége.   Ôss nāwakhta
day.   Biā rāsha.   Dā sōk day.   Da haghuh kōr
charta day.   Da haghé mōr charta wah.   Saray
bāhar woh.   Zamā salām warkra.   Warta wo
wāya chi dalta rāshi.   Zuh ba dāktar wo balam.
Mardān kharāp zāi nuh day.   Dā lār khahar
ta talé dah.   Déra kha dah.*

(IV)

دوه تن سړي ولاړ وو ۔ يو بادشاه ځما مُلك ته راغیَ ۔ دَ بادشاه څوی ناجوړ شو۔ دوه كال پس هغه مړ شو ۔ دَ كور پۀ څواكښې يو جماعت دیَ ۔ دَ كلی خلق ډير ښۀ دی ۔ هغوی ټول پۀ كورډنو كښې اوسیږی

خمول سپاهيان اوس آرام كوي ۔ څما طلب چرته دی ۔ كمان افسرصاحب
نه سوی دی ۔ خمول افسران نه دی ۔ دهغو پلتن اوس په كراچي
كښں ده ۔ زرلاورشه بيا دلته مه راخه ۔ زر زر كار كوه۔ زه دفتر ته خم ۔ په
خلور بجى به بير ته راخم ۔

*Dawa tana sari walār woo. Yao bādshāh zamā
mulk ta rāghay. Da bādshāh zōi, nājōr sho
Dwa kāla pas hagha mar sho. Da kōr puh khwā
ké yao jumait day. Da kali khalq dair khuh di
Haghūi tōl puh kōrūno ké oségi. Tōl spāhyān
oss arām kawi. Zamā talab ḍharta day. Kamān
afsar sāhib khuh saray day. Tōl afsarān khuh
di. Da hagho paltan oss puh Karāchai ké dah.
Zar lārsha biā dalta muh rāza. Zar zar kār
kawa. Zuh daftar ta zam. Puh salōr bajé ba
biartā rāzam.*

Section 3.

There is no article in Pushtu, corresponding
to the "a" or "an" in English, the article being
inherent in the noun itself.

يو = *Yau* = one, which is an indefinite numeral,
is some times used as an article, as :—

يو بادشاه = *Yau bādshāh* = A king.

PERSONAL PRONOUNS.

زۀ	*Zuh*	I	
تۀ	*Tuh*	Thou	Singular.
هغه	*Hagha*	He, she. it or that	

مُونږ	*Mūng*	We	
تاسو	*Tāso*	You	Plural.
هغوی	*Haghūi*	They (Masculine and Feminine)	

POSSESSIVE PRONOUNS.

څما	*Zamā*	My or mine	
ستا	*Stā*	Thy or thine	
دَ هغۀ	*Da haghuh*	His	Singular.
دَ هغی	*Da haghé*	Her	

څمُونږ	*Zamūng*	Our or ours	
ستاسو	*Stāso*	Your or yours	Plural.
دَ هغوی	*Da haghūi*	Their or theirs (m. or f.)	

THE VERB "TO BE."

Present Tense.

زۀ یم	*Zuh yam*	I am	
تۀ یی	*Tuh yé*	Thou art	
هغه دی	*Hagha day*	He is	Singular.
هغه ده	*Hagha hah*	She is	

مُوْنٍر يُو	*Mūng yū*	We are	
تَاسوٗئِیی	*Tāso yai*	You are	Plural
هَغوٖی دی	*Haghūi di*	They are (M. and F.)	

FUTURE TENSE.

زَه بَه يَم	*Zuh ba yam*	I will be or I shall be	
تَه بَه یی	*Tuh ba yé*	Thou wilt be	Singular
هغَه بَه يِر	*Hagha ba yi* or	He, she, it will be	
هغَه بَه وی	*Hagha ba wi*		
مُوْنٍر بَه يُو	*Mūng ba yū*	We will be	
تَاسوٗ بَه يِي	*Taso ba yai*	You will be	
هغْیَ بَه يِي	*Haghūi ba yi* or	They will be (M. and F.)	Plural.
هغْیی بَه وی	*Haghūi ba wi*		

PAST TENSE.

زَه وَم	*Zuh wam*	I was	
تَه وی	*Tuh wé*	Thou wast	
هغَه وٚہ	*Hagha woh*	He was	Singular
هغَه وَہ	*Hagha wah*	She was	
مُوْنٍر وٝر	*Mūng woo*	We were	
تَاسوٗوٝی	*Taso wai*	You were	
هغوٖی وٝر	*Haghūi woo*	They were	Plural.
هغوٖی ؛یـٚ	*Haghūi wé*	They were (Feminine)	

Section 4.

PREPOSITIONS AND POST-POSITIONS

A preposition is composed of two parts and the noun or pronoun qualified is placed in the middle, while a postposition is always placed after the noun or pronoun.

NOTE :—The inflected form of ‮زه‬ = *Zuh* is ‮ما‬ = *mā*; and ‮ته‬ = *tuh* is ‮تا‬ = tā, of ‮هغه‬ = *hagha* . is ‮هغۀ‬ = *haghuh* and in the case of feminine singular ‮هغه‬ = *hagha* becomes ‮هغي‬ = *haghé*; while in 1st 2nd and 3rd person plural the pronouns remain uninflected, as :—

‮لۀ نه‬ = *Luh-na* from

‮لۀ ما نه‬ *Luh mā na*	from me	⎫
‮لۀ تا نه‬ *Luh tā na*	from thee	⎬ Singular
‮لۀ هغۀ نه‬ *Luh haghuh na*	from him	⎬
‮لۀ هغي نه‬ *Luh haghé na*	from her	⎭
‮لۀ موږ نه‬ *Luh mūng na*	from us	⎫
‮لۀ تاسو نه‬ *Luh tāso na*	from you	⎬
‮لۀ هغوی نه‬ *Luh haghūi na*	from them	⎬ Plural
‮لۀ هغوی نه‬ *Luh haghūi na*	from them (Feminine)	⎭

NOTE:—Either of the two parts can be used to express the same meaning as above, but the first part can only be used with nouns and pronouns ending in consonants, in which case

Zabar = _a_, should be put over the last consonant letter of the noun and pronoun, instead
of نه = _na_, as :—

له پیښور نه _Luh pekhawar na_ ⎫
پیښور نه _Pekhawar na_ ⎬ From Peshawar.
له پیښور _Luh pekhawara_ ⎭

ته = _ta_ له = _la_ لره = _lara_ or وته = _wata_ = to as :—

ماته	_mā ta_	to me	⎫
تاته	_tā ta_	to thee	⎪
هغه ته	_haghuh ta_	to him	⎬ Singular.
هغی ته	_haghé ta_	to her	⎭
موُنږ ته	_mūng ta_	to us	⎫
تاسو ته	_tāso ta_	to you	⎪
هغوی ته	_haghūi ta_	to them	⎬ Plural.
هغوی ته	_haghūi ta_	to them (Feminine)	⎭

NOTE :—Decline the personal pronouns with
the following post or prepositions as above :—

په-کښس _puh-ké_   In
په ماکښس _puh mā ké_   In me etc.

NOTE :—The last part of above can also be
used to express the same meaning as:—

په پیښور کښس or _puh pekhawar ké_ ⎫
یا   or   ⎬ In Peshawar.
پیښور کښس _pekhawar ké_ ⎭

په-باند _puh-bandé_   On.
په ما باند _puh mā bandé_   On me etc.

NOTE :—Either of the two parts of above can be used to express the same meaning as :—

پۀ ميز باند	*Puh méz bānde*	
پۀ ميز	*Puh méz*	} On the table.
ميز باند	*Méz bānde*	
لاند	*Lānde*	Beneath, below, under.
ماالاند	*Mā lānde*	Beneath, below or under me etc.

NOTE :—Certain post-positions can also be used with the noun or pronoun in the Genitive Case *e. g.* :—

د دلاند يا	*da-da lānde*	} Beneath, below or under.
د لاند	or *da-lāndé*	
څما دلاند	*zamā da lānde*	Under me.
څما لاند	*Zamā lānde*	Under me.
څما ميز دلاند	*Zamā méz da lānde*	Under my table.
څما ميز لاند	*Zamā méz lānde*	Under my table.
سره	*Sara*	With.
ماسره	*Mā sara*	With me.
	or	
د سره	*da sara*	With.
څما سره	*Zamā sara*	With me etc.
دپاره	*Dapāra*	} For
د دپاره	*Da dapāra*	
ما دپاره	*Mā dapāra*	} For me etc.
څما دپاره	*Zama da pāra*	

پشان	Pashān	⎫ Like
دَپشان	Da pashān	⎭
ما پشان	Mā pashān	⎫ Like me
څما پشان	Zamā pashān	⎭
کره	Kara	⎫ In the house of
دَ-کره	Da kara	⎭
ما کره	Mā kara	⎫ In my house etc
څما کره	Zamā kara	⎭
پوری	Pōré	Near or by
ما پوری	Mā poré	Near or by me etc.
ته نیزدی	Ta nizdé	Near
ما ته نیزدی	Mā ta nizdé	
سخه	Sakha	⎫ Near; it is also used for
دَ-سخه	Da sakha	⎬ the possessive case in ⎭ the verb to have.

EXAMPLE I

ما سخه	Mā sakha	⎫
یا	or	⎬ Near me etc:
څما سخه	Zamā sakha	⎭

EXAMPLE II

ما سخه کتاب دی	Mā sakha kitāb day	⎫ lit near
یا	or	⎬ me book
څما سخه کتاب دی	Zamā sakha kitāb day	⎭ is = I have a book.
تا سخه کتاب دی	Tā sakha kitāb day	⎫ lit near thee book
or	or	⎬ is = thou
ستا سخه کتاب دی	Stā sakha kitāb day	⎭ hast a book.

هغۀ سخه کتاب دی	*Haghuh sakha kitāb day*	lit near him book is = he has a book.
یا	or	
دَ هغۀ سخه کتاب دی	*Da haghuh sakha kitab day*	

NOTE:—سخه *sakha*, can only be used when the object is light and moveable as well as to denote owner-ship otherwise the possessive case should be used as :—

ما سخه یو قلم دی	*Mā sakha yau qalam day*	I have a pen
ملک سخه یوه اسپه ده	*Malak sakha yawa aspa dah*	The malik owns a mare
ستا څو کوروند دی	*Stā so korūna dee*	How many houses have you?
ستا څو ورونړه دی	*Sta so vrūnra dee*	How many brothers have you?

دَ پاسَ	*Da pāsa*	above.
دَ...دَ پاسَ	*da...da pāsa*	
ما دَ پاسَ	*Mā dapāsa*	above me etc.
څما دَ پاسَ	*Zamā dapāsa*	
دَ...په مینځ کښ	*da...pa mianz ké*	in the middle of or through, among.
دَ باغ په مینځ کښ	*da bāgh pa mianz ké*	Through the garden.
لۀ...نه وراندِ	*luh na varāndé*	before (in place)
دَ...دَ وراندِ	*da...da varāndé*	

لۀ مانه وراند *luh mā na vrāndé*
or
ځما دَوراند *Zamā da vrāndé*
} before me (etc).

لۀ...نه ورو_مبی *luh-na vrūmbay* or   before (in time.)
یا الۀ_نه اول *awal*

لۀ ما نه وروـمبی *luh mā na vrūmbay*
لۀ ما نه اول *luh mā na awal*
} before me

لۀ...نه ورستو *luh-na vrosto*
دَ...دَ ورستو *da...da vrosto*
} b e h i n d (in
place)

لۀ ما نه ورستو *Luh mā na vrosto*
یا
ځما دَ ورستو *Zmā da vrosto*
or
} behind me.

لۀ...نه پس *Luh-na pas*   after (in time).

لۀ ما نه پس *Luh mā na pas*   after me etc.

NOTE:—پس = *Pas*, does not inflect any noun
of time.

پسی = *Pasé* = after (in the case of a person or
business).

ما پسی *Ma pasé*   after me.

څۀ پسی *suh pasé*   after what
business).

لۀ...نه دی خوا *Luh-na dé khwa*   this side of.

لۀ دفتر نه دی
خوا *Luh daftar na dé
khwa*   this side of the
office.

لۀ...نه هغه خوا *Luh-na hagha khwa*   beyond.

لۀ دفتر نه هغه
خوا *Luh daftar na
hagha khwa*   Beyond the
office.

لۀ...نه گیرچاپیره *Luh-na gér chapéra*   around.

لۀ ښهر نه گیر
چاپیره *Luh khahar na gér
chapéra*   Around the
City.

دَ...پۀ باب کښې	Da...puh bāb ké	About, concerning.
ځما پۀ باب کښې	Zma puh bāb ké	About me etc.
دَ...پۀ سبب یا	Da...puh sabab or	Owing to, on account of or
دَ...پۀ وجه	Da puh waja	by reason of
دَ باران پۀ سبب یا	Da bārān puh sabab	Owing to the rain
or		
دَ باران پۀ وجه	Da bārān puh waja	
دَ...پۀ موجب	Da...puh mūjeb	According to
دَ حکم پۀ موجب	Da hukam puh mūjeb	According to order
بی لۀ...نه	bé luh...na	Without, except, besides.
بی لۀ ما نه	bé luh mā na	Without me etc.
دَ...پۀ شا	Da...puh sha	At the back of
دَ کور پۀ شا	Da kor puh sha	At the back of the house.
دَ	Da	Of
دَ میجر صاحب آس	Da maijar sāhib ass	The Major's horse.

The particles ﺍﺭ = Ra, ﺩﺭ = Dar, ﻭﺭ = War are used with post positions and with the 2nd part of prepositions as well as with some verbs denoting the singular and plural both numbers and they have the force of personal pronouns :—

ﺍﺭ   Ra   For 1st   person   singular   and plural.

ﺩﺭ   Dar   For 2nd   ,,   ,,   ,,

در	*War*	For 3rd person singular and plural.

as :—-

را نه	*Rā na*	From me or from us.
درنه	*Dar na*	From thee or from you.
ورنه	*War na*	From him or from them, her, or it.
را باند	*Rā bāndė*	On me or on us.
در باند	*Dar bāndė*	On thee or on you.
ور باند	*War bāndė*	On him or on them, her or it.
را ته	*Rā ta*	To me or to us.
در ته	*Dar ta*	To thee or to you.
ورته	*War ta*	To him or to them.
را سره	*Rā sara*	With me or with us.
در سره	*Dar sara*	With thee or with you.
ور سره	*War sara*	With him or with them, her or it.
و تل	*Watal*	To go out.
را و تل	*Rā watal*	To come out towards me or us.
در و تل	*Dar watal*	To come out towards thee or you.
ور و تل	*War watal*	To come out towards him or them, her or it.

Section 5.

THE NOUN.

A noun is a word denoting a person, place or thing, and has two Genders—Masculine and

Feminine and two numbers—Singular and Plural :—

ENDINGS OF MASCULINE NOUNS.

I. Nouns ending in ی = *ay*. are masculine as :—

سړی   *Saray*   A man.

کلی   *Kalay*   Village.

پوړی   *Paray*   Rope.

سپی   *S̩ay*   Dog.

مړی   *Maray*   Dead body.

کانړی   *Kānray*   Stone.

II. Nouns ending in consonants are masculine as :—

چرګ   *Charg*   Cock.

هلک   *Halak*   Boy.

میز   *Méz*   Table.

کور   *Kōr*   House.

دفتر   *Daftar*   Office.

مَلک   *Malak*   Head man.

EXCEPTIONS:—

لر   *Lār*   Road.

پلتن   *Paltan*   Regiment.

ورځ   *Vraz*   Day.

وریځ   *Woriaz*   Cloud.

مياشت   *Miasht*   Month, half moon.

بوستن   *Brastan*   Quilt.

لهر من   *Sarman*   Skin, leather.

خنغل   *Sangal*   Elbow.

دُر شل   *Durshal*   Frame of a door.

رُ منز.   *Gumanz*   Comb.

ستن   *Stan*   Needle. Pillar, Telegraph Post.

لمن   *Lman*   Skirt.

ميچن   *Mechan*   Hand Mill.

III. Nouns ending in ی=*i*, denoting profession are masculine as :—

مالی   *Mali*   Gardener.

دوبی   *Dobi*   Washerman.

نابی   *Nayi*   Barber.

قاضی   *Qazi*   Judge.

موچی   *Mochi*   Shoe Maker.

IV. Nouns ending in ه=*uh*. (Hard) are masculine as :—

وادة   *Waduh*   Marriage.

نيكة   *Nikuh*   Grand father.

كارغة   *Karghuh*   Crow.

مارغة   *Marghuh*   Bird.

EXCEPTIONS :—

چارة   *Charuh*   Knife (Fem).

تيارة   *Tyaruh*   Darkness (Fem).

ENDINGS OF FEMININE NOUNS.

I.   Nouns ending in $'$ = h (soft) are feminine as :—

ونه	*Wana*	Tree.
تبَه	*Taba*	Fever.
ښځه	*Khaza*	Woman or wife.
چغه	*Chagha*	Pursuit party.
مږه	*Maga*	Rat.
خټه	*Khata*	Mud.

II.   Nouns ending in ۍ = *ai* are feminine as:—

جنۍ	*Janai*	Girl.
چټۍ	*Chitai*	Letter.
ټوکرۍ	*Tokrai*	Basket.
ګلۍ	*Galai*	Hail-storm, Hail-stone.
نالۍ	*Nalai*	Quilt.
سيلۍ	*Silai*	Sand or dust-storm.
څپلۍ	*Saplai*	Sandals.

III.   Nouns ending in ي = *i* denoting qualities are feminine as :—

دوستي	*Dosti*	Friendship.
بدي	*Badi*	Enmity, feud.
دُشمني	*Dushmani*	Enmity.
غريبي	*Gharibi*	Poverty.

نیکی   *Neki*   Goodness.

نا مردی   *Namardi* Cowardice.

IV.   Nouns = ending in ‏ا‎ = ā (*alif*) are feminine as :—

بلا   *Bala*   Calamity.

قلا   *Qala*   Fort.

سزا   *Saza*   Punishment.

نبا   *Nia*   Grand-mother.

ژړا   *Jhara*   Crying, weeping.

خندا   *Khanda* Laughter.

EXCEPTIONS —

ملا   *Mula* A priest   ملایان *Mulayan* Priests.

گدا   *Gada* A beggar   گدایان *Gadayan* Beggars.

کک   *Kaka* An uncle (Polite term of calling an
          old man کک کاگن *Kakagan* Uncles.

سنډا   *Sanda*   Male buffalo.

سنډ گان   *Sandgan* Male Buffaloes.

V.   Nouns ending in ‏و‎ = o, are feminine as :—

پیشو   *Pisho*   Cat.

بیزو   *Bizo*   Monkey.

ور شو   *Warsho*   Grazing ground.

لنبو   *Lanbo*   A swim.

FORMATION OF FEMININE FROM MASCULINE.

I. Nouns ending in ي = *ay*, form their feminine by changing this letter in ۍ = *ai* as :—

سپی *Spay*	Dog.	سپۍ *Spai*	Bitch
چیلی *Chelay*	He goat.	چیلۍ *Chelai*	She goat.
نوسی *Nwasay*	Grand son	نوسۍ *Nwasai*	Grand daughter.
اوسی *Osay*	Antelope.	اوسۍ *Osai*	Female antelope

II. Nouns ending in consonants form their feminine by adding ه = *h* (soft) as : —

چرګ *Charg*	Cock	چرګه *Charga*	Hen
خر *Khar*	He ass	خره *Khara*	She ass
ګډ *Gad*	Male sheep	ګډه *Gada*	F. sheep
غل *Ghal*	Thief	غله *Ghla*	F. thief
اس *Ass*	Horse	اسپه *Aspa*	Mare.

(Persian = اسپ = *Asp* = horse)

III. Nouns ending in ی = *i* form their feminine by changing this letter into نره = *nra* (or *narah*) as :—

دوبی *Dobi*	Washerman.
دوبنره *Dobanra*	Washer woman.
نائی *Nai*	Barber.
نائینره *Nayanra*	Barber's wife.

مالي *Mali* Gardener.

مالنره *Malanra* Gardener's wife, f. gardener.

بنګی *Bangi* Sweeper.

بنګنره *Banganra* Sweeper's wife.

NUMBER OF MASCULINE NOUNS.

I. Nouns ending in ـَي = *ay* form their oblique singular and nominative plural by changing this letter into ـِي = *i* as:—

سړي *Saray* A man.   سړي *Sari* Men.

سپي *Spay* A dog.   سپي *Spi* Dogs.

له سړي نه *Luh Sari na* from a man (ob. s.)

II. Nouns ending in consonants denoting animate objects and those ending in ـِي = *i* remain un-changed in the oblique singular and form their nominative plural by adding آن = *ān,* and those denoting time, measure, and weight, form their plural by adding —— *zabar* over the final letter as :—

هلک *Halak* Boy.   هلکان *Halakān* Boys.

مَلک *Malak* Head Man   مَلکان *Malakān* Head men.

د ملک *da malak* of the head man (remains un-changed).

Singular.			Plural.		
کال	*Kal*	Year.	کال	*Kala*	Years.
ګز	*Gaz*	Yard.	ګز	*Gaza*	Yards.

Singular.			Plural.		
من	*Man*	Maund.	مَن	*Mana*	Maunds
سیر	*Sér*	Seer.	سیَر	*Séra*	Seers.
میل	*Mïl*	Mile.	میلَ	*Mïla*	Miles.
قدم	*Qadam*	Pace.	قدمَ	*Qadama*	Paces.
جیرب	*Jirub*	½ acre.	جیربَ	*Jiruba*	Jiribs.
ملټ	*Mélat*	Minute.	ملټَ	*Mélata*	Minutes

III. Nouns ending in consonants denoting in-animate objects remain unchanged in the oblique singular and form their nominative plurals by adding ونه = *ūna* as:—

کور	*Kōr*	House.	کورونه	*Korūna*	Houses
کتاب	*Kitāb*	Book.	کتابونه	*Kitābūna*	Books.
میز	*Méz*	Table.	میزونه	*Mézūna*	Tables
په کور کښ	*Pa kōr ké*	In the house (ob.s.)			

IV. Nouns ending in و = *ū*. They remain unchanged in the oblique singular and form their nominative plural by adding ګان = *gān* as:—

بابو	*Bābū*	Clerk.	بابوګان	*Bābūgān*	Clerks.
میلو	*Mélū*	Bear.	میلوګان	*Mélūgān*	Bears.
پارو	*Pārū*	Snake charmer.	پاروګان	*Pārūgān*	Snake charmers
تارو	*Tārū*	Francolin.	تاروګان	*Tārūgān*	Francolins.
دبابو	*Da bābū*	of the clerk. (ob. s.)			

V. Nouns having $=u$· in the last syllable,
change the $=u$ into ا$=a=$ (alif) and $=H$ (hard)
after it to form their nominative plural and
they remain unchanged in the oblique singular:—

پښتُون *Pukhtūn* Pathan.　پښتانۀ *Pukhtā- Pathans
nuh*

شپُون *Shpūn* Shepherd,　شپانۀ *Shpānuh* Shepherds.
سور *Sŏr*　Horse man,　سوارُه *Swāruh* Riders.
rider.

دَ پښتُون *Da pukhtūn* of the Pathan. (ob. s.)

VI. Some nouns form their nominative
plural irregularly as :—

ورور	*Vrŏr*	Brother	وروڼه	*Vrūnrah*	Brothers
ځوي	*Zŏi*	Son	ځامن	*Zāman*	Sons.
ترۀ	*Truh*	Uncle	ترۀڼه	*Trūna*	Uncles (Paternal)
ماما	*Māmā*	Uncle	ماما ګان	*Māmā gān*	Uncles. (Maternal)
اس	*Ass*	Horse	اسُونه	*Assūna*	Horses.
غل	*Ghŭl*	Thief	غلۀ	*Ghluh*	Thieves.
میلمه	*Mĕlma*	Guest	میلمانۀ	*Mĕlmānuh*	Guests.
زړۀ	*Zruh*	Heart	زړُونه	*Zrūna*	Hearts.

VII. Some nouns, are only used in the plural
as :—

شراب　*Sharap*　Wine.
غنم　*Ghanam*　Wheat.
جوار　*Jowār*　Maize.

پیې	*Pai*	Milk.
ما ستۀ	*Māstuh*	Curds.
کچ	*Kuch*	Butter.
تیل	*Tail*	Oil.
اپیم	*Apim*	Opium.
ما غزۀ	*Māghzuh*	Brain.
زهر	*Zahar*	Poison.
بانړۀ	*Bānruh*	Eye-lashes
اوړۀ	*Oruh*	Flour.
سکاړۀ	*Skāruh*	Charcoal.
ریښم	*Rékham*	Silk.

NUMBER OF FEMININE NOUNS.

1. Nouns ending in ٔ = *h* (soft) form their oblique singular and nominative plural by changing this letter into ي = *é* as :—

| ونه | *Wana* | Tree | ونی | *Wané* | Trees. |
| تبه | *Taba* | Fever | تبی | *Tabé* | Fevers. |

دَونی *Da wané* of the tree. (ob. s.)

NOTE :—In the locative case feminine singular they are not inflected.

| پۀ ونه کښس | *Puh wana ké* | In the tree. |
| پۀ ونه باند | *Puh wana bāndé* | On the tree. |

EXCEPTION.

Feminine nouns ending in ي = *i*.

| دوستی | *Dōsti* | Friendship. |
| پۀ دوستۍ کښس | *Puh dōstai ké* | In friendship. |

II. Nouns ending in ‫ی‬ = *i* form their oblique singular and nominative plural by changing this letter into ‫ئ‬ = *ai*, as :

‫دوستی‬ *Dōsti* Friendship ‫دوستئ‬ *Dōstai* Friendships

‫دشمنی‬ *Dush* Enmity ‫دشمنئ‬ *Dush* Enmities.
mani   manai

‫په دوستئ کښ‬ *Puh dostai ké* In friendship (Ob. S.)

III. Nouns ending in consonants form their oblique singular and nominative plural by adding ‫ی‬ = *é*, or <u>zer</u> under the final letter.

‫یوه ورځ‬ *Yawa vraz* One ‫دوورځ‬ *Dwa* Two days.
day   *vrazé*

‫پلټن‬ *Paltan* Regiment ‫پلټنی‬ *Paltané* Regiments.

‫د ورځی‬ *Da vrazé* of the day (idiomatic "in the day time") Ob. S.

IV. Nouns ending in ‫ئ‬ = *ai*, remain unchanged in the oblique singular and nominative plural as :—

‫جنئ‬ *Jinai* Girl or girls ‫جنکئ‬ *Jinakai* Girls.
               (In Khalil and Mohmand.)

‫درئ‬ *Darai* Carpet or Carpets.

‫څپلئ‬ *Saplai* Sandal or Sandals.

‫د جنئ‬ *Da jinai* of the girl. (Ob. S.)

V. Nouns ending in ‫ا‬ = *ā* (alif) remain unchanged in the oblique singular and nominative plural in Yusafzai, but in Khalil and Mohmand add ﮔﺎﻧﯽ = *gāné* as :—

قلا *Qalā* Fort or Forts.

(Khalil and Mohmand قلا ﮔﺎﻧﯽ = *Qalā gāné* = Forts.)

نيا *Niā* Grand mother or Grand mothers.

(In Khalil and Mohmand نيا ﮔﺎﻧﯽ = *Niā gāné* = Grand mothers)

په قلا كښس *Puh qalā ké* In the fort.

VI. Some nouns form their plural irregularly as :—

لور *Lūr* Daughter لوڼه *Lūnra* Daughters

مور *Mōr* Mother ميندى *Méndé* Mothers

خور *Khōr* Sister خويندى *Khwéndé* Sisters.

ترور *Trōr* Aunt ترورياني *Trōryāné* Aunts

VII. Some nouns are only used in the plural as :—

اوربشي *Orbashé* Barley

شوملى *Shōmlé* Butter milk.

وريژي *Vrijhé* Rice (in shop)

شولى *Shōlé* Rice (in field)

توكانړى *Tukānré* Spittle.

اوبه *Obuh* Water.

OBLIQUE PLURAL.

All masculine and feminine plural nouns

form their oblique plural by adding ﺭ = "o" to
the last consonant letter of the word as :—

لَه سَرو نه	*Luh sarō na*	From men.
پهٔ ښځو باندې	*Puh khazō bāndé*	On the women
ماليانو ته	*Māliāno ta*	To the gardeners
پهٔ کورونو کښې	*Puh korūno ké*	In the houses.

CASE OF NOUN.

There are eight cases of noun in Pushtu :—

1. Nominative.   Subject always, but object in
the past tenses of a transitive
verb.

2. Accusative   Object in the present and
future.

3. Agentive   Subject in past tenses of a
transitive verb.

4. Genitive   Possessive (د = *da* = of)

5. Dative   In direct object (ته = *ta*, له = *la*
or لره = *lara* = to)

6. Ablative   Distance from a place (له-نه =
luh-na = from)

7. Locative   Remaining in a place :
(پهٔ-کښې   *pa-ké*   in)
(پهٔ-باندې   *puh-bāndé*   on)

8. Vocative   Used in calling.

INFLECTION OF MASCULINE NOUNS.

I. Nouns ending in سَرَی = *ay* are thus inflected :—

Singular.   Plural.

1. Nominative :

سَرَی *Saray* A man   سَرِی *Sari*   men

2. Accusative :

سَرَی *Saray* The man   سَرِی *Sari*   The men

3. Agentive :

سَرِی *Sari* By a man   سَرو *Saro*   by men

4. Genitive :

د سَرِی *Da sari* Of a man   د سَرو *da saro* of the men

5. Dative :

سَرِی ته *Sari ta* To a man   سَرو ته *Sarō ta* To men

6. Ablative :

لـه سَرِی نه *Luh sari na* From   لـه سَرو نه *Luh saro na* From
              a man   men

7. Locative :

پـه سَرِی کښې *Puh sari ké* In a   پـه سَرو کښې *Puh saro ké* In
              man   men

8. Vocative :

اى سَرِیه *Ay sariya*   اي سَرو *Ay saro* Oh men !
      Oh man!

NOTE :—The nominative and accusative are the same in both Singular and plural, therefore if one knows nominative, then one will know the accusative, and if one knows the agentive one will also know all the rest.

II. Nouns ending in consonants denoting animate objects are thus inflected :—

	Singular.	Plural.
Nominative هلک	*Halak* Boy	هلکان *Halakān* Boys
Agentive هلک	*Halak* by boy	هلکانو *Halakāno* by boys.

III. Nouns ending in consonants denoting in animate objects are thus inflected :—

	Singular.	Plural.
Nominative کور	*Kōr* House	کوروﻧﻪ *Korūna* Houses
Agentive کور	*Kōr* by house	کوروﻧﻮ *Korūno* by houses.

INFLECTION OF FEMININE NOUNS.

I. Nouns ending in ه = *h*, are inflected thus:--

	Singular.	Plural.
Nom ونه	*Wana* Tree	وﻧﯥ *Wané* Trees.
Agent وﻧﯽ	*Wané* by tree	وﻧﻮ *Wanō* by trees

II. Nouns ending in ي = *i*, are inflected thus:-

	Singular.	Plural.
Nom دوسﺗﯽ	*Dōstī* Friendship	دوسﺗﯥ *Dostai* Friend-ships.
Agent دوسﺗﯥ	*Dostai* by Friendship	دوسﺗﻮ *Dōsto* by Friendships.

III.   Nouns ending in consonants are inflected thus :—

	Singular.		Plural.	
Nom	ورځ *Vraz*	Day	ورځي يا ورځ، *Vrazé*	Days.
Agent	ورځى *Vrazé*	by day	ورځو *Vrazō*	by days.

IV.   Nouns ending in ۍ = *ai*, are declined
thus :—

	Singular.		Plural.	
Nom	جنۍ *Jinai*	girl	جنۍ *Jinai* or جنكۍ *Jinakài*	girls.
Agent	جنۍ *Jinai*	by girl	جينو *Jino* or جنكو *Jinakō*	by girls.

V.   Nouns ending in ا = a (*alif*) are declined
thus :—-

	Singular.		Plural.	
Nom	قلا *Qala*	Fort	قلا *Qalā* or قلا گاني *qalāgané*	forts.
Agent	قلا *Qalā*	by fort	قلاؤ *Qalāo* or قلا گانو *Qalāganō*	by forts.

Section 6.

THE ADJECTIVE.

The adjective follows the rules of the noun
for Gender, number and case. It is generally
placed before its noun.

EXAMPLE :

1.   نرى سرى   *Naray saray*   A thin Man.

نري سري   *Nari sari*   thin men.

ﺩ ﻧﺮﻯ ﺳﺮﻯ   *Da nari sari* of a thin man (m. ob. s)

ﺩ ﻧﺮﻭ ﺳﺮﻭ   *Da narō sarō* of thin men (mas. ob. plu).

ﻧﺮﻯ ﺧﺰﻩ   *narai khaza* thin woman.

ﻧﺮﻯ ﺧﺎﺷﻰ   *narai khazé* thin women.

ﺩ ﻧﺮﻯ ﺧﻨﺸﻰ   *da narai khazé* of a thin woman (f. ob. s.)

ﺩ ﻧﺮﻭ ﺧﺸﻮ   *da narō khazō* of thin women (f. ob. plu.)

II.   But note:—Expressing sympathy.

ﺳﺮﻯ ﻧﺮﻯ ﺩﻯ   *saray naray day* the man is thin.

ﺧﺰﻩ ﻧﺮﻯ ﺩﻩ   *khaza narai dah* the woman is thin.

ﺳﺮﻯ ﻧﺎ ﺟﻮﺭ ﺩﻯ   *saray nā jora day* the man is (unfortunately) ill.

2.   The following adjectives ending in ﻯ = *ay* change ﻯ = *ay* into ﻱ = *i.* in the nominative plural and form their feminine singular and plural by changing ﻯ = *ay* into ﻱ = *é* as:—

m. s.	f. s. & f. p.	
ﻧﻮﻯ *naway*	ﻧﻮﻱ *nawé*	new.
ﺗﺮﻯ *tagay*	ﺗﺮﻱ *tagé*	thirsty.
ﻏﻠﻰ *ghalay*	ﻏﻠﻱ *ghalé*	silent.
ﺧﻮﺷﻰ *khūshay*	ﺧﻮﺷﻱ *khushé*	useless.
ﺍﻭﺯﻯ *ogay*	ﺍﻭﺯﻱ *ogé*	hungry.

وروکَی *warūkay*	ورُوکِي *warūké*	small.
ورکوتَی *warkōtay*	ورکوتِي *warkōté*	small.
کمزورَی *kamzōray*	*kamzōré*	weak.

3. Adjectives ending in consonants do not change in the nominative plural and follow the rules of nouns for feminine singular and plural as:—

خراپ سړی *kharāp saray*		A bad man.
خراپ سړي *kharāp sari*		Bad men.
خراپه ښځه *kharāpa khaza*		A bad woman.
خراپی ښځی *kharāpé khazé*		Bad women.

4. The following adjectives remain unchanged except in the oblique plural :—

خائيسته *Khāiesta*		beautiful or handsome.
ناکاره *nā kāra*		bad, ugly.
خپه *khapa*		unhappy.
دروغ *darogh*		lie.
رښتیا *rikhtiā*		true.
څینی *ziné or bāzé*		some.
پوره *pūra*		complete.
بی حیا *bé hayā*		shameless.
بی وفا *bé wafā*		faithless.
وریا *wéryā*		free, gratis.
مفت *muft*		free, gratis.
ټکره *takra*		strong.

5. The following adjectives are irregular
as :—

M. S.	M. P.	F. S.	F. P.	
مر Mar	مرُہ mruh	مرہ mra	مری mré	dead
لُند lŭnd	لؤندہ lăunduh	لؤندہ launda	لؤندی laundé	wet.
کوٴر kōg	کار۔رہ kāguh	کرہ kaga	کری kagé	crooked.
درؤند drūnd	درانہ drānuh	درنہ drana	درنی drané	heavy.
مور mōr	مارہ māruh	مرہ mara	موری maré	rich, replete.
پروت prōt	پراتہ prātuh	پرتہ prata	پرتی prate	prostrate.
زور zōr	زارہ zāruh	زرہ zara	زری zaré	old.
تود tōd	تاودہ tāuduh	تودہ tauda	تودی taudé	hot.
تریو trīw	تاروہ tārwuh	تروہ trawa	تروی tarwé	sour
خور khōg	خواگرہ khwā-guh	خوگہ khwaga	خوری khwagé	sweet.
تریکس trikh	تارخبہ tārkhuh	تارخہ tārkha	ترخی tarkhé	bitter
وروست vrōst	وراستہ vrāstuh	ورستہ vrasta	ورستی vrasté	rotten.
شین shin	شنہ shnuh	شنہ shna	شنی shné	green.

رُوند *rūnd* راندهٔ *rānduh* رنده *randa* رندی *randé*
blind.

کُونْر *kūnr* کانْرهٔ *kānruh* کنرہ *kanra* کنْرِی *kanré*
deaf.

پوښ *pōkh* پاښهٔ *pākhuh* پښہ *pakha* پښی *pakhé*
cooked, ripe.

6.   COMPARISON OF ADJECTIVE.

There is no special form for the Comparative Degree in Pushtu. Comparison is expressed by using the Positive Degree with the Ablative case as :—

أس لهٔ اوښ نه ګرندی دی = *Ass luh ūkh na garanday day* the horse is swifter than the Camel.

SUPERLATIVE.

There is no special form for the superlative degree in Pushtu. It is expressed by using the positive degree with the following phrases as :—

لهٔ ټولو نه *luh tōlō na* Used by Khalils.
لهٔ وارو نه *luh wārō na* } than all „ „ Yusafzais
لهٔ جمله ونه *luh jumlaō na* „ „ Afghans.

as :—

دا هلک لهٔ ټولو نه هوښیار دی *dā halak luh tōlo na hukhyār day*

This boy is the cleverest

Section 7.

THE NUMERAL CARDINAL NUMBERS.

1	—	١	يو	*Yau.*
2	—	٢	دوﮦ	*dwa.*
3	—	٣	دري	*dré.*
4	—	۴	څلور	*salōr.*
5	—	۵	پنځه	*pinzuh.*
6	—	٦	شپږ	*shpag.*
7	—	٧	اوﮦ	*owuh.*
8	—	٨	اتﮥ	*atuh.*
9	—	٩	نهﮥ	*nahuh.*
10	—	١٠	لس	*las.*
11	—	١١	يو لس	*yaolas.*
12	—	١٢	دو لس	*dōlas.*
13	—	١٣	ديارلس	*diārlas.*
14	—	١۴	څوارلس	*swārlas.*
15	—	١۵	پنځه لس	*pinzalas.*
16	—	١٦	شپارس	*shpāras.*
17	—	١٧	اولس	*owalas.*
18	—	١٨	اتلس	*atalas.*
19	—	١٩	نولس	*nūlas.*
20	—	٢٠	شل	*shal.*
21	—	٢١	يو ويشت	*yau wisht.*
22	—	٢٢	دوﮦ ويشت	*dwa wisht.*
23	—	٢٣	در ويشت	*dar wisht.*
24	—	٢۴	څلريشت	*salréisht.*
25	—	٢۵	پنځه ويشت	*pinza wisht.*

26	—	۲٦	شپږ ویشت	*shpag wisht.*
27	—	۲۷	اوۀ ویشت	*owuh wisht.*
28	—	۲۸	اتۀ ویشت	*atuh wisht.*
29	—	۲۹	نهۀ ویشت	*nahuh wisht.*
30	—	۳۰	دیرش	*dérsh.*
31	—	۳۱	یو دیرش	*yau dérsh.*
32	–	۳۲	دوه دیرش	*dwa dérsh.*
33	—	۳۳	درې دیرش	*dré dérsh.*
34	—	۳۴	څلور دیرش	*salŏr dérsh.*
35	—	۳۵	پنځۀ دیرش	*pinzuh dérsh.*
36	—	۳٦	شپږ دیرش	*shpag dérsh.*
37	—	۳۷	اوۀ دیرش	*owuh dérsh.*
38	—	۳۸	اتۀ دیرش	*atuh dérsh.*
39	—	۳۹	نهۀ دیرش	*nahuh dérsh.*
40	—	۴۰	څلویښت	*salwékht.*
50	—	۵۰	پنځوس	*panzōs.*
60	—	٦۰	شپېتۀ	*shpétuh*
70	—	۷۰	اویا	*auyā.*
80	—	۸۰	اتیا	*atyā.*
90	—	۹۰	نوي	*navi.*
100	—	۱۰۰	سلَ	*sal.*
200	—	۲۰۰	دوه سوَ	*dwa swa.*
1000	—	۱۰۰۰	زرَ	*zar.*
2000	—	۲۰۰۰	دوه زرَ	*dwa zara.*
100000		۱۰۰۰۰۰	لک	*Lak.*

پۀ سلګونو	*Puh salgūnō*	Hundreds of
پۀ زر ګونو	*Puh zargūnō*	Thousands of.
پۀ لکونو	*Puh lakūnō*	"Laks" of.

Numerals (both cardinal and ordinal) are used in Pushtu as adjectival nouns. When governed by any preposition and post position they are put into the Oblique Plural as :—

په څلورو سړو باندې *Puh saloro saro bāndé* On four men.

يو = *Yau* becomes يوه = *Yawa* in the case of Feminine as :—

يوه ښځه *Yawa Khaza* One woman.

The Ordinal numbers are formed (with the exception of اول = *Awal* = 1st and دويم = *Dwém* = 2nd) by adding م = *m* to the Cardinals. They form the Feminine by the addition of ه = *h* (soft).

CARDINAL.

Masculine.	Feminine.
دري سړي *Dré sari* three men	درى ښځي *Dré khazé* three women

ORDINAL.

Masculine.	Feminine.
دريم سړى *Drém saray* 3rd man.	دريمه ښځه *Dréma khaza* 3rd woman
څلورم *saloram* 4th	
پنځم *pinzam* 5th	
شپږم *shpagam* 6th	

In Pushtu only the simpler fractions can be expressed :—

EXAMPLES.

1/4	پاؤ	*Pāw*
1/2	نيم	*Nim*
3/4	درى پاؤ	*Dré Pāwa*
1¼	پنځۀ پاؤ	*Pinzuh Pāwa*
1½	يو نيم	*Yau Nim*
1¾	پاؤ کم دوه	*Pāw kam dwa*
2¼	پاؤ باند دوه	*Pāw bāndé dwa*
2½	دوه نيم	*dwa nim*

Some times the villagers count by *Shal* = a score the plural of which is *Shalé* as

دوه شلى *dwa shalé*   two scores 40.

درى شلي *dré shalé*   three scores 60

پنځۀ دا پاس درى شلي *Pinzuh dapāsa* 5 over 3 scores dréshalé   65.

پنځۀ کم درى شلي *Pinzuh kam* 5 less of dréshalé   3 scores 55.

وارۀ *Wāra* all.   put after a cardinal number indicates universality.

دوارۀ *dwāra*   both.

درى وارۀ *dré wāra*   all three.

څلور وارۀ *salōr wāra*   all four.

Multiplication by degree is expressed by using the particle په = *Puh* between the cardinal يو = *yau* and any other cardinal as :—

يو په دوه *yau puh dwa*   twice as much.

يو په درى *yau puh dré*   thrice as much.

يو په څلور *yau puh salōr*   four times as much.

Some times the word چه = *chand* is used after
any cardinal number to express the same
meaning as above.

دو چند *do chand*	twice as much.
دری چند *dré chand*	thrice as much.
څلور چند *salōr chand*	four times as much.

Section 8.

PRONOUNS.

1st Person.

Singular.			Plural.		
Nom :	زٔه *zuh*	I.	مُونږ *mūng*	we.
Acc :	ما *mā*	me.	مُونږ *mūng*	us.
Agent :	ما *mā*	by me.	مُونږ *mūng*	by us.
Gent :	زما *zamā*	my.	زمُونږ *zamūng*	our.
Dat :	ما ته *mā ta* to me.	مُونږ ته *mūng ta*	to us.
Abl :	له ما نه *luh mā* from	له مُونږ نه *luh mūng* from
	na me.	*na* us.

Loc :—
په ما کښې *puh mā* in me په مُونږ کښې *puh mūng* in us.
ké *ké*

Voc :—
ای زٔه *ay zuh* oh me! ای مُونږ *ay mūng* oh us!

2nd Person.

Singular.			Plural.		
Nom :	ته *tuh*	thou.	تا سو *tā so*	you.
Acc :	تا *tā*	thee.	تا سو *tā so*	you.
Agent :	تا *tā*	by thee	تا سو *tā so*	by you

Singular.			Plural.		
Gent:	ستا *stā*	thy.	ستاسو	*stā so*	your.
Dat :	تاته *tā ta*	to thee.	تا سوته	*tā so ta*	to you.
Abl:	له تا نه *luh tā na*	from thee.	له تا سونه	*luh tā_ so na*	from you.
Loc :—					
پۀ تا کښ *puh tā ké*		in thee.	پۀ تاسو کښ *puh tāso ké*		in you.
Voc :—					
اي تۀ *ay tuh*		oh thou	اى تا سو *ay tāso*		oh you

3rd Person.

Singular.			Plural.		
Nom :	هغه *hagha*	he	هغوي *haghūi*		they.
Acc :	هغه *hagha*	him.	هغوي *hughūi*		them.
Agent:	هغۀ *haghuh*	by him	هغوي *haghūi*		by them.
Gent:	دَ هغۀ *da haghuh*	his.	دَ هغوي *da haghūi*		their.
Dat :—					
هغۀ ته *haghuh ta*		to him	هغوي ته *haghūi ta*		to them.
Abl :—					
له هغۀ نه *luh haghuh na*		from him.	له هغوي نه *luh hughūi na*		from them.
Loc :—					
پۀ هغۀ کښ *puh haghuh ké*		in him.	پۀ هغوي کښ *puh haghūi ké*		in them.
Voc :—					
اى هغۀ *ay haghuh*		oh him !	اي هغوي *ay haghūi*		oh them.

NOTE:—A. Some times ‌دَی‌ = *day* is used for هغه = *hagha*, when the object is close at hand and it is inflected thus :—·

	Singular.		Plural.	
Nom:	دَی *day*	he	دوی *dui*	they
Agent:	دَ *duh*	by him	دوی *dui*	by them.

B. The following particles are used as pronouns in three cases, accusative, agentive and genitive.

Singular.   Plural.

م *mé* me, by me or my   مو *mō* us, by us or our.

دَ *dé* thee, by thee or thy   مو *mō* you, by you or yours

یې *yé* him, by him or his   یې *yé* them, by them or their

EXAMPLE :

Accus : هغه م وهي *hagha mé wahi*   He beats me

Agent : هغه م ووهلو *hagha mé wo wahalo*
                         I beat him

Geni : کتاب م *kitab mé*   My book

Ordinarily in Pushtu sentences the subject is placed first, the object second and the Verb last, but where the above particles are used, in the case of a transitive verb Past-Tense, the object is put first and the subject second.

هغه م و لیدلو *hagha mé wo lidalo*   I saw him.

C. The following particles are used as prepositions and have the force of personal pronouns :—

پرِ *pré* on him, on them, on her, or on it.

ترِ *tré* from him, from them, from her or from it.

There was only one chair in the room and he himself was sitting on it.

پهٔ کمره کښې خالي يوه کُرسَي وَه   " *puh kamra ké khāli yawa*
او هغه پخپله پرِناست وَه   *kursai wah aw hagha*
pakhpala pré nast woh ".

DEMONSTRATIVE PRONOUNS.

There are only three Demonstrative Pronouns in Pushtu which are inflected thus :—

Nom دا *dā* this or these   دغه *dagha* this or these.

هغه *hagha*   that or those.

Agent دې *dé* by this   د غي *daghé* by this
or these   or these.

هغي *haghé*   by that or by those.

دا ځما نوکر دی *dā zamā* this is my servant.
naukar day

لهٔ دې هلک نه *luh dé halak na* from this boy.

دغه څوک دیَ *dagha sōk day* who is this.

دَ دغي هلک *da daghé* this boy's father is

پلار مِ نوکر دیَ *halak plār mé* my servant
naukar day

هغه ځما کلیَ دیَ *haghá zamā* that is my village.
kalay day

دَ هغیِ کای نه هغه څوا *da haghé kali* beyond that
na hagha khwā village.

THE INTERROGATIVE PRONOUNS.

څوک *sok* who.

څه *suh* what.

کوم *kum* which

کوم یو *kum yau* which one.

څو یا څو مره *sō or somra* how many or how much.

څوک *sōk* is inflected thus :—

Nom څوک *sōk* who	used in singular and
Agent چا *chā* by whom	plural both numbers.

m. s.	m. p.	f. s.	f. p.	ob. p.
کوم سړیَ	کوم سړی	کومه ښځه	کومیِ ښځی	دَ کومو خلقو
kum saray	*kum sari*	*kuma khaza*	*kumé khazé*	*da kumo hhalqo*
which man.	which men	which woman	which women	of which people.

THE RELATIVE PRONOUNS.

There is only one relative pronoun in Pushtu
چه = *Chi,* which is also used as a conjunction
for joining two sentences. It also makes any
interrogative word relative as :—

1. هغه سړی۰راوبله چه *hagha saray* Call that man
   پرون دلته وه *rā wōbala chi* who was here
   parūn dalta yesterday.
   woh

2. هغهٔ و چه نوم مٰ *haguh wō* he said that my
   احمد دی *wé chi nūm* name is Ahmad
   mé Ahmad (direct speech)
   day he said his
   name was
   Ahmad.

3. څوک چه *sōk chi* he who.
   هر څوک چه را شي *har sōk chi* whoever may
   rāshee come.
   کوم چه دِ خوښ وي *kum chi dé* whichever you
   khwakh wé like.
   کوم یو چه د خوښ وي *kum yau chi* which ever one
   dé khwakh wé you like.
   څهٔ چه کوی *suh chi kawé* whatever you
   do.

THE CORRELATIVE PRONOUNS.

Interrogative			Correlative		
که	*kuh*	if	نو	*no*	then.
چه	*chi*	} when.	نو	*no*	then.
کله چه	*kala chi*		نو	*no*	then.
څومره چه	*sōmra chi*	as much as	دومره	*dōmra*	that much.
څنګه چه	*sanga chi*	what ever	هسے	*hasé*	thus.

EXAMPLE.

كه ستا خوهند	*kuh stā khwakha*	
وي نو لارشه	*wī nō lārsha*	go if you like.
چه يا كله چه	*chi or kala chi mā*	he also spoke
ما وو نو هغه	*wo wé no haghuh*	when I spoke.
هم و و	*hum wo wé*	
څو مره چه	*sōmra chi ghwāré*	take as much as
غوارى دومره	*dōmra wākhla*	you want Liter-
واخله		ally: as much as
		you want take so
		much.
څنګه چه د	*sanga chi dé khwa-*	do as you like.
خوښه وي	*hha wi hasé kawa*	Literally: what-
هسى كوه		ever you wish,
		thus do.

INDEFINITE PRONOUNS.

In Pushtu the simple indefinite pronouns
are :—

څوك	*sōk*	some one.
څه	*suh*	some, something or anything.
څينى	*ziné*	some.
هيڅ	*hiss*	no, or nothing. anyone, any-
		thing which is followed by
		a negative *e. g.*

هيڅڅوك نشته *hiss sōk*
    nishta there is no body.

هيڅ نشته *hiss nishta* there is nothing.

څوك *sōk* becomes چا *chā* in the oblique case *e. g.*

هيڅ چا ته مۀ وايه یا   *hiss chā ŧa muh wāya*   Don't tell any one

هيڅا ته مۀ وايه   *hichā ŧā muh wāya*   ,, ,, ,, ,,

څينی = *ziné* takes the regular inflection and څۀ = *suh* and هيڅ = *hiss* are indeclinable.

EXAMPLE.

څوک په دی کور کښی شته   *sōk puh dé kor ké shta*   is there anyone in this house?

څوک خو شته   *sōk kho shta*   there is someone (*Kho* = really.)

څۀ شیَ راکه   *suh shay rākra*   give me something.

څینی هوښیاردي څینی کم عقل   *ziné hukhyār di ziné kam akal*   some are clever, some foolish.

څينو خلقو ته   *zinō khalqō ta*   to some people.

Numerous compound indefinite pronouns are formed from the above thus :—

هر = *har* every, combining with څوک = *sōk*, څۀ = *suh* and یو = *yau* makes:— هرڅوک = *har sōk* every one هرڅۀ = *har suh* every thing

هر یو = *har yau* every one and similarly بل = *bal* another and نور = *nōr* more or others make:— بل څوک = *bal sōk* anyone else.

نور څوک = *nŏr sŏk* any others بل څه = *bal suh*
anything else نور څه = *nŏr suh* something more.

نور هيڅ = *nŏr hiss* nothing else بل يو = *bal yau*
another.

VERBAL NOUNS.

In Pushtu the verbal nouns can be formed
in two ways Viz:—

1. By changing the final ل = L of the
infinitive into نه = *na* which is always feminine
singular as :—

تړل *taral*   to bind.   تړنه *tarana* binding

هيرول *hérawal* to forget هيرونه *herawana* forgetting.

ښودل *khodal* to show. ښودنه *khŏdana* showing

2. The infinitive itself can be used as a
verbal noun as :—

تړل *taral*   to bind or binding.

هيرول *hérawal* to forget or forgetting.

NOTE :—This form of the verbal noun is
always masculine plural. So when it is governed
by a preposition or post position the oblique
plural should be used as :—

په تړلو کښ *puh taralo ké*   in binding.

په هيرولو باندِ *puh hérawalo* on forgetting
bándé

The Noun of agency is formed by changing
the final ل = *l*, of the infinitive into ونکی = *ŭnkay*

which is declinable as :—

ليکل *likal* to write ليکونکی *likūnkay* writer.

دَ ليکو نکي نوم *da likūnki* the name of the writer
nūm

In the case of an intransitive verb it also
expresses the meaning of "to be about to" as:—

را تلل *rātlal* to come هغه را تلونکی دی *hagha rā-*
tlūnkay day
He is about
to come.

NOTE :—To express "to be about to" use the
preposition *pa-ké* with verbal-noun as :—

هغه پۀ تلو کښ دي *hagha puh*   he is about to go.
tlo ké day

ABSTRACT OR DERIVED NOUNS.

(Substantive and Adjective.)

Secondary nouns are derived from primary
by the following suffixes : — ا = *a*, ي = *i*

ستيا = *stia* توب = *tōb* والی = *walay* ګلي = *gali.*
تون = *tūn* تيا = *tia* :—

غل *ghal*   a thief   becomes   غلا *ghla* theft.

خوښ *khwakh* pleased   „   خوښي *khwakhi*
pleasure.

سپاهي *spahi* soldier   „   سپاهي توب *spahi tōb*
توب soldiering.

شين *shin* green   „   شينوالي *shin walay*
green-ness

پيژندل *péjhandal* knowing becomes پيژندګلى *péjhandgali*
كلى acquain-
tance.

بيل *bial*   separate ,,   بيلتون *bīltūn*
separation.

ناجوړ *nājōr*   ill   ناجوړتيا *nājōrtiā*
illness.

ميلمه *mèlma*   guest   ميلمستيا *mèlmastia*
hospitality

Section 9.

THE VERB.

As regards their formation, the Pushtu verbs
are devided into seven different classes: —

1. Regular transitive.
2. Regular intransitive.
3. Irregular transitive.
4. Irregular intransitive.
5. Compound transitive.
6. Compound intransitive.
7. Verbs which are irregular in the formation of the present Tense and Tenses derived
from it.

Class. I.

REGULAR TRANSITIVE.

All verbs in Pushtu end in ل = *l* :—

وهل ;   *Wahal*   to beat, strike.

تړل	*taral*	to bind, tie.
ليکل	*likal*	to write.
بلل	*balal*	to call.
خوړل	*khwaral*	to eat.
سکل	*skal*	to drink.
منل	*manal*	to obey, agree, accept.
ساتل	*satal*	to keep, guard, cherish
استول يا ليږل	*astawal* or	
	légal	to send.
کرل	*karal*	to sow.
ګنډل	*gandal*	to sew.
خريل	*khrayal*	to shave.
ګنړل	*ganral*	to consider.
چيچل	*chichal*	to bite.
ښيل	*khayal*	to show or direct.

THE PRESENT TENSE.

Change the final ل = L of the infinitive into:—

1st P.	م *m*			ؤ *oo*	
2nd P.	ې *é*	} Singular.		ئ *ai*	} Plu.
3rd P.	ي *ee*			ي *ee*	

as

زۀ وهم	*zuh waham*	I beat	
تۀ وهې	*tuh wahé*	thou beatest	} Sing.
هغه وهي	*hagha wahee*	he beats.	

عءؤ نِر وهؤ   *M ūng wahoo*   We beat

تا سو وهيِ   *tāso wahai*   you beat   } Plu.

هغؚرى وهيِ   *hagh ʊi wahee* they beat

THE FUTURE TENSE.

Prefix به = *Ba*, to the Present tense as :—

زؤ به وهم   *zuh ba waham*   I will beat

تؤ به وهى   *tuh ba wahé*   thou wilt beat

هغه به وهى   *hagha ba*   he will beat
             wahee

} Sing.

مؤ نِر به وهؤ   *M ūng ba*   we will beat
             wahoo

تا سو به وهيِ *tāso ba wahai* you will beat   } Plu.

هغوى به وهيِ   *haghui ba*   they will
             wahee   beat.

THE AORIST (PRESENT SUBJUNCTIVE.)

Prefix :— و = *wo*, to the present tense as :—

زؤ ووهم   *zuh wo waham*   I may beat

تؤ ووهى   *tuh wo wahé*   thou mayst beat

هغه ووهيِ   *hagha wo*   he may
             wahee   beat

} Sing.

مؤنِر وو هؤ   *M ūng wo wahoo* we may beat

تا سو ووهيِ   *tāso wo wahai*   you may beat.   } Plu.

هغوِ ووهبِ   *haghūi wo*   they may beat.
             wahee

THE IMPERATIVE.

Is formed by changing the final ر = *m* of the
aorist into ه = *a* (H. soft) to form singular and
into ي = *ai* to form plural as :—

و وهﻪ   *wo waha*   beat (thou)

و وهﻰ؛   *wo wahai*   beat (you)

THE PROHIBITIVE.

Is formed by changing the first و = *wo* of the
imperative into مﻪ = *muh* as : —

مﻪ وهﻪ   *muh waha*   don't beat (thou)

مﻪ وهﻰ؛   *muh wahai*   don't beat (you)

THE IMPERFECT TENSE.

Add to the infinitive the following suffixes :—

1st P. ر *m* ⎫   ﻭ *oo* ⎫
2nd P. ي *é* ⎬ Singular.   ﻯ *ai* ⎬
3rd P. و *ō* ⎭   infinitive ⎬ Plural.
3r P. F. ه *h*   ي *é* ⎭

NOTE :—(A) The verb agrees with the subject
in the present and object in all past tenses.

(B) Object in the past tenses is always put
into the nominative form as :—

هﻐﻪ زﻩ وهﻠم   *haghuh zuh*
                wahulam   he was beating
                            me

هﻐﻪ تﻪ وهﻠﻰ   *haghuh tuh*
                wahalé   he was beating
                            thee

هﻐﻪ هﻐﻪ وهﻠو   *haghuh hagha*
                wahalō   he was beating
                            him   Sing.

هﻐﻪ هﻐﻪ وهﻠﻪ   *haghuh hagha*
                wahalō   he was beating
                            her

هغهٔ موزِ, وهلؤ *haghuh mūng* he was beating
wahaloo   us

هغهٔ تاسو وهلي *haghuh tāso*   he was beating
wahalai   you

هغهٔ هغوی وهل *haghuh haghūi* he was beating
wahal   them

هغهٔ هغوی وهلي *haghuh haghūi* he was beating
wahalé   them (fem.)

} Plu.

ما هغه وهلو *mā hagha wahalō*   I was beating
him.

موزِ, هغه وهله *mūng hagha wahala* We were beating her.

PAST HABITUAL.

Prefix به = *ba* to the imperfect tense as :—
Singular.

هغهٔ زِ به وهلم *haghuh zuh*   he used to beat me or
ba wahalam   he would beat me.

هغهٔ تهٔ به وهلي *haghuh tuh*   do.   thee
ba wahalé

هغهٔ هغه به وهلو *haghuh hagha*   do.   him
ba wahalō

هغهٔ هغه بهٔ وهله *haghuh hagha*   do.   her
ba wahala

Plural.

هغهٔ موزِ, به وهلؤ *haghuh mūng* he used to beat us or
ba wahaloo   he would beat us

هغهٔ تاسو بد وهلي *haghuh tāso*   do.   you
ba wahalai

هغهٔ هغوی به وهل *haghuh haghūi*   do.   them
ba wahal

هغهٔ هغوِي بهِ وهلي *haghuh haghui* he used to beet them *ba wahalé* or he would beat them (fem.)

ما هغوِي بهِ وهل *mā haghui ba wahal*   I used to beat them.

PAST DEFINITE.

Prefix و = *wo*, to the imperfect tense as :—

هغهٔ زهٔ و وهلم *haghuh zuh wō wahalam*   he beat me ⎫

هغهٔ تهٔ و وهلي *haghuh tuh wō wahalé*   do. thee ⎪

هغهٔ هغهٔ و وهلو *haghuh hagha wō wahalo*   do. him ⎬ Sing.

هغهٔ هغهٔ و وهله *haghuh hagha wō wahalah*   do. her ⎭

هغهٔ مؤنږ و وهلو *haghuh mūng wō wahaloo*   he beat us. ⎫

هغهٔ تاسو و وهلي *haghuh tāso wō wahalai*   do you. ⎪

هغهٔ هغوِ و وهل *haghuh haghū wō wahal*   do them. ⎬ Plu.

هغهٔ هغوِي و وهلي *haghuh haghui wō wahalé*   do them. (feminine). ⎭

جنۍ هلک و وهلو *jinai halak wō wahalo*   the girl beat the boy.

هلک جنۍ و وهله *halak jinai wō wahāla*   the boy beat the girl.

THE PAST PARTICIPLE.

Is formed by adding ی = *ay*, to the infinitive as :—

وهلی *wahalay*   beaten.

This is used as an adjective and is inflected as nouns ending in ‌ی = *ay* as :—

و هلی سری	*wahalay saray*	beaten man.
و هلی سری	*wahali sart*	beaten men:

د و هلو سرو	*da wahalo saro*	of the beaten men (Ob. Plu.)
و هلی جنی ته	*wahalé jinai ta*	to the beaten girl (F. Ob. S.)
و هلو ښځو ته	*wahalo khazo ta*	to the beaten women (F. Ob. P.)

PERFECT TENSE.

Conjugate the present tense of the verb to be after the past participle as :—

هغه زۀ و هلی یم	*haghuh zuh wahalay yam*	he has beaten me	
هغه تۀ و هلی یې	*haghuh tuh wahalay yé*	he has beaten thee	Sing
هغه هغه وهلی دی	*haghuh hagha wahalay day*	he has beaten him.	
هغه هغه و هلی ده	*haghuh hagha wahalé dah*	he has beaten her.	
هغه مۇږ وهلی یؤ	*haghuh mūng wahali yū*	he has beaten us.	
هغه تاسو وهلی یي	*haghuh tāso wahali yai*	he has beaten you.	
هغه هغوی وهلی دی	*haghuh haghui wahali dee*	he has beaten them.	Plu.
هغه هغوی وهلی دی	*haghuh haghui wahalé dee*	he has beaten them (Feminine.)	

خَښى سوى وهلى *khazé saray*   the woman has
دى   *wahalay day*   beaten the man.

سوى خَښه وهلى ده *sari shaza*   the man has beaten
wahalé dah   the woman.

هلكا نو هندو وهلى *halakāno*   the boys have
hindū   beaten a Hindu.
wahalay day

PLUPERFECT TENSE.

Conjugate the past tense of the verb to be
after the past participle as :—

هغهٔ زهٔ وهلى وم *hāghuh zuh*   he had beaten
wahalay wam   me.

هغهٔ تهٔ وهلى وى *hāghuh tuh*   he had beaten
wahalay wé   thee.   } Sing

هغهٔ هغه وهلى وهٔ *haghuh hagha*   he had beaten
wahalay woh   him.

هغهٔ هغه وهلى وهٔ *haghuh hagha*   he had beaten
whalé wah   her.

هغهٔ مونږ وهلى وو *haghuh mūng*   he had beaten
wahali woo   us.

هغهٔ تاسو وهلى وى *haghuh tāso*   he had beaten
wahali wai   you.

هغهٔ هغوى وهلى وو *haghuh*   he had beaten
haghui   them.   } Plu.
wahali woo

هغهٔ هغوى وهلى *haghuh*   he had beaten
haghui   them
دى *wahalé wé*   (feminine).

هلک خَشَ وهلی زَه *halak khaza*   The boy had
          wahalé wah   beaten the
                             woman.

خشی هلک وهلَی ژه *khazé halak*   The woman had
          wahalay woh   beaten a boy

PRESENT POTENTIAL.

Add ي = *ay* to the infinitive and conjugate the word شم = *sham* after it according to the present personal terminations as :—

زَه وهلَی شم *zuh wahalay*
         sham   I can beat.

تهٔ وهلَی شی *tuh wahalay* Thou canst
        shé   beat.   Sing.

هغه وهلَی شی *hagha*
     wahalay shee He or she can
                beat.

مؤنږ وهلَی شؤ *mung*
     wahalay shoo We can beat.

تاسو وهلَی شی *tāso wāhalay*
        shai   You can beat.   Plu.

هغوی وهلَی شی *haghui*
     wahalay shee They can beat
                M. & F.

هغه ما وهلَی شی *hagha mā*
یا *wahalay shee* or
هغه م وهلَی شی *hagha mé*
     wahalay shee He can beat me.

زهٔ هغه وهلَی شم *zuh hagha*
یا *wahalay sham* or
زهٔ یی وهلَی شم *zuh yé wahalay*
     sham   I can beat him.

THE PAST POTENTIAL.

Add ی = *ay* to the infinitive and conjugate the word شوم = *shwam* afrer it according to the past personal terminations :—

هغۀ زۀ وهلی شوم	*haghuh zuh wahalay shwam*	He could beat me or he was able to beat me.	
هغۀ تۀ وهلی شوی	*haghuh tuh wahalay shwé*	He could beat thee.	Sing
هغۀ هغه وهلی شو یا شۀ	*haghuh hagha wahalay sho or shuh*	He could beat him.	
هغۀ هغه وهلی شوه یا شوله	*haghuh hagha wahalay shwa or shwala*	He could beat her.	
هغۀ موږ وهلی شوو یا شو	*haghuh mūng wahaly shwoo or shoo*	He could beat us.	
هغۀ تاسو وهلی شوی	*haghuh tāso wahalay shwai*	He could beat you.	Plu.
هغۀ هغوی وهلی شوو یا شول	*haghuh haghūi wahalay shwoo or shwal*	He could beat them,	
هغۀ هغوی وهلی شوی یا شوئی	*haghuh haghūi wahalay shwé or shwalé*	He could beat them (Feminine.)	
ځما نوکر هغه وهلی شو	*zamā naukar hagha wahalay sho*	My servant could beat him	
هلک جنۍ وهلی شوه	*halak jinai wahalay shwa*	The boy could beat the girl.	

Diagram showing all the tenses of regular transitive verb. It is quite clear that ز = wo and به = ba are added twice, once to the present to form aorist and future. Then to the imperfect to form past and habitual. All one needs to now are the Present, Imperfect, and Past participle. From these three principal parts of the verb all the other tenses are formed.

PERFECT
وهلی یم = *Wahaley yam* — Have beaten.

S. P.
yam ga
ye yai
dey dee
dah dee f.

PLUPERFECT
وهلی وم = *Wahaley wam* — Had beaten.

S. P.
woo woom
wai woo
woo wai
wah woo f.

PRESENT POTENTIAL
وهلی شم = *Wahaley sham* — Can beat.

S. P.
sham shwam
she shwai
she sho
she f. shwah f.

PAST POTENTIAL
وهلی شوم = *Wahaly shwam* — Could beat.

PAST PARTICIPLE
وهلی = *Wahaley* — Beaten.

S. P.
shwam shwoo
shwe shwai
sho shwal
shwa shwala f.

Add ی = ay to inf.

HABITUAL
به وهلم = *Ba wahalam* — Used to beat.

IMPERFECT
وهلم = *Wahalam* — Was beating.

PAST
وهلم = *Wahalam* — (Did)beat.

REGULAR TRANSITIVE VERB.
وهل = *Wahal* — To beat.

add to inf.

PROHIBITIVE
مه وهه = *Mah waha* — Don't beat.

IMPERATIVE
وهه = *Wo waha* — Beat.

AORIST
وهم = *Wo waham* — (I) may beat.

FUTURE
به وهم = *Ba waham* — Will beat.

PRESENT
وهم = *Waham* — (I) beat.

Change the final ل = l of the inf. into (1) ه...

REGULAR INTRANSITIVE VERBS CLASS II.

رسيدل *rasédal* to arrive خ‍يدل‍ذ *sasédal* = to leak.

اوسيدل *osédal*   to live.

بهيدل *bahédal*   to flow.

زغليدل *zghalédal*   to run.

تﻬتيدل *takhtédal*   to flee.

زليدل *zalédal*   to shine.

خوزيدل *khwazédal* to move.

رپيدل *raŗédal*   to tremble.

كړيدل *karédal*   to pine.

غزريدل *ghwarédal* to spread.

غوريدل *ghurédal*   to thunder.

From the above examples it is quite clear that all regular intransitive verbs end in ‍يدل = *édal*.

PRESENT TENSE.

Change the final د = *d* of the infinitive into ‍ر = *g* and apply the rules of regular transitive verb as :—

زﮦ رسيږم *zuh raségam*   I arrive.

تﮦ رسيږي *tuh raségé*   thou arrivest.

هغﮦ رسيږي *hagha raségee*   he arrives.   } Sing.

" " "   she "

موﮊ رسيږو *mūng raségoo*   we arrive.

تاﺳو رسيږي *tāso raségai*   you arrive.

هغوى رسيږي *haghūi raségee* they arrive. } Plur.

" " " " " (f.)

NOTE :—See syntax rule No. 3 for explanation of the formation of transitive from intransitive verbs of class II.

67

DIAGRAM OF THE INTRANSITIVE VERB.

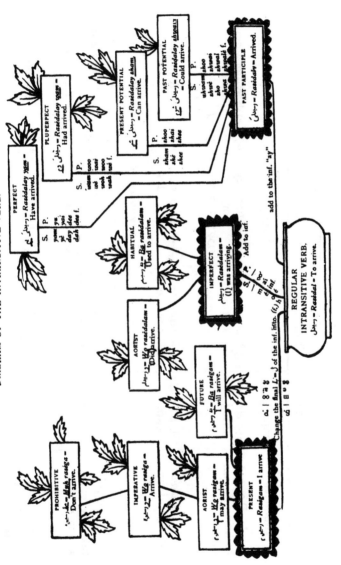

THE MODERN PUSHTO INSTRUCTOR

IRREGULAR TRANSITIVE VERBS CLASS III.

Infinitive.	Imperative.	Prohibitive.	Past participle.	Past.
راوړل Rāwral to bring (in animate.)	راوړه Rāwra bring.	مه راوړه muh rāwra don't bring.	راوړلى rāworalay or راوړى rāworay } brought.	راوړلم Rāworalam or راوړم Rawram brought.
راوستل Rāwastal to lead. animate.	راوله Rāwala lead.	مه راوله muh rāwala don't lead.	راوستلى rāwastalay or راوستى rāwastay } Led.	راوستلم Rāwastalam or راوستم Rāwastam Led.
وړل Vral to take away. inanimate.	يوسه Yausa take away.	مه وړ muh vra don't take away.	وړى woray or وړلى woralay } led away taken away	يوړلم Yawralam or يوړم Yauram took away.
بيول Biwal to lead away. animate.	بوز Bōza lead away.	مه بيايه muh biyaya don't lead away	بيولى biwalay } led away	بوتلم Botlam led away.

کېښودل kėkhodal to place or put.

کول kawal to do.

1. Imperfect راوړلم rāworalam was bringing.
2. Habitual به راوړلم ba rāworalam used to bring.

کېږده Kėgda place.   مه ږده muh gda don't place.

کړه Kra do.   مه کوه muh kawa don't do.

1. Aorist راوړم rāworam may bring.

---

1. Present:— راوړم rāworam I bring.
2. Future:— به راوړم ba rāworam will bring.

کېښودلی kėkho-dalay or ایښی ikhāy

کړی kāray

{ placed }
{ done }

1. Perfect:— راوړلی yam rāworalay yam have brought.
2. Pluperfect. راوړلی وم rāworalay wam had brought.
3. Present poten راوړلی شم rāworalay sham can bring.
4. Past.poten. راوړلی با راوړی rāworalay or rāworay shwam = could bring.

کېښودلم kėkho-dalam placed.

کرلم kralam or کرم kram did.

{ placed }
{ done }

GRAMMAR

IRREGULAR INTRANSITIVE VERBS CLASS IV.

Infinitive.	Imperative.	Prohibitive.	Past Participle.	Past.
تلل *tlal* to go.	لارشه *larsha* go.	مه زه *muh za* don't go.	تلی *talay* gone.	لارم *lārm* I went.
راتلل *ratlal* to come.	راشه *rasha* come.	مه راځه *muh raza* don't come.	راغلی *rāghalay* come.	راغلم *rāghlam* I came.
کېناستل *kénastal* to sit.	کېنه *kéna* sit.	مه کېنه *muh kéna* don't sit.	کېناستلی *kénasta-lay* sat.	کېناستلم *kénāsta-lam* I sat.
سملاستل *samlastal* to lie down.	سمله *samla* lie down.	مه سمله *muh samla* don't lie down.	سملاستلی *samlāst-alay* laid down	سملاستلم *samlāsta-lam* I lay down.
کېدل *kédal* or شول *shwal* to become.	شه *sha* be or become.	مه کېږه *muh kéga* dont be or don't become.	شوی *shwaay* been or become.	شوم *shwaam* I became.

69a

Imperfect.	Aorist.	Present, Future.	Perfect.
1. Imperfect. تلم *tlam* or *talalam* was going.	1. Aorist. لارشم *larsham* may go.	1. Present. ځم *zam* I go.	1. Perfect. تللی *talay yam* have gone.
2. Habitual. به تلم *ba tlalam* or به تلم *ba talam* used to go.		2. Future. به ځم *ba zam* will go.	2. Pluperfect. تللی وم *talay wam* had gone.
			3. Present Potential. تللی شم *tlay sham* can go.
			4. Past Potential تللی *tlay* *shwam* could go.

NOTE:—In the verbs "to come, become and do" ی=*ay*, should be added to the infinitive to form their potential mood and their irregular past participles should not be used as:—

راتلی=*ratlay* کیدلی=*kedalay* کولی=*kawalay* شم=*sham* and شوم=*shwam* and (not) (راغلی)=*raghalay*, شوی=*shaway* or شوی=*shaway*, کړی=*karay*, شم=*sham* and شم=*shwam*.)

COMPOUND VERBS CLASS V & VI.

The Compound verbs are formed by adding adjectives and nouns to کول = *Kawal* and کیدل = *Kédal*.

Transitive.		In Transitive.	
ورکول *war kawal*	to give	ورکیدل *war kédal*	to be given,
مړکول *mar kawal*	to kill or put out.	مړکیدل *mar kédal*	to die or to be put out.
جوړکول *jōr kawal*	to make, build.	جوړکیدل *jōr kédal*	to be made, to be built.
پوه کول *pōh kawal*	to inform instruct.	پوهکیدل *poh kédal*	to understand, to be instructed
لوکول *law kawal*	to harvest.	لوکیدل *law kédal*	to be harvested
اوبهکول *obuh kawal*	to irrigate.	اوبه کیدل *obuh kédal*	to be irregated
خراپکول *kharāp kawal*	to spoil.	خراپ کیدل *kharāp kédal*	to be spoilt.
لرى کول *laré kawal*	to open	لرى کیدل *laré kédal*	to be opened.
پورىکول *pōré kawal*	to shut.	پورىکیدل *pōré kédal*	to be shut.
تپوسکول *tapōs kawal*	to ask	تپوس کیدل *tapōs kédal*	to be asked.
پُښتنه کول *pukhtana kawal*	to ask	پُښتنه کیدل *pukh-tana kédal*	to be asked.

برباد کول *barbād to
kawal* destroy. برباد کیدل *barbād to be
kédal* destroyed

کنډر کول *kandar to
kawal* burgle. کنډر کیدل *kandar to be
kédal* burgled

ژوبل کول *jhōbal to wound
kawal* ژوبل کیدل *jhōbal to be
kédal* wounded

ځوړ کول *khūg to hurt.
kawal* ځوړ کیدل *khūg to be
kédal* hurt.

بل کول *bal to light.
kawal* بل کیدل *bal to be lit.
kédal*

پری کول *pré to cut.
kawal* پری کیدل *pré to be
kédal* cut.

مات کول *mat to break.
kawal* مات کیدل *mat to be
kédal* broken.

NOTE:—See syntax Rule No. 5. for full explanation of the formation of derivative verbs from Class V & VI.

CLASS VII.

Verbs which are irregular in the formation of Present and tenses derived from it.

Infinitive		Present.	
غوښتل *ghukhtal*	to want.	غوارم *ghwāram*	I want.
راغوښتل *rāghukh-tal*	to send for.	راغوارم *rāghwā-ram*	I send for
پریوتل *préwatal*	to fall.	پریوځم *préwo-zam*	I fall.
پوریوتل *pōréwatal*	to cross.	پوریوځم *pōréwo-zam*	I cross.

پریښودل *prékhō-dal*	to leave, let off.	پریږدم *prégdam*	I leave.
پیژندل *péjhan-dal*	to recognize.	پیژنم *péjha-nam*	I recognize.
موندل *mūndal*	to get, obtain, receive, find.	مومم *mūmam*	I get, obtain, receive, find.
ویشتل *wishtal*	to shoot.	ولم *wōlam*	I shoot.
وژل *wajhal*	to kill.	وژنم *wajhnam*	I kill.
لوستل *lwastal*	to read.	لولم *lwalam*	I read.
لیدل *lidal*	to see.	وینم *winam*	I see.
کتل *katal*	to look.	گورم *gōram*	I look.
اوریدل *aurédal*	to hear.	اورم *auram*	I hear.
اخستل *akhistal*	to take.	اخلم *akhlam*	I take.
اغوستل *aghustal*	to wear, to put on, to dress.	اغوندم *aghun-dam*	I put on. etc.
ختل *khatal*	to climb.	خیژم *khéjham*	I climb.
الوتل *alwatal*	to fly.	الوځم *alūzam*	I fly.
کنودل *kanōdal*	to dig.	کنم *kanam*	I dig.
اوریدل *aurédal*	to hear.	اورم *auram*	I hear.
ویل *wayal*	to say, speak, tell.	وایم *wāyam*	I say, speak, tell.
وتل *watal*	to go out.	وځم *wozam*	I go out.
راوتل *rāwatal*	to come out.	راوځم *rawozam*	I come out.
ویستل *wistal*	to take out.	وباسم *wobā-sam*	I take out.
ننوتل *nanawa-tal*	to go in.	ننوځم *nanawo-zam*	I go in.

ننويستل *nanawis*-to take in.   ننباسم *nanabā*- I take in.
tal   sam

خندل *khandal* to laugh.   خاندم*khāndam* I laugh.

ژړل *jharal*   to cry,   ژارم *jhāram* I cry, I
              weep.   weep.

نښتل *nakhatal* to be ca-   نښلم *nakha-*   I am
             ught.   lam   caught.

چاودل *chāwdal* to split,   چرم *chwam*   I am
             burst.   burst.

لنبل *lānbal*   to bathe.   لانبم *lānbam* I bathe.

نيول *niwal*   to catch,   نيسم *nīsam*   I catch
             seize,   etc :—
             arrest, hold.

زنګل *zangal*   to swing.   زانګم *zāngam* I swing.

پاخيدل *pāsédal* to get up.   پاخم*pāsam* or I get up.
                           pāségam

راښکل *rākhkal* to pull.   راکږم *rākāgam* I pull.

نغښتل *nghakh-* to wrap-   نغارم *nghāram* I wrap-
tal   up.   up.

پرانتل *pranatal* to untie.   پرانځم *prana-* I untie.
                           zam

Section 10.

THE SYNTAX RULES.

1. Verbs commencing with ا = *rā* در = *dar*
ور = *war* پا = *pā* پري = *tré* پوری = *pōré* کی = *ké*
نن = *nan* بې = *bé* تې = *té* do not take "و = *wo*" in their
past, aorist and imperative:—

راوتل *rāwtal*   to come out towards
                                 (me or us)

در وتل *dar wtal*   to come out towards
                                    (thee or you)
وروتل *war watal*   to come out towards
                                    (him or them, her, it)
پاخیول *pasédal*   to get up.
تیرباسل *térbāsal*   to mislead.
پریوتل *préwatal*   to fall.
پوریوتل *poréwatal*   to cross.
کیښودل *kékhōdal*   to put, place.
ننوتل *nanawatal*   to go in, enter
بیلل *bélal*   to lose.
راهکل *rākhkal*   to pull.

EXAMPLE.

I got up زه پاخیسم = *zuh pāsédam* (Not *wo pāsé-dam*) past).

May I get up پاخم = *pasam* (aorist)
Get up پاخه = *pasa* (The imperative)

EXCEPTIONS.

Which take *wo* after the ٳ = *rā* در = *dar* and
رر = *war* :—

راغوښتل *rāghukhtal*   to send for.
رابلل *rābalal*   to call for, recall.
رازغلیدل *rāzghalédal* to run towards me or us.
راتښتیدل *rā takhtédal* to flee towards me or us.
راویستل *rā wistal*   to bring out, towards me
                                    or us.

راوتل *rā watal*   to come out towards me or us.

راگرزيدل *rā garzédal*   to return.

رانغښتل *rā nghakhtal* to wrap up.

راگرزول *rā garzawal* to bring back, to make to return.

راشړل *rā sharal*   to drive back towards me or us.

EXAMPLES.

ما هغه را و غوښتلو = *Mā hagha rā wo ghukhtalo* = I sent for him (past).

زه يى را و غوړم = *Zuh yé rā wo ghwāram* = May I send for him? (aorist)

را و يى غوړه = *Rā wo yé ghwāra* = Send for him! (imperative).

NOTE :—Verbs which take را = *rā*, in the 1st person, take در = *dar*, and ور = *war* in the 2nd and 3rd person singular and plural as well as :—

هغه را و زغليدلو *hagha rā wo zghalédalo*   he ran towards me or us.

هغه در و زغليدلو *hagha dar wo zghalédalo*   he ran towards thee or you.

هغه ور و زغليدلو *hagha war wo zghalédalo*   he ran towards him or them, her, it.

2 The subject of the following verbs although they are intransitive, is put in the Agentive case and the verb always goes into the 3rd person masculine plural in past tenses :—

دزهل	*dangal*	to jump.
غپل	*ghapal*	to bark.
خندل	*khandal*	to laugh.
ژړل	*jharal*	to weep.
زنهل	*zangal*	to swing.
تؤ کل	*tūkal*	to spit.
توخل	*tōkhal*	to cough.
لنبل	*lanbal*	to bathe.
جار باسل	*jārbāsal*	to vomit.

Examples as :—

ما و دزهل	*mā wō dangal*	I jumped.
سړی و دزهل	*sari wō dangal*	The man jumped.
جنی و دزهل	*jinai wō dangal*	The girl jumped.
سړو دزهلي دي	*saro dangali di*	The men have jumped.
ښځی دزهلي دی	*khazé dangali di*	The woman has jumped.
ما دزهلي وو	*mā dangali woo*	I had jumped.

In the absence of an object the following verbs also follow the above rules

لیکل	*likal*	to write.
لوستل	*lwastal*	to read.
و یل	*wayal*	to say, speak. tell.
کتل	*katal*	to look.
لیدل	*lidal*	to see.

غوښتل	ghukhtal	to wish, want.
اوريدل	aurédal	to hear.

As :—

ما وا وريدل	Mā wā wrédal	I heard.
تا وا وريدل	Tā wā wrédal	Thou heard
هلك وا وريدل	Halak wā wrédal	The boy heard.
جينۍ وا وريدل	Jinai wā wrédal	The girl heard.
سړو وا وريدل	Saro wā wrédal	The men heard
ښځو وا وريدل	Khazo wā wrédal	The women heard.
ما اوريدلي دي	Mā aurédali di	I have heard.
ما اوريدلي وؤ	Mā aurédali woo	I had heard.
جينۍ اوريدلۍ وؤ	Jinai aurédali woo	The girl had heard.
هلك اوريدلي وؤ	Halak aurédali woo	The boy had heard.
ما و ليكل چه	Mā wo likal chi...	I wrote that...
ما پۀ اخبار کښې ولوستل	Mā puh akhbār ké wo lwastal	I read in the paper.
ما پۀ اخبارکښې لوستلي دي	Mā puh akhbār ké lwastali di	I have read in the paper.

3. To form transitive from class II, Regular intransitive verbs, change يدل = édal of the infinitives into ول = awal as : —

رسيدل	rasédal	to arrive	رسول	rasawal	to make to arrive
اوسيدل	osédal	to live	اوسول	osawal	to make to live

پاخیدل *pāsédal* to get up پاخول *pāsawal* to make to
get up.

NOTE :—In conversation some times the
present tense of Class II is formed irregularly.

رسیدل *rasédal*	to arrive	رسم *rasam*	I arrive
اوسیدل *osédal*	to live	اوسم *ōsam*	I live
زغلیدل *zghatédal*	to run	زغلم *zghalam*	I run
تښتیدل *takhtédal*	to flee	تښتم *takhtam*	I flee
خوزیدل *khwazédal*	to move	خوزم *khwazam*	I move
رپیدل *rapédal*	to tremble	رپم *rapam*	I tremble
څښیدل *sasédal*	to leak	څښم *sāsam*	I leak.

4. Compound verbs formed from adjectives
never take و = *wo*, in their past, aorist and imperative and those formed from nouns always
do as :—

ما میز صاف کړلو *mā méz sāf kralo* I cleaned the table.

ستا بوټونه صاف کړم *stā būtūna sāf* May I clean your
kram ? boots ?

لوکوټی یې صاف کړه *lūkūti yé sāf kra* Please clean them.

ما کار و کړلو *mā kār wo kralo* I worked.

زه کار و کړم *zuh kār wo kram* May I work ?

خپل کار و کړه *khpal kār wo kra* Do your work.

5. Compound verbs formed from some
adjectives are Derivative Verbs which are
formed by leaving out the first letter ک = *k* of
کول = *kawal* and کیدل = *kédal* and add *zabar* over

the last letter of the adjective only in case of
transitive verb, as : —

from صاف كول *saf kawal* صافول *safawal* to clean.

from صاف كيدل *saf kédal* صافيدل *saféđal* to be
cleaned.

from پوه كول *pōh kawal* پوهول *pōhawal* tø inform

from پوه كيدل *pōh kédal* پوهيدل *pōhédal* to understand.

EXAMPLES.

زه صافوم	*zuh sāfawam*	I clean.
زه به صافوم	*zuh be sāfawam*	I will clean.
مه صافوه	*muh sāfawa*	don't clean.
ما صافولو	*mā safawalo*	I was cleaning.
زه صافولی شم	*zuh sāfawalay sham*	I can clean.

NOTE :—In the Past, Aorist, Imperative and
Past Participle of Derivative Verbs however
كول = *kawal*, and كيدل = *kédal*, are conjugated in
full.

EXAMPLES.

ما ميز صاف كړلو	*mā méz saf kralo*	I cleaned the table.
صاف كړم ؟	*sāf kram* ?	my I clean ?
هو صاف كړه	*ho sāf kra*	yes, clean.
ميز تيار شو	*méz tayār sho*	the table was (be-came) ready.
تيار شم ؟	*tayār sham* ?	may I became ? ready ?

هو تیار شه *ho tayār sha*   yes, be ready.

Not : ما میز و صافوله *mā méz wo sāfawalo*.

وصافوم = *wo sāfawam* or وصافوه = *wo sāfwa*

The list of adjectives from which the derivative Verbs are formed.

Adjective.		Verbs.	
خراپ *kharāp*	خراپول *kharapawal*	to spoil.
جوړ *jor*	جوړول *jorawal*	to make, build.
پوه *poh*	پوهول *pohawal*	to inform or instruct.
موړ *mōr*	موړول یا *mōrawal* or	
	مړول *marawal*	to feed.
لوند *lūnd*	لوندول *lūndawal*	to make wet.
کوږ *kōg*	کوږول با *kōgawal* or	to make
	کږول *kagawal*	crooked.
دروند *drūnd*	دروندول *drundawal*	
	یا دړول or *dranawal*	to make heavy.
تود *tōd*	تودول *tōudawal*	to make hot.
پوخ *pōkh*	پښول یا *pakhawal* or	
	پوښول *pokhawal*	to cook.
تریو *triw*	تریوول *triwawal*	to make sour.
خوږ *khōg*	خوږول یا *khōgawal* or	
	خوږول *khwagawal*	to make sweet.
تریخ *trikh*	تریښول یا *trikhawal* or	
	ترخول *tarkhawal*	to make bitter.

Adjective.		Verbs.	
خُږ khūg	خُږَوَل khūgawal		to hurt.
وروست vrōst	وروسْتَوَل يا vrostawal or		
	ورسْتَوَل vrastawal		to make rotten.
شین shin	شینَوَل shinawal		to make green
رُوند rūnd	رُوندَوَل يا rūndawal or		
	رَنْدَوَل randawal		to make blind.
سپین spin	سپینَوَل spinawal		to make white.
زیر ziar	زیرَوَل ziarawal		to make yellow.
بند band	بنْدَوَل bandawal		to close.
لوی loi	لویَوَل loyawal		nurse up or make bigger.

PRESENT CONTINUOUS.

6. When the action is continuous use simple present in the first sentence and simple future in the second, the 1st: sentence commences with که = *kuh* if, and the 2nd: with نو = *no* then.

EXAMPLE.

که هغه راځي نو زه به ځم = *kuh hagha rāzee, no zuh ba zam*
If he keeps on coming, I shall keep on going.

PAST CONTINUOUS.

7. Use imperfect in the first sentence and Habitual in the 2nd as:—

كۀ هغه راتلو نوزهٔ به تلم *kuh hagha rātlo, nō zuh ba tlam*
If he had kept on coming I would have kept on
going.

PRESENT CONDITIONAL.

8 Use aorist in the first sentence and aorist
preceded by به = *ba* in the 2nd as: —

كۀ هغه راشي نوزهٔ به لارشم *kuh hagha rāshee, no zuh ba
lārsham* If he comes I will go.

NOTE:—Some times in the present conditional idiomatically, the Past tense is used
instead of the aorist, in the first clause when the
condition is assumed to be realised, as :—

كۀ تا دا كار وكړلو نو انعام به دركړم *kuh tā dā kār wokralo, no
inām ba darkram*
If you do this work I will reward you.

PAST CONDITIONAL.

9. Use the word وى = *way* unchangeably
after the uninflected Past Participle in the first
sentence and pluperfect preceded by به = *ba*, in
the 2nd: as: —

كۀ هغه راغلى وى نوزهٔ به تلى وم *kuh hagha rāghalay
way, nō zub ba talāy wam*
If he had come, I would have gone.

PAST POTENTIAL CONDITIONAL.

10. Use the word شوى = *shway*, unchangeably after the original uninflected Past participle

in the first half and Pluperfect tense preceded
by به = ba, in the 2nd as :—

كه زۀ راتلی شوی نوزۀ به را غلی وم	*kuh zuh rātlay shway, no zuh ba rāghalay wam*	If I could have come, I would have
كه م وهلی شوی نو به م وهلی وۀ	*kuh mé wahalay, shway, no ba mé wahalay woh*	If I could have beaten him, I would have done so.

PASSIVE VOICE.

11. In Pushtu the Passive Voice is only
used in those cases wnen the subject of the
verb is not mentioned at all.

Formation :—

Conjugate the required tense of كيدل = *kédal*,
after the uninflected Past Participle of an other
Verb as :—

دودۍ خوړلی كيږي	*dodai khwaralay kégi*	The bread is being eaten.
دودۍ به خوړلی کيږي	*dodai ba khwaralay kégi*	The bread will be eaten.
دودۍ خوړلی شوی ده	*dodai khwa- ralay shawé dah*	The bread has been eaten.

NOTE :—To form Passive Past and Aorist add ﺩی = *ay* to the Past Tense 3rd. Person masculine Plural with ﻛیﺪﻝ = *kédal* conjugated after it *e. g.*

هغه و وهلی شو	*hagha wo wahalay sho*	He was beaten.
كه هغه و وهلی شی	*kuh hagha wo wahalay shi*	If he is beaten.
كتاب يوړلی شو	*kitāb yauralay sho*	The book was taken away.
كه كتاب يوړلی شی	*kuh kitāb yauralay shi*	If the book is taken away.
آس بوتللی يا بوتلی شو	*ass bōtlalay* or *bōtlay sho*	The horse was taken away.
كه آس بوتللی يا بوتلی شی	*kuh āss bōtlalay* or *botlay shi*	If the horse is taken away.
كار وكړی شو (يا وكړای شو)	*kār wo kray sho* or *kār wo kralay shō*	The work was done.
كه كار وكړی شی يا وكړلی شی	*kuh kār wo kray shi* or *wo kralay shi*	If the work is done.
ميز صاف كړی شو يا كړلی شو	*méz sāf kray sho* or *kralay sho*	The table was cleaned.
كه ميز صاف كړی يا كړلی شی	*kuh méz sāf kray* or *kralay shi*	If the table is cleaned.

NOTE :—كړی = *kray*, is a short form of كړلی *kralay*.

12. The Infinitive of Purpose is always inflected and it is followed by the Post Position
د دَ پاره = *da dapāra* as :—

زهٔ د رپوټ کولو دَ پاره ا غلَی یم	*zuh da rapōt kawalo dapāra rāghalay yam*	I have come to make a report.

13. In the Negative Past and Aorist, the
نهٔ—*nuh,* is placed after the following Particles:—

را *rā*	در *dar*	ور *war*	پا *pa*	پری *pré*	پوری *pōré*
و *wo*	وا *wa*	لا *lā*	کی *ké*	بی *bé*	نن *nan*
پرا *prā*, as :—					

هغه را غلو	*hagha rāghlo*	He came.
هغه را نهٔ غلو	*hagha rā nuhghlo*	He did not come.
زهٔ لارم	*zuh lāram*	I went.
زهٔ لا نهٔ رم	*zuh lā nuh ram*	I did not go.
تهٔ پا خیدلی	*tuh pasédalé*	You got up.
تهٔ پا نهٔ خیدلی	*tuh pa nuhsédalé*	You did not get up.
ما و ویل	*mā wo wayal*	I said, spoke or told
ما و نهٔ ویل	*mā wo nuh wayal*	I did not say etc.
مؤنږ وا خستلو	*mūng wā khistalo*	We took it.
مؤنږ وا نهٔ خستلو	*mūng wā nuh khistalo*	We did not take it.
تا سو کیښو دلو	*tāso kékhōdalo*	You placed it.
تا سو کینهٔ ښودلو	*tāso ké nuh khōdalo*	You did not place it.

هغوی ننوتل	*haghui nanawatal*	They entered.
هغوی نننۀ وتل	*haghui nana nuh watal*	They did not enter.
چا پرا نتلو	*chā prānatlo*	Who opened it ?
چا پرا نۀ نتلو	*chā prānuh natlo*	Who did not open it ?

14. In the case of all verbs commencing with ‍ا = *ā*, (alif) the sound of ‍و = *wo*, becomes ‍وا *wā*, in their Past, Aorist and Imperative as :—

ما یو کتاب واخستلو   *mā yau kitāb wākhistalo*   I took a book.

15. When an infinitive is used after an imperative, the last part of the sentence should be put into the aorist preceded by ‍چه = *chi* as :—

ورته و وایه چه   *warta wō wāya*
لاړ شي   *chi lārshee*   Tell him to go.

16. Use the word ‍ځان = *zān*, self or ‍خپل ځان *khpal zān* oneself when the person of the subject is concerned as :—

یو کتاب م د ځان سره وا خستلو	*yau kitāb mé da zān sara wākhistalo*	I took a book with me.
څۀ اوبۀ د ځان سره واخله	*suh obuh da zān sara wākhla*	Take some water with you.

17. The words ‍تنه = *tana* or ‍کس = *kasa* = individuals, are used before persons as :—

شل تنَ سړي راغلل	shal tana sari rāghlal	Twenty men came
څلور تنَ ښځى	salōr tana khazé	l'our women.
پنځهُ كسَ ښځى	pinzuh kasa khazé	Five women.
څو كسَ	sō kasa	How many persons ?

18. When a possessive pronoun refers to the nominative of the sentence it should always be translated by خپل = *khpal.* own :—

زهٔ خپل كور ته ځم	zuh khpal kōr ta zam	I go to my house.
ټول خپلو خپلو	tōl khpalo	Each man went.
كورونو ته لاړل	khpalo korūnō ta lāral	to his own house, or they all went to their own houses.
زهٔ خپله كمرهٔ كښى دم	zuh khpala kamra ké wam	I was in my room

19. The particle د = *dé.* is used before the aorist tense at the end of a sentence only in the 3rd person singular and plural to express command and permission, but to show negation, permission and continuation use Present Tense as :—

هغهٔ د لاړ شی	hagha dé lārshee	He should go.

د هغهٔ خور د هم لاړه شي	*da haghuh khŏr dé hum lāra shee*	His sister should also go.
هغه د نۀ راخي	*hagha dé nuh rāzee*	He should not come.
هغه د راخى يا را خى د	*hagha dé rāzee* or *rāzee dé*	He may come or he is allowed to come or let 'him come.
هغه د مدام راخى راخى	*hagha dé mudām rāzee*	He should always come.

NOTE (A)—لاړ = *lār* is used as an adjective declinable .

NOTE (B)—د = *dé* with لكه = *laka* after it is used after the subject of the verb in all persons to express the following idioms *e. g.*

تۀ دلکه خوب کوې او زۀ د لکه ستا بوټونه صافوم	*tuh dé laka khŏb kawé aw zuh dé lakā stā būtūna sāfawam*	Is it reasonable that you should go to sleep and I should cleam your boots.

20. Use the word پکار دي = *pakār di* it is necessary, after the uninflected infinitive at the end of a sentence and the subject of the verb should be put into the dative case to express should, must or ought as :—

ما له تلل پکاردي	*mā la tlal pakār di*	lit To me going necessary is I must go.

تا له تلل پكاردي *ta la tlal pakar di* You should go.

موز,لهپۀخار (نهر) *mung la puh khar* We must live in

كښ اوسيدل‌پكاردي *ké osédal pakar di* The city.

21. Use the word پكار دي چه = *pakar di chi* at the beginning of a sentence followed by the aorist tense to express the same meaning as above as :—

پكاردى چه زٱ پريږ *pakar di chi zuh*   I must go on
تہ لٱرشم   *paraid ta lārsham*   parade.

پكار دى چه تا سو *pakar di chi taso*   You must go
وختى لٱرشئ   *wakhti lārshai*   earlier.

22. To express should have or ought to have, use پكار ؤو چه = *pakar woo chi* at the beginning of a sentence followed by وى = *way* after the uninflected past participle at the end of a sentence as :—

پكار ؤو چه زٱ تلَى *pakar woo chi zuh*   I ought to have
وى   *talay way*   gone.

پكار ؤو چه هغه *pakar woo chi*   He should have
راغلَى وى   *hagha rāghalay*   come.
   way

23. وى = *wi* the aorist tense of the verb "to be", is only used in the 3rd person singular and plural to express doubt, continuation, present conditional in the verb "to be" and general statement as :—

كُنِد هغه هلته وي	gunde haga haltā wi	Perhaps he is there.
هغه مدام پۀ ښهر کښں وي	haga mudām puh khahar ké wi	He is always in the city.
کۀ هغه پۀ مردان کښں وي	kuh hagha puh mardān ké wi	If he is in Mardan.
نو زۀ به ورسره خبرې وکړم	no zuh ba warsara khabaré wo karm	I will speak to him.
پۀ دی وطن کښں هر رنگ ښکار وي	pa dé watan ké har rang khkār wi	There are all kinds of shooting in this country.

24. Aorist preceded by به = ba is called strong future, which stands for certainty and fixed time as :—

هغه به صبا راشی	hagha ba sabā rāshee	He will (certainly) come tomorrow.
هغه به پۀ کور کښں وي	hagha ba puh kōr ké wi	He will (certainly) be in the house.

25. The Imperative formed from the Present Tense denotes continuation, or habit as :—

هره ورځ ښما کورته راځه	hara wraz zamā kōr ta rāza	Come to my house every day.
هره ورځ مدرسی ته ځه	hara wraz madrasé ta za	Go to the school every day.

26. The Plural of Onomatopœic Nouns is formed by adding هار—ahār, which takes the verb to be into 3rd person masculine singular, as :—

دز *daz*	sound of a shot.	دزهار *dazahār*	sound of shots.
کرپ *krap*	foot fall	کرپهار *krapahār*	sound of footfalls.
شرنگ *shrang*	chink of money.	شرنگهار *shranga- hār*	chink of rupees.
پس *pus*	sound of whisper	پسهار *pasah.ār*	whisper- ing.
هینر *henr*	neigh of a horse.	هینرهار *hénrahār*	neighing of horses.

27. Use the word لگیا = *lagyā* = busy, as an adjective with the subject of the Verb, when the action is continuous as :—

زۀ لگیا یم پښتو زده کوم *zuh lagyā yam pukhtu zda kawam*   I am busy learn- ing Pushtu.

هغه لگیا دی چټي لیکي *hagha lagyā day chitai likee*   He is busy writ- ing letters.

مونږ لگیا یۇ غنم کوو *mūng lagyā yū ghanam karoo*   We are busy sowing wheat.

28. The following words take the Genitive Case followed by the Verb to be (بدي = *badi* is the only one which takes the aorist of " to be- come ".)

خوښ *khwakh*   pleasant.

پكار *pakār*   required.

بدي *badi*   unpleasant.

پيرزو *pérzo*   wish.

EXAMPLES.

دا كتاب ځما خوښ *dā kitāb zamā*
دى *khwakh day*   I like this book.

ځما درى روپئي پكار *zamā dré rupai*   I requirè three
دى *pakār dee*   rupees.

دَ هغهٔ ورور ځما بدي *da haghuh vror*
شي *zamā badi shee*   I hate his brother.

تا پهٔ ځما انعام دا *dā ināam zamā*   I wish you to
پيروز دى *puh tā pérzo day* have this reward.

29. The word معلوم = *malūm* = known, takes
dative case followed by the Verb to be as:—

دا ما ته معلوم دي *dā mā ta malūm*   I know this.
     day

30. The phrases given below are followed
by the aorist tense :—

راځه چه *rāza chi*   Let us.

پريږده چه *prégda chi*   Let him, them, her, it.

EXAMPLES.

راځه چه دغه كلي *rāza chi dagha*   Let us go to that
ته لارشو *kali ta lārshoo*   village.

پريږده چه لارشي *prégda chi lārshee* Let him go.

31. The verbs "to sell" and "sell for" always take the preposition پۀ باند = *puh bāndé* on as :—

ما خپل آس پۀ هغۀ *mā khpal ass*
باند پۀ لس روپئ *puh haghuh*
خرڅ کړو *bāndé puh las*   I sold my horse
rūpai khars   to him for 10
kralo   rupees.

32. The verb "to understand" takes پۀ = *puh* as :—

زۀ پۀ پښتو پوهېږم *zuh puh pukhtu*   I understand
pōhégam   Pushtu.

33. پس = *pas* = after (in time) does not inflect any nouns of time as :—

درى مياشتى پس *dré miāshté pas*   After three
months.

څلور کال َ پس *salōr kāla pas*   After four years.

34. پسى = *pasé* after (position or business) inflects its nouns or pronouns e. g.

ما پسى دفتر ته راشه *mā pasé daftar*   Come after me to
ta rāsha   the office.

زۀ نوکرئ پسى راغلى يم *zuh naukarai*
pasé rāghalay   I have come
yam   after a job.

35. The following Verbs take Ablative Case (نه ـ لۀ = *luh - na*) from.

تپوس کول يا پښتنه کول *tapōs kawal* or
pukhtana kawal To ask.

ويريدل	*veyarédal*	to fear.
پوريوتل	*pōréwatal*	to cross.
هير کيدل	*hér kédal*	to be forgotten.

EXAMPLES.

لۀ هغۀ نه تپوس وکړه	*luh haghuh na tapòs wokra*	Ask him.
لۀ سيند نه پوريوتلم	*luh sind na pōré-watalam*	I crossed the river.
را نه کتاب هير شو	*rā na kitāb hér shō*	I forgot the book.

36. When the action is unintentional an Intransitive Verb with the Ablative case should be used as :—

گلاس را نه مات شو	*galās rā na māt shō*	I broke the glass (by accident).

37. To do something by means of any thing, the indirect object is always governed by باند - پۀ = *puh - bāndé* on as :—

زۀ پۀ قلم باند ليکم	*zuh puh qalam bāndé likam*	I write with a pen.
زۀ یې پۀ لرګی و وهلم	*zuh yé puh largi wo wahalam*	He beat me with a stick.

38. For the Pluperfect Tense after "when" the past tense should be used and for Perfect, the Aorist as :—

کله چه ما خپل کار و کړلو یا وکړ	*kala chi mā khpal kār wo kralo* or *wo kar*	When I had done my work

و دودئ ژه چه كله *kala chi zuh dodai* When I have
خورم   *wo khuram*   eaten my food.

39. "Until" at the beginning of an English sentence is always translated by تر خو پورى چه = *tar sō pōrė chi.* and followed by the Negative Aorist tense as :—

خما چه پورى خو تر *tar sō pōrė chi* Until you come
دفتر له راشه شى *zamā daftar la* to my office.
                rā nuh shė

40. "Since" (in the sense of time) at the beginning of an English sentence, is translated by كله راسى چه = *kala rāsė chi,* as :—

كله راسى چه هغه *kala rāsė chi*
خما نوكردى *hagha zamā* Since he has been
           naukar day in my service.

41. To express "See if" the negative tense with خو *kho,* before it, should be used as :—

گوره چه خما كتاب په *gora chi zamā* See if my book
ميز باند خو نشته *kitāb puh mėz* is on the table.
             bāndė kho
             nishta

42. To express Present Optative, change the last م = *m,* of the past tense 1st. person singular into ى = *ay,* for all persons.

To express Past Optative, use the word *way,* unchanged after the uninflected past participle and to form Past Potential Optative, use the word شوی = *shway.* unchanged after the original uninflected past participle. All these Optative expressions commence with :—

| ار مان دیَ چه | *armān day chi* | I wish that (Lit : I regret.) |

EXAMPLE.

ار مان دیَ چه زهٔ	*armān day chi*	I wish I could
لاریَ	*zuh lāray*	go.
ار مان دیَ چه زهٔ	*armān day*	I wish I had
تلیَ ویَ	*chi zuh talay way*	gone.
ار مان دیَ چه زهٔ	*armān day chi*	I wish I could
تلیَ شویَ	*zuh tlay shway*	have gone.

43. To express compulsion, کم نا کم = *kām nā kām* or خوا مخواه = *khwā makhwāh* = some-how or other, should be used as :—

زهٔ خوا مخواه لاړم	*zuh khwā makhwāh lāram*	I had to go.
ما کم نا کم نوم کت کړو	*mā kām nā kām nūm kat kro*	I had to resign.
زهٔ به خوا مخواه ځم	*zuh ba khwā makhwāh zam*	I will have to go.

44. Adverbial phrases of time and place are sometimes put before the subject of the verb as :—

| پهٔ شپږ بجی زهٔ | *puh shpag bajé* | I will go to the |
| به د دفترته لارشم | *zuh ba daftar ta lārsham* | office at 6. |

45. شته = *shta* Is there or are there ? It is
also used for a question and an answer to a
question in the verb to have, but in case of
using any interrogative, Adjective and Adverb
in the sentence, شته = *shta* can not be used as :—

تا سخه کتاب شته	*tā sakha kitāb shta*	Have you a book ?
هو ما سخه کتاب شته	*ho mā sakha kitāb shta*	Yes, I have a book.
خو ما سخه قلم نشته	*kho mā sakha qalam nishta*	But I have not a pen.
تا سخه څومره کتابونه دی	*tā sakha sōmra kitabūna di*	How many books have you ?
تا سخه کوم کتاب دي	*tā sakha kum kitāb day*	What book have you?
تا سخه ډیر دولت دي	*tā sakha dér daulat day ?*	Have you much wealth ?

46.   The post position سخه = *sakha* = In the
possession of, can be used when the object
possessed, is light and moveable and can be
carried about.

In the case of parts of the body, relations
and heavy property the possessive case should
be used as:—

ما سخه یو قلم دی	*mā sakha yau qalam day*	I have a pen.
ملک سخه یوه اسپه ده	*malak sakha yawa aspa dah*	The headman owns a mare.

خما يوه سترگه ده zamā yawa
starga dah   I have one eye.

ستا ورور شته stā vror shta ? Have you a
brother ?

ستا کور شته stā kōr shta   Have you a house ?

47. The use of two similar numerals together denotes "each" as :—

يو يو ته دوه دوه انی yau yau ta dwa   Give them two
ورکړه dwa ané warkra annas each.

48. The Past Conditional of the verb to be
is formed by using the word ری = way (indecline-
able) at the end of a sentence as :—

که زه هلته وی kuh zuh halta
way   If I had been there.

که ته هلته وی kuh tuh halta If you had been
way   there.

که خان هلته وی kuh khān halta If the khan had
way   been there.

49. In the Negative Tenses formed from
the Past Participle, the Past Participle in
conversation is sometimes put last as :—

هغه نه دی راغلی hagha nuh day
rāghalay   He has not come.

خان نه وه راغلی khān nuh woh The Khan had
rāghalay   not come.

زه نه شم راتلی zuh nuh sham
rātlay   I cannot come.

خزه يه لار نه شوه *khaza puh lāra*   The woman could
تلَی *nuh shwa tlay*   not go on the road.

50. In Yusafzai Pushtu the last لو = *lo*, of
the 3rd. person Masculine singular of the past
tense is left out as : —

كينا ستلو *kénāstalo* or كيناست *kénāst*   He sat.

خملا ستلو *samlāstalo* or خملاست *samlāst* He lay
down.

51. The following nouns take the verb in
the 3rd. person masculine singular :—

مال *māl*   Cattle.

يرغمل *yarghamal*   Hostage or Hostages.

فوځ *fauz*   Troops, Army.

ملاتړ *mlā tar*   Followers, Fighting men.

دښمن *dukhman*   Enemy (in War.)

52. The following words take the verb in
the 3rd ; person Masculine Plural :—

دروغ *darōgh*   Lie.

رښتيا *rikhtiā*   Truth.

كنزل *kanzal*   Abuse,

څه *suh*   What, anything.

هيڅ *hiss*   Nothing (takes negative tense.)

53. To forget = هير كول = *hér kawal*, is only
used transitively if the act of forgetting is
delibrate ; ordinarily = هير كيدل = *hér kédal.* with
the ablative case is used e. g.

ما مه هيروه = *mā muh hérawa* = Don't forget me

يٿ دفتر كښ كتاب *puh daftar ké*
رانه هير شو *kitab rā na her sho* I forgot the book in the office.

Lit : — In the office the book from me was forgotten.

54. (A) Terms of politeness used in addressing the following are :—

Old man كاكا جي يا *kāka ji* or *kāka* Uncle.
Blind man حافظ *hāfiza* The man who knows the Quran by heart.
Stranger ځوان *zowāna* Young man.
Known person هلك *halaka* Boy.
Father بابا *bābā* Father.
Mother ادي *adé* Mother.
Brother للا *lala* Brother.
Sister (older) بى بى *bébé* Sister.
Uncle چاچا *chāchā* Uncle.
Grand-mother نانا *nā nā* Grand-mother.
Maternal uncle ماما *māmā* Maternal uncle.
Wife or husband ري *way* Oh !
Urdu knowing person مرزا صاحب *mirzā sāhib* Urdu writer.
English knowing person بابو صاحب *bābū sāhib* Clerk.
A sweeper جمعدار *jamādar* Jemadar.
Mali چودري *chōwdhri* Manager.

(B) The following are the terms of calling and driving away different kinds of animals etc :—

	Calling.	Driving away.
Dog	تو تو تو *to to to*	کوری شه یا چغَی شه *kurésha* or *chakhaysha*
Cat	پیش پیش پیش *peesh peesh peesh*	پشی شه *pashéysha.*
Cow or Bullock	شو شو شو *sho sho sho*	هاوشه *hawsha*
Buffalo	تی تی تی *té té té*	هي شه *hai sha*
Hawk	بیا بیا بیا *biā biā biā*	سُو سُو سُو *sū sū sū* or هان هان هان *hān hān hān*
Goat	بچی بچی بچی *baché baché baché*	کچی شه *kaché sha*
Sheep	درزی درزی درزی *darray darray darray*	درزی شه *darray sha*
Horse or Donkey	کوڑ کوڑ کوڑ *koor koor koor*	تپو شه *tpo sha*
Hen or Cock	پاپ پاپ پاپ *pāp pāp pāp*	کړی شه *kƶré sha*
Camel	پش پش پش *pash pash pash*	لؤ شا *oosha*
Crow	آ آ آ *ā ā ā*	دو شه *dōsha*

(C) Driving a person out شه ورک = *vraksha* = Confound you, go and lose yourself.

(D) When speaking of any defective person use the word معذور = *mazūr* = the one who has objection.

هغهٔ په يوه سترګه hagha puh yawa
معذور دى starga *mazūr* He has only one
day Eye.

هغهٔ په لس معذوردى hagha puh lās He has only one
mazūr day hand.

هغهٔ په ښپه معذوردى hagha puh khpa He has only one
mazūr day foot or leg.

55. When two similar post positions are used together, their meaning is intensified as :—

ورستو ورستو راغه vrosto vrosto
rāza Come far behind.

لاند لاند lāndé lāndé Right underneath,
the lower most
ones.

پورته پورته pōrta pōrta Upper most ones.

مخ کښى مخ کښى خه makhké makhké
zah Go right ahead.

56. The following words have an additional meaning derived from the characteristic of the language and the people as :—

پښتو pukhtu Pashto or modesty.

پښتون pukhtūn Pathan or modest, self respect-
ing, firm.

EXAMPLES.

پۀ هغۀ کښې هيڅ پښتو نشته	*puh haghuh ké hiss pukhtō nishta*	He has no modesty (shame) in him.
کرنیل صاحب یو پښتون سړی دی	*karnél sāhib yau pukhtūn saray day*	The colonel is a modest yet firm person.

57. The following words are used as regular adjectives with the verb to be :—

ناست	*nāst*	Sitting.
و لاړ	*walār*	Standing.
ملا ست	*mlāst*	Lying.
اودۀ	*ūduh*	Sleeping.

EXAMPLE

هغه پۀ کُرسۍ نا ست دی	*hagha puh kursai nāst day*	Lit: he is seated on the chair = he is sitting on the chair.
جنۍ پۀ کُرسۍ ناسته ده	*jinai puh kursai nāsta dah*	The girl is sitting (seated) on the chair.

58. خندل=*khandal*, to laugh takes پورې=*poré* as :—

هغۀ ما پورې و خندل	*haghuh mā poré wo khandal*	He laughed at me
ما هغۀ پورې و خندل	*mā haghuh poré wo khandal*	I laughed at him.

59. The future perfect and past dubious
are formed by conjugating the future tense of
the verb to be after the past participle of another verb as :—

هغه به راغلیْ وی *hagka ba*   He must, will, or
          rāghalay wee may have come.

NOTE :— به = *ba* the sign of the future can be
put anywhere after the subject of the verb,
so long as it is before the verb as :—

زهٔ به پهٔ پنخهٔ بجی *zuh ba puh pinzuh*
دَ کرنیل صاحب سره *bajé da karnail* I will go for shoot-
        sāhib sara khk- ing with the colo-
ښکار دَ پاره ځم *ār da para zam* nel at 5 o'clook.

60. To express "to be about to" either
change the final ل = *l* of the infinitive into
ونکیْ = *ūnkay* or use the preposition پهٔ-کهٔ = *puh-ké*
with the verbal nouns as :—

هغه راتلوُنکیْ دیَ *hagha rātlūnk-*   He is about to
       ay day   come.

هغه په راتلوکښ دیَ *hagha puh rātlo* He is about to
       ké day   come.

61. To express "to be about to be"
conjugate the verb راتلل = *rātlal* = to come or
کیدل = *kédal* = become after the verbal nouns
governed by پهٔ-بندیَ = *puh-bāndé* as :—

کوهیَ پهٔ ډکیدلو راغیْ *kuhy puh dakédalo*   ) the well
               rāghay | is about
کوهیَ په ډکیدلو شو   ,,   ,,   ,, *sho* | to
                                 | become
کوهیَ په ډکیدلو دیَ   ,,   ,,   .   ,, *day*   ) full

62.   To express "either......or," use يا = *yā* at
the beginning of both sentences and to express "neither nor," use نه = *nuh* at the begin-
ing of both sentences as :—

يا دا واخله يا   *yā dā wākhla*
هغه واخله   *yā hagha* take either this
                wākhla or that.

زه نه دا اخلم نه هغه   *zuh nuh dā*
اخلم   *akhlam nuh*   I will take neith-
          hagha akhlam   er this nor that.

63.   ياد كول = *yād kawal*   to remind and
ويل = *wayal* to say, speak or tell, take the dative
case ته = *ta* = to.

ما ته ياد كړ   *mā ta yād kra*.   Remind me.
ورته و وايه   *war ta wo wāya* Tell him.

64.   In some districts the imperfect tense
3rd. person masculine singular and plural of
the Class II, III, IV and VII verbs, is formed
by changing the final ل = *l*, of the infinitive into
ه = *uh*, as :—

هغه رسيده   *hagha raséduh* He was arriving.
هغوى رسيده   *haghui raséduh* They were arriving.
ما هغه راوسته   *mā hagha*
                rāwastuh   I was bringing him.
ما هغوى راوسته   *mā haghui*   I   was   bringing
                rāwastuh   them.
هغه مړ كيده   *hagha mar*
                kéduh   He was dying.

هغوی مړهٔ کیدهٔ	*haghui mruh kéduh*	they were dying.
ما کتاب لو ستهٔ	*mā kitāb lwastuh*	I was reading a book.
ما کتا بونه لوستهٔ	*mā kitābūna lwastuh*	I was reading books.

In Class I. Verbs the above rule applies only to 3rd. person masculine singular as :—

ما هغهٔ و وههٔ	*mā hagha wo wahuh*	I beat him, struck him.
ما هغوی وهل	*mā hughui wo wahal*	I beat them, struck them.

Some times the imperfect tense 3rd person masculine singular is formed irregularly :—

هغهٔ تهٔ	*hagha tuh*	He was going.
هغهٔ را تهٔ	*hagha rātuh*	He was coming.

65. Sometimes in forming the potential mood the final ل = *l*, of the past participle is dropped.

زهٔ ر سیدی شم	*zuh raséday sham*	I can arrive.
زهٔ او سیدی شم	*zuh oséday sham*	I can live.
زهٔ رسیدی نهٔ شم	*zuh raséday nuh sham*	I cannot arrive.
زهٔ کینا ستی شوم	*zuh kénāstay shwam*	I could sit.
زهٔ راوری شم	*zuh rāwray sham*	I can bring.
ما راوری شو	*mā rawray sho*	I could bring.

66. The past tense of the following verbs is sometimes formed thus :—

راتلل = *ratlal* = to come,

Singular.	Plural
راغم *ragham* (I) came	راغو *raghū* (we) came.
راغې *raghè* (thou) came	راغئ *raghai* (you) came.
راغى *raghay* (he) came or *ragho*	راغه *raghuh* (they) came.
راغه *ragha* (She) came (F)	راغى *raghè* (they) came. (F. P.)

کول = *kawal* = to do.

(زۀ یې مۀ) کړم (*zuh yé mar*) kram	(He killed) me.
(تۀ یې مۀ) کړې (*tuh yé mar*) krè	(he killed) thee.
(هغه یې مۀ) کړو (*hagha yé mar*) kro	(He killed) him.
(هغه یې مۀ) کړه (*hagha yé mra*) kra	(He killed) her (F. S.)
(موږبولي مۀ) کړو (*mūng yé mruh*) kroo	(He killed) us.
(تا سو ئي مۀ) کړئ (*tāsō yé mruh*) krai	(He killed) you.
(هغوى یې مۀ) کړه (*haghui yé mruh*) kruh	(He killed) them.
(هغوى یې مرى) کړى (*haghui yé mrè*) krè	(He killed) them (F. P.)

کیدل = *kédal* = to become.

شولم *shwalam* (I) became. شولو *shwaloo* (we) become.

شولی *shwalé* (thou) become. شولي *shwalai* (you) became.

شولوباشۀ *shwalo* (he) or *shuh* become. شوہ *shwuh* (they) became.

شوله *shwalah* (she) became. شوي *shwé* (they) became. (F. P.)

وبل *wayal* to say, speak, tell.

ما وو وې *má wo wé* I said, spoke, or told.

ر ما وې *má wé* I was saying. (Imperf. tense.)

67. To express "unless or until" use the negative aorist tense of the required verb as :—

که تۀ پخپله رانۀ شی *kuh tuh pakh-pala rā nuh shé* Unles you come yourself.

را زۀ چه پورې تر سو *tar so pōré chi zuh rā nuh sham* Until I come my-self. نۀشم

68. داره = *dāra* raid or raiding party and جرم = *jurm* fine (on the village or tribe) both take the verb to fall = پریوتل = *préwatal*.

زما پۀ کلی باندې *zamā puh kali bāndé dāra préwatala* My village was raided. داره پریوتله

زما پۀ کلی باندې *zamā puh kali bāndé jurm préwatalo* My village was fined. جرم پریوتلو

69. افسوس = *afsōs*, sorrow. must always be
used with کول = *kawal* = to do, as :—

زه افسوس کوم = *zuh afsōs kawam*,   I am sorry.

70. Nouns ending in consonants governed
by ablative case sometimes take ﹷ *zabar* over
the last consonant letter of the noun instead
of نه = *na*, the second Part of the Post position
as :—

له کور نه *luh kōr na* or   له کورَ *luh kōra*
                                 From the house.

له مسکوټ نه *luh miskōt na* or له مسکوټَ *luh miskota*
                                 From the Mess.

71. بل = *bal*, next or other (stands for
number) Its Plural is نور = *nòr*, = more or others
(Stands for both number and quantity) as :—

بل سړی راغی   *bal saray*   Another man
                 rāghay   came.

نور اوبه نشته . *noré obuh*   There is no more
                 nishta   water.

72. څو = *so*, how many (stands for number.)
څومره = *somrā*, how many or how much (Stands
both for number and quantity) e. g.

څو هلکان دی *so halakān di*   How many boys
                              are there.

پۀ ګلاس کښ *puh gélās ké*   How much water
څومره اوبه دی. *sōmra obuh di*   is there in the
                              glass.

73. When an adjective is used to qualify two or more nouns of different Genders the verb agrees with last one as :—

يو سړى او دوه *yau saray aw* One man and two
ښځي ناستي وى *dwa khazé nāsté wé* women were sitting.

74. When two or three or more than three nouns of different genders are used in the sentence, the verb agrees with the last one and if two nouns of different genders in the singular number are used, the verb goes into the 3rd person masculine plural. In the case of the verb "to be" however agreement is with the last noun as :—

هلته دوه سړي او *halta dwa sari* There were two
درى هلكان او *aw dré halakān* men and three
درى ښځي وى *aw dré khazé wé* boys and three women three.

په کور کښ څلور *puh kōr ké salōr* There were four
ښځي او دوه *khazé aw dwa* women and two
سړي وُو *sari woo* men there in the house.

يو هلک او يوه *yau halak aw* One boy and one
جنۍ ولاړ وُو *yawa jinai walār woo* girl were standing

هلته يو هلک او *halta yau halak* There are one
يوه جنۍ ده *aw yawa jinai dah* boy and one girl there.

زما په خيال کښ *zamā puh kheyāl* I think there were
يوه جنۍ او يو *ké yawa jinai aw* one girl and one
هلک وه *yau halak woh* boy there.

75. خپل = *khpal* Own—comes under the rules of regular adjectives ending in consonants and is used as a reflexive pronoun as :—

زۀ خپل کورته ځم	*zuh khpal hŏr ta zam*	I go to my house.
ځما خپل کورونه دی	*zamā khpal kŏrūna di*	They are my own houses.
ځما خپله لور دَه	*zamā khpala lūr dah*	She is my own daughter.
ځما خپلی لوڼی دی	*zamā khpalé lūnra di*	They are my own daughters.
دَ خپلی اسپی زین راوړه	*da khpalé aspé zin rāwra*	Bring the saddle of your mare.
خپلو اسپونه واښۀ واچوه	*khpalo aspo ta wākhuh wāchawa*	Give grass to your mares.
مونږ خپلو کورونو ته ځو	*mūng khpalo kŏrūno ta zoo*	We are going to our houses.

NOTE :—When the particle پۀ = *pa* is prefixed to خپل = *kapal*, the ه = *h* of the particle پۀ = *pa* is placed after the same word :—

پخپله = *pakhpala* = Myself, yourself, himself, herself, itself, etc.

زۀ پخپله ځم	*zūh pakhpala zam*	I go or will go myself.
هغه به پخپله راشی	*hagha ba pakhpala rāshi*	He will come himself.

76. The Causative verbs are formed by using the preposition پ‍ه‍-ب‍ان‍د = *puh-bandé* with a transitive verb as :—

ما پ‍ه م‍ن‍ش‍ى ب‍ان‍د *mā puh munshi*
چ‍ٹ‍ى و‍ل‍ی‍ك‍ل‍ه *bandé chitai* I made the munshi
wo likalah write a letter.

77. The interrogative is often used to indicate strong negative as :—

ما س‍خ‍ه روپ‍ی چ‍ر‍ت‍ه‍دی *mā sakha* I have no money
rupai charta di? at all.

78. The past participle of any verb can be used as an adjective as :—

ت‍خ‍ت‍ی‍د‍ل‍ى آس *takhtédalay ass* Run away horse.

و‍ه‍ل‍ى ش‍و‍ى س‍ر‍ى *wahalay*
shaway saray The beaten man.

79. Prefix د = *da* = of, (the genitive) to a noun to use it as an adjective as :—

د م‍ی‍و‍ى د‍و‍ك‍ان *da mewé dūkān* The fruit shop.

د ك‍ور خ‍او‍ن‍د *da kŏr khawand* The owner of the house.

80. ل‍و‍ك‍و‍ت‍ی = *lūkūti* or ل‍گ = *lag* = little, is used at the beginning of a sentence to express "Please" as :—

ل‍و ك‍و‍ت‍ی ز‍ر ر‍اش‍ه *lūkūti zar rāsha* Please come quickly.

لوُ كوُنٍّ اوبهٔ راوره *lukūti obuh*   Please bring
                      rāwra   some water.

لږى اوبهٔ راكړه *lagé obuh rakra* Please give me
                                 some water.

81.   غوندى = *ghundé* Like, added to adjectives
signifies "Somewhat" :—

ووړوكَى غوندي *warūkay ghundé* somewhat small or
                              smallish.

سپين غوندي *spin ghundé*   somewhat white or
                              whitish.

82.   The plural is used for the 2nd and 3rd
person singular for politeness, but if the name
of the person is mentioned then the Verb remains singular as :—

تا سو كله راغلٍ يِيْ *tāso kala rāghali*
                    yai   instead of.

تهٔ كله راغلَى يِيْ *tuh kala rāghalay* When have you
                  yé   come ?

هغوْى كله راغلٍ دِى *haghūi kala*
                  rāghali dĭ   Instead of.

هغهٔ كله راغلى دَى *hagha kala*   (lit) when has
                 rāghalay day   he come, when
                                    did he come ?

افضل خان كله تلَى *afzal khān kala* when did Afzal
          دىَ *talay day*   Khan go ?

83.   پهٔ مخه راتلل = *puh makha rātlal* to meet.
When using this in a sentence, the subject of
the English verb is always left out as :-

هغه پۀ مينه راغلو *hagha puh makha*
            rāghlo   I met him.

هغه پۀ مينه درغلو *hagha puh makha*
            daraghlo   Thou met him.

هغه پۀ مينه ورغلو *hagha puh makha*
            waraghlo   He met him.

84. To express strong negation in question form repeat, the tense in affirmative after the negative tense with خو = *kho* before it as :—

زۀ ستا نوکر خو نۀيم *zuh stā naukar*
چه نوکريم *kho nuh yam*   I am not your
         chi naukar yam servant am I ?

85. The expression "Will you" the sign of a question or force after an imperative in English is always translated by کۀ نه = *ka na* = if not, or not as :—

دا واخله کۀ نه *dā wākhla ka na* take this will you ?
but when used with هو = *ho*, it means "Of course" as :—

هو کۀ نه *ho ka na* of course, certainly.

86. For blessing and cursing use د = *dé* before the imperative for 2nd person singular as :—

خدای دے لاټ کړه *khudāi dé lāt* May God make
        kra   you a lord.

خدای د خوار کړه *khudāi dé* May God make
        khwār kra   you poor.

NOTE : — For the rest of the persons use the
following particles.

$ف$ = mé ⎫
$د$ = dé ⎬ Singular.
$ی$ = yé ⎭

$م$ = mo ⎫
$م$ = mo ⎬ Plural.
$ئ$ = yé ⎭

before the aorist tense 3rd, person with $د$ = dé
before it as :—

خدای م د خان کړی	khudāi mé dé khān kri	May God make me a Khan.
خدای مو د خوار کړی	khudāi mō dé khwār kri	May God make you poor.
خدای د یی خوار کړی	khudāi dé yé khwār kri	May God make him (them) poor.

NOTE :— The above particles are idiomatically used after :—

$را$ = rā $در$ = dar $ور$ = war $پ$ = pa $پری$ = pré
$پوری$ = póré $کی$ = ké $و$ = wo $وا$ = wā $نن$ = nan
$بی$ = bé, e. g.

را یی نۀ کړ	rā yé nuh kar	He did not give it to me.
پا یی نۀ څولو	pa yé nūh sawalo	He did not make him get up.
و م نۀ ویل	wo mé nuh wayal	I did not say.

كيم نۀ ږو دلو *ké mé nuh*
khŏdalo   I did not place it.

رايى نۀ ورو *ra yé nuh vro*   He did not bring it.

87. An inanimate object can never be used in the Agentive case. The verb is changed into intransitive governed by the Ablative case as : —

ستا چقى مہ ولوستله او وز نه پوه شوم چه تۀ نوره نوکرى نه کوى

sta chitai mé wo lwastalah aw war na poh shwam chi tuh nŏra naukari nuh kawé

I read your letter which made me think that you were not going to serve any more.

لۀ دى سيند نه ځمنوزر، ټوله زمکه اوبۀ کېږى

luh dé sind na zamung tŏla zmaka obuh kégi

This river irrigates all our land.

ځمونږر بټو له پۀ وله کنس اوبۀ راځى يا لۀ ولى نه اوبۀ راځى

zamung patŏ la puh wala ké obuh razee or *luh walé na obuh razee*   The irrigation channel brings water to our fields.

88. The first letter of a noun is changed into ‪م‬ = *m* and then it is repeated for emphasis and etc. but when the noun begins with ‪م‬ = *m* it should be repeated without any alteration as :—

تا سخه کتاب متاب *ta sakha kitab mitab shta*   Have you any book etc ?
شته

پۀ کمره کنس ځه ميز *puh kamra ké suh méz méz shta*   Is there any table etc. in the room ?
ميز شته

NOTE :—-The following are the exceptions :—

غږ غوږ	*ghag ghūg*	Human voice (in answer)	
هان هون	*hān hūn*	,, ,, ,,	
تس تُس یا	*tas tūs* or		
دز دوس	*daz dūz*	Sniping.	
غلا غَلتیا	*ghlā ghultia*	Theft etc.	
کانړی بوټی	*kānri būti*	Stones etc.	
کرُو کور	*karū kōr*	Rendered homeless.	
چنگ رباپ	*chang rabāp*	Squandered.	
خل پل	*khal pal*	Leaves and twigs.	
غال بُول	*ghal būl*	Harum scarum.	
ټیل ما ټیل	*tail mātail*	Pushing each other.	
درب درُوب	*drab drūb*	Fisticuffs.	
گار گُور	*gār gūr*	Thunder and lightning.	

89.   The use of خو = *kho* = but

دغه کتاب خو راکړه	*dāgha kitāb kho rākra*	Just hand me that book please.
زۀ خو دا کار نۀ کوم	*zuh khō dā kār nuh kawam*	I shall not do this really.
دا سړی خو ځما نوکر وو	*dā saray khō zamā naukar woh*	I believe this man was my servant.
هغه خو به پاس شی	*hagha khō ba pāss shi*	He will certainly pass.
آخر گوره خو چه دَ دې به څۀ نتیجه وی	*ākher gora kho chi da dé ba suh natija wee*	Any way do at least wait and see what the result of it will be.

تُه نا جوړ خو نه يى	*tuh nā jŏr kho nuh yé*	I hope you are not ill. (you look as if you are.)
جوړ خوئى كه نه	*jŏr kho yé ka na*	I hope you are well. (you look as if you are not.)
كم عقل.خو دىَ خو غل نهٔ دىَ	*kam aqal khŏ day kho ghal nuh day*	Admitted that he is a fool but he is not a thief.
دا خو رښتيا خبره دهٔ	*dā kho rikhtiā khabara dah*	This indeed is true.
زهٔ خو نهٔ ځم	*zuh khŏ nuh zam*	I (as you know) am not going.

پښتو خو پښتو ده چه زهٔ پهٔ انګريزي هم نهٔ پو هيږم

pukhtŏ kho pukhtŏ dah chi zuh puh angrézai hum nuh pŏhégam

or

پښتو خو پريږده چه زهٔ پهٔ انګريزي هم نهٔ پو هيږم

pukhtŏ kho prégda chi zuh puh angrézai hum nuh pŏhégam

Let alone (or to say nothing of) Pushtu I do not even understand English.

ښه دا كار خو وشو	*kha dā kār khŏ wo shŏ*	Well that is done.
يو خو هغهٔ غريب دىَ بل بد خوئى دىَ	*yau khŏ hagha gharib day, bal bad khūi day*	For one thing (or first) he is poor, and for another (or secondly) bad tempered,

90. When a noun is repeated, it denotes entirety plurality and variety as :—

ما هغه کټ پۀ کټ ولتولو	*mā hagha kat puh kat wo latawalo*	I searched for him in each and every bed.
رښتيا رښتيا وايه	*rikhtiā rikhtiā wāya*	Speak the truth and nothing but the truth (i. e. the whole truth.)
مؤ نۀ پۀ سرک سرک راغلۇ	*mūng puh sarāk sarāk rāghlū*	We came by the road the whole way.
اوس هغه درپۀ در ګرځي	*us hagha dar puh dar garzee*	Now he wanders about begging from door to door

91. When a personal or pronominal adjective is repeated, it denotes plurality, variety and distribution.

تا څۀ څۀ وليدل *tā suh suh wo lidal*

What various things did you see ?

پۀ هغه وخت هلته څوک څوک موجود وو *puh hagha wakht halta sōk sōk maujūd woo.*

What people were individually present there at that time ?

کوم کوم چه وګټي نوانعام به ومومي *kum kum chi wo gati no inām ba wo mūmee*

Every one of those who wins will get a reward.

څيني څيني سړي هلته پاتي دي *zinė zinė saray halta patė day*

There were only a few people left there.

بعضي بعضي په کښ ډير   *bazé bazé pa ké dér*
مُنصف وه   *munsif woh*

Some of them (considered individually) were very just.

هر سړی خپل خپل کور ته لاړ   *har saray khpal khpal kōr ta lār*

Everyone of them went to his own house.

ټول خپلو خپلو کورونو ته لاړل   *tōl khpalō khpalō kōrūno ta lāral*

All went to their respective houses.

ما هغه هغه یا داسی داسی   *mā hagha hagha or dāsé*
خیزونه ولیدل چه ورته حیران   *dāsé sizūna wo lidal*
   chi war ta hairan pāté
پاتی شوم   *shwam*

I was astonished to see such things.

څه څه یا څه نا څه   *suh suh* or *suh nā suh*

Somewhat or to some extent.

هغه څه نا څه	*hagha suh nā*	He can speak
انګریزی ویلی	*suh angrezi*	English a little
شي	*wayalay shee*	(to some extent.)
اوس هغه څه	*os hagha suh*	He is somewhat
نا څه جوړ دی	*nā suh jōr day*	better now.

92. څوک = *sōk* = who, څه = *suh* = what, repeated in negative sentences have the additional idiomatic meaning of all or whole. as :—

هلته څوک څوک   *halta sōk sōk* Who was not present
نه وه ؟   *nuh woh*   there ? (name them individually) ? or every body was there.

‌ما څه څه ورنه‌ *ma suh suh*   I saw everything (lit :
ليدل ؟   *wo nuh lidal*   what was it that I
did not see?)

93. When an adjective is repeated it
denotes plurality, entirety, and variety or
distribution.

پۀ هر طرف اوچت	*puh har taraf*	There were tall
اوچت کورونه ؤو	*ūchat ūchat*	houses on every
	korūna woo	side.
لۀ سرک نه پورى	*luh sarak na*	Beyond the road
غاړه لوى لوى	*poré ghāra lŏi*	there were many
پټى ؤو	*lŏi pati woo*	large fields.
لۀ چاونۍ نه باهر	*luh chāwnrai*	Outside the cant-
شنۀ شنۀ فصلونه	*na bāhar*	onment there are
دى	*shnuh shnuh*	many green crops.
	faslūna di	

دَ هغوى لنډى لنډى ګيرى دي   *da haghūi landé landé*
giré wi
They have (generally) short beards.

ورته تازه تازه پۍ ورکوه   *war ta tāza tāza par*
war kawa
Give him (or them) very fresh milk or give him
milk while it is still fresh.

يخه يخه هوا الوزي   *yakha   yakha   hawā*
alūzee
A nice cool breeze is blowing (continued and
agreeable intensity).

ورته پنځۀ پنځۀ انى وکړه   *war ta pinzuh pinzuh*
ané war kra
Give them five annas each.

صاحب سخه ډېر ښ ډېر جامى دي *sāhib sakha khé khé*
jāmé di

The sahib has many good clothes.

ورسخه خرځ ډ پاره لس لس *war sakha khars da para*
روپۍ دي *las las rupai di*

Each of them has ten rupees to spend.

تا سو ټولو ته به پاؤ بانډ څلور *tāso tōlo ta ba paw*
څلور روپۍ ملاؤ شي *bandé salōr salōr rūpai*
milāw shi

Everyone of you will get Rs. 4/4/-.

94. When an imperfect tense or a verbal
noun is repeated it denotes continuity.

تلم تلم کابل ته ورسېدم *tlam tlam kābal ta wo*
rasédam

I went on till I reached Kabul.

هغه پۀ لوستو لوستوکښ لېونۍ شو *hagha puh lwasto*
lwasto ké léwanay sho

By continually reading he went mad.

پۀ ناستى ناستى ستړی شوم *puh nāsté nāsté staray*
shwam.

I became tired of continued idleness.

پۀ ملاستى ملاستى یی روټۍ *puh mlāsté mlāsté yé*
وخوړله *rōtai wo khwarala*

He ate his food lying down all the time.

پۀ لیدو لیدو مې زړۀ باغ باغ *puh lido lido mé zruh*
کیږي *bāgh bāgh kégee*

By continuously looking I am delighted.

خپ خپ چه را نه یی غوښتل ما   *suh suh chi rā na yé*
به ورکول   *ghukhtal mā ba*
                              warkwal

I gave him whatever he asked me for.

95.   Note the force of repetition in the following :—

زر زر راځه   *zar zar rāza*   Come on quickly.

ورو ورو ځه   *vro vro za*   Go on slowly.

مخ کښې مخ کښې ځه   *makh ké makh*   Go ahead or take
                   ké za   the lead.

کله کله دلته راځی   *kala kala dalta*   He comes here
                    rāzee   occasionally.

تۀ چرته چرته   *tuh charta*   What various
وګرزیدی   *charta*   places have you
               wo garzédé   been to ?

هوائي جهاز اوس لاند لاند راځی   *Hawāi jéhāz oss lāndé*
                                lāndé rāzee

The aeroplane is now gradually coming down.

چرته چرته چه لوړه ژوره وي نو   *charta charta chi lwara*
هغه برابره کړه   *jhawara wee no hagha*
                           barābara kra

Level the ground wherever it is rough.

اول اول هغۀ ماسره ښۀ سلوک   *awal awal haghuh mā*
کولو   *sara khuh salūk kawalo*

In the beginning (i. e. early days) he treated me
very well.

ورستو ورستو را پسی راځه   *vrusto vrusto rā pasé*
                          rāza

Follow me closely.

هغه كلیِ ته نيزدی نيزدی مال *hagha kali ta nizdé* خروه *nizdé māl sarawa*

Keep on grazing your cattle near that village.

دَ سيند پهٔ غاړه غاړه يوه كچه لاړده *da sind puh ghāra ghāra yawa kacha lār dah*

There is an unmetalled road along the bank of the river.

خپلی كمپنی سره سره روان اوسه *khpalé kampanai sara sara rawān osa*

Keep on with your company.

In this connection, note the following idioms :—

كلیِ پهٔ كلیِ *kalay puh kalay*	Village to village or village by village
كال پهٔ كال *kāl puh kāl*	Yearly.
جمعه پهٔ جمعه *jūma puh jūma*	Weekly.
ورځ پهٔ ورځ *vraz puh vraz*	Daily.
فصل پهٔ فصل *fasal puh fasal*	Half yearly.
ديوال پهٔ ديوال *déwāl puh déwāl*	Next door to.
څهٔ نا څهٔ *suh nā suh*	Something or other
څوک نه څوک *sōk na sok*	Someone or other.
چرته نا چرته *charta nā charta*	Somewhere or other.
كور پهٔ كور *kōr puh kōr*	In each house.
لاس پهٔ لاس *lās puh lās*	hand to hand or very quickly.
ناسته پهٔ ناسته *khpa puh khpa*	Sitting doing nothing (idly).

جوړ پﮥ جوړ *jŏr puh jŏr*   Like servant like master (or wife and husband both are of the same nature)

96. To form a question in the absence of any interrogative word use کﮥ نﮧ = *kuh na* = or not, at the end of a sentence. Also, as in other languages a rising intonation at the end of a remark implies a question.

خان اوس پﮥ هسپتال کﮥﮯ دﮮ   *Khān oss puh haspatāl*
کﮥ نﮧ ؟   *ké day kuh na*
Is the Khan in the hospital now ?

97. کﮥ نﮧ = *kuh na* = or not, is some times put at the end of a sentence to make it interrogative and invites an answer accordingly as the rest of the sentence is couched e. g. if the rest of the sentence is put affirmatively the answer is expected to be in the affirmative, but if it is worded negatively, the answer is expected to be in the negative as :—

تﮥ خو بﮧ صبا ﮊﮯ کﮥ نﮧ   *tuh kho ba sabā zé kuh na*
I believe you will go tomorrow, wont you ?

بیا خو بﮧ داسﮯ کارنﮥ کوﮮ کﮥ نﮧ   *biā kho ba dāsé kār nuh kawé ka na*
Well, I hope you will not do so in future, will you ?

98. The names of places ending in ي = ِ are considered masculine plural, therefore when governed by any preposition they should be put into the oblique plural as :--

خوا دى پبونه لهٔ *luh pabo na dé*   This side of
     khwa   Pabbi.

ځم متنوته زهٔ صبا *sabā zuh matano*   I am going to
     ta zam   Mattani tomorrow.

99. To show dislike or anger add ے = *ay*, ݢے = *gay*, to proper nouns and titles ending in consonants or vowels respectively.

احمد *ahmad*   احمدے *ahmaday*

ملا *mula*   ملاݢے *mulagay*

100. To animate or inanimate articles add ݢے = *gay*, to express smallness or poor quality as :—

ټټو *tattu* Pony   ټټوݢے *tatugay* Small pony.

تم تم *tam* Tonga   تم تمݢے *tam*   Ordinary kind
     tam   *tamgay* of tonga.

101. Generic Plural Animals etc. when seen in numbers from a distance are sometimes referred to as feminine plural and sometimes as masculine plural regardless of their actual sex.

e. g. Feminine Plural.

ميښے *Mékhé*   Buffaloes.

ګډے *gadé*   Sheep.

کونتزے *köntaré*   Pigeons.

Masculine Pural.

ميلۇ ګان	*mélūgān*	Bears.
اوښان	*ukhān*	Camels.
ڊنګر	*ḋangar*	Cattle.
ها تیان	*hāthiān*	Elephants.
قار غان	*qārghār*	Crows.
ټپۇ ښان	*tapūsīn*	Kites.
طو طیان	*tōtyān*	Parrots.
امزَری	*amzari*	Tigers.
بیزو ګان	*bizōgān*	Monkeys.

102. لرل = *laral* to have. is rarely used except in the present and imperative.

زۀ یو کتاب لرم	*zuh yau kitāb laram*	I have a book.
ټول رسد تیار لره	*tōl rasad tayār lara*	Have all supplies ready.

103. ماره = *māra*, give me, the imperative, has no infinitive, it only derived from Persian Dative case مارا *mā rā* = to me as :—

دا کتاب مارا	*dā kitāb māra*	Give me that book.

104. مینه کېدل = *mina kédal* to have a desire for, takes Dative case and is followed by the genitive case :—

څما تلو تۀ مینه کېږی	*zamā tlo ta mina kégee*	I have a desire to go.

105. The following nouns are masculine in the singular and feminine in the plural :—

مرز	*maraz*	Quail	مرزى	*maraze*	F. P.
كندر	*kandar*	ruined house	كندرى	*kandare*	F. P.
كوتک	*kōtak*	big stick	كوتكى	*kōtake*	F. P.
دز	*daz*	Gun shot (report)	دزى	*daze*	F. P.

106. Some nouns are feminine in the singular and masculine in the plural as :—

گناه *gunāh* Sin   گناهونه *gunāhūna* Sins M. P.

107. خدمت كول = *khidmat kawal* = To serve (without payment) takes genitive case as :—

مونږ د سركار خدمت كړى دى *mūng dā sarkār khidmat karay day*
We have served Government.

108. Use simple imperfect when the desire of a person i. e. subject of the verb is expressed as :—

كه هغه راتلو نو را د شي *kuh hagha rātla no rā dé shee*
Let him come if he wishes to come.

109. In the imperative of a transitive verb the direct object must be expressed as :—

را يى كړه *rā yé kra*   Give it to me.
ورى كړه *war yé kra*   Give it to him.

وهه ويى   *wo yé waha*   Beat him.

كيم نوه   *ké mé nawa*   Make me sit.

110.   When the intention of the subject in the conditional form is expressed, use the original uninflected past participle in the 1st sentence and the required tense in the 2nd; half as :—

كه هغه راتلئ نو به راغلئ وه   *kuh hagha rātlay nō ba rāghalay woh*

If he meant to come he would have come.

111.   To express "nearly" or "about" use يو = *yau* = one. before the required numerals as :—

يو دوه سوَ   *yaw dwa sawa*   nearly two hundred.

112.   List of common female animals and their male young.

غوا	*ghwā*	Cow	سخی	*skhay*	calf.
ميښه	*mékha*	Buffalo	كتی	*katay*	Buffalo calf.
اسپه	*aspa*	mare	كوْ چانزی	*kūcha nray*	Colt.
گډه	*gada*	Sheep	اورَی	*oray*	Lamb.
چيلئ	*chélai*	She goat	بکری	*bakray*	Kid.
اوښ	*ūkha*	Female camel	جوْنۍ	*jōngay*	young camel.
سپئ	*spai*	Bitch	كوْترى	*kūtré*	pup.

113. پﮧ قهر کیدل = *puh qahar kédal* to be enraged with. takes Dative case as :—

| ما ته پﮧ قهر شو | *mā ta puh qahar sho* | He got angry with me. |

114. خپه کیدل = *khapa kédal* to be angry with, takes لﮧ-نﮧ = *luh-na* as :—

هغه رانه خپه شو *hagha rā na*

یا هغه له ما نه *khapa sho* or

خپه شو *hagha luh mā na khapa sho* He got angry with me.

لﮧ ما نه مﮧ خپه *luh mā na* Don't be angry کیږه *muh khapa kéga* with me.

115. بلا = *balā* = calamity, when used before plural nouns means innumerable and before singular number, denotes greatness, the biggest size and the best qualification of a person as :—

پﮧ جماعت کښ *puh jumāit ké* There are innu-
بلا خلق دی *balā khalq dee* merable people in the mosque.

هغه بلا سړی دی *hagha balā saray day* He is an exception-able person.

116. The Definite Habitual expressing a condition is formed by prefixing بﮧ = *ba* to the past definite as :—

چه ښهر ته به راغلو نو زﮤ به یی *chi khahar ta ba rāghlo*
و لیدم او بیا به لاړو *no zuh ba yé wo lidalam aw biā ba lāro*

Whenever he came to the city, he would come to see me and then go back.

117.   The Potential Habitual in the form of conditional in the 2nd half is formed by prefixing به = *ba*, to the past potential.

كه سركار ټول وطن ته د ټوپكو ساتلو اجازت وركړې وی ۔ نو څنګه به مـ ټول په قابو کښې ساتلی شول	*kuh sarkār tōl watan ta da tōpakō sātalō ijāzat warkaray way, nō sanga ba mé tōl puh qābū ké sātalay shwal.*

If the Government had allowed the whole country to keep rifles, how could I keep them all in hand.

118. هسې نه وی چه = *hasé nuh wi chi* = Lest. is followed by the *A*orist tense as :—

هسې نه وی چه هغه راشی   *hasé nuh wi chi hagha rāshee*

Lest he should come.

NOTE :—Also the use of چرته = *charta*, in this connection.

چرته هغه را نه شی   *charta hagha rā nuh shee.*

I hope he will not come (i.e. I fear lest he should come.)

119. Politely speaking when referring to the son of gentleman call him صاحبزاده = *Sahibzāda*, or برخوردار = *Barkhurdār* and when referring to ones own son, call him غلام = *ghulām* = Slave. Similarly when talking about the house of a gentleman (other than your own) you will call it

دولت خانه = *daulat khāna* = (abode of wealth) and
when talking of your own house, you will call it.

غريب خانه = *gharib khāna* = Humble cottage,
as :—

ستا سو دَ برخوردار نوم څۀ دی   *stāso da burkhurdār*
nūm suh day

What is the name of your son ?

داستاسو غلام به جواب درويږي   *dāstaso ghulām ba*
jawāb dar wree

This son of mine lit your slave will bring you
the answer.

ستا سو دولت خانه چرته ده   *stāso daulat khāna*
charta dah

Where is your house ?

ځما غريب خانه پۀ ښهر کښ ده   *zamā gharib khāna puh*
khahar kė dah

My house is in the city.

120. When visiting a patient, or referring
to an unpleasant subject, say, first :—

نصيب دشمنان   *nasibé dushmanān*

May it (disease) fall to the lot of your enemies.

When praising something or somebody
belonging to another person say :—

ماشاء الله   *mā shā allāh*   As God wills.

چشم بد دور   *chéshmé bad dūr*   Far be the evil eye.

نصیب دشمنان دا کله راسی ناجوړ
شوی یی

*nasibé dushmanān da
kala rāsé nā jora
shaway yé*

May your disease become the lot of your
enemies. How long have you been ill ?

ماشاء الله ستا سو برخوردار پۀ
جماعت کښې اول لمبر دی

*mā sha allah stāso
barkhurdār puh jamāat
ké awal lambar day*

By God's will your son is first in the class.

چشم بد دوړ ستا سو موټر دَ
چاونرئ دَ موټرونو پلار دی

*cheshmé bad dūr stāso
mōtar da chāunrai da
mōtarūno plār day*

Far be the evil eye, your motor is the best in the
cantt; (lit: is the father of motors in the Cantt.)

121. Strong Negation is sometimes expressed by using خاوري = *khāwré* = dust, with the
subject of the verb as :—

هغه به پۀ دی خاوري پوه
شی څۀ

*hagha ba pa dé khāwré
poh shee suh*

How on earth can he understand this ?

122. Interrogatives are often used to express
strong negation, surprise and impossibility as :—

زۀ پۀ دی کښې څۀ کولی شم

*zuh pa dé ké suh
kawalay sham*

What can I do in this matter! (or it is impossible
for me to do anything in this matter).

زۀ څنګه هلته لاړشم

*zuh sangā halta lār
sham*

How can I go there or I cannot go there or it is
impossible for me to go there.

تهٔ پهٔ دی څهٔ پوهیږي   *tuh pa dé suh pohégé*

How do you know of this ? (you know nothing
of this).

هغه کله کابل ته تلی دی   *hagha kala kabal ta
talay day*

When has he been to Kabul ? (i e. he has
never been to Kabul).

123. Many Arabic and Persian adverbs
are commonly used :—

اتفاقاً	*ittefāqan*	by chance.
خصوصاً	*khusūsan*	especially.
تخميناً	*takhminan*	nearly.
قريباً	*qariban*	nearly.
فوراً	*fauran*	at once.
جبراً	*jabran*	by force.
مثلاً	*masalan*	for instance.
عموماً	*umūman*	generally.
ارادتاً	*irādatan*	intentionally.

etc :—

124. Some idiomatic uses of چرته—*charta*
where.

چرته زهٔ او چرته تهٔ   *charta zuh aw charta tuh*
there is all the difference between you and me
(lit : where am I and where are you.) ?

چرته هغه بادشاهی او چرته دا غریبی   *charta hagha bādshāhi
aw charta dā gharibi*

Once there was such a good time and now there
is this poverty.

زۀ چرته او تۀ چر ته *zuh charta aw tuh charta*

We were far apart from each other or you found me merely by luck.

چر ته یې کیږ ده *charta yé kégda*

Place it somewhere.

ګوره که چر ته څوک راشي *gōra kuh charta sōk rāshee*

Wait and perchance someone may come.

ما چر ته ایښی دی *mā charta ikhay day*

I have placed it somewhere.

پهم کوه چه چر ته نا جوړنه شی *paham kawa chi charta nā jōra nuh shé*

Be careful lest you should fall ill.

چر ته ورک شوی خو نۀ دی *charta vrak shaway kho nuh day*

I hope he or it has not been lost by any chance.

125. Direct narration is always used in place of indirect narration as :—

هغۀ و وچه څما نؤم جان دی *haghuh wō wé chi zamā nāu Jān day*

He said his name was John.

هغۀ و چه زۀ بۀ لاړ شم *haghuh wo wé chi zuh ba lār sham*

He said that he would go.

126. The required tense of کیدل = *kédal* with the ablative can be used to express Potential mood.

دا كارلۀ تا نه كيږي *dā kar luh tā*
na kégee   You can do this.

دا كارلۀ ما نه نۀ كيږي *da kar luh mā*
na nuh kégee   I cannot do this.

داسي كارلۀ ما نه نۀ *dāsé kar luh*   I could not do
كيدو *mā na nuh kédo* such work.

لۀ ماٰنه دانۀ اوچتيږي *luh mā na dā*   I cannot lift this
nuh ūchatégee up.

127. The negative potential mood with the
ablative case is also used to express impossibility and strong negation as :—

لۀ ما نه نۀ شى كيدى   *luh mā na nuh shi*
kéday

I am not going to do it or it is impossible for me
to do it. (lit: from me it cannot become).

128. Pathans themselves are often puzzled
to know which is the subject and which is the
object in sentences with a transitive verb, where
the subject and object both are singular in
number and the subject remains uninflected in
form in the agentive case.

To distinguish the subject لرى كيدل *= lagé*
kédal to act, is conjugated after it as :—

احمد خان لرى شو محمد خان   *Ahmad Khan lagé sho,*
Muhamad Khan yé wo
يى ووهلو   *wahalo*

Ahmad Khan beat Muhamad Khan.

NOTE:—Normally the subject in the sentence is put first, but colloquially this is often disregarded.

129. The following nouns take ورکول = *war kawal* to give.

شکست ورکول	*shikast war kawal*	To defeat.
مدد ورکول	*madad war kawal*	To help.
قرض ورکول	*qarz war kawal*	To lend.
لاس ورکول	*lās war kawal*	To shake hands, help.
رنگ ورکول	*rang war kawal*	To colour, dye.
گُذار ور کول	*guzār war kawal*	To give a blow.
رنج ور کول	*rabar war kawal*	To trouble.
سزا ور کول	*sazā war kawal*	To punish.

130. The following nouns take اخستل = *akhistal* = to take.

ساه اخستل	*sāh akhistal*	To breathe.
پناه اخستل	*panāh akhistal*	To take refuge.
لُـنه پور اخستل	*luh-na por akhistal*	To borrow.
لُـنه څولہ اخستل	*luh-na khuluh akhistal*	To kiss.

131. The following nouns take لږول = *lagawal* = to add, to put, to apply etc, as :—

لاس لږول	*lās lagawal*	To fight, touch.
اور لږول	*aur lagawal*	To set fire to.
قُلپ لږول	*qulp lagawal*	To lock.

ديل لږَول	*dïl lagawal*	To delay.
زور لږَول	*zōr lagawal*	To exert strength.
پته لږَول	*pata lagawal*	To trace.
ګلونه لږَول	*gulūna lagawal*	To arrange flowers (in vases)
ميز لږَول	*méz lagawal*	To arrange table.
روپي لږَول	*rupai lagawal*	To spend money.
ډيره لږَول	*dèra lagawal*	To pitch a tent, or encamp.
دوكان لږَول	*dūkān lagawal*	To open shop.

132. The following nouns take لږيدل=
lagédal = to be applied.

پښ۔باند اور لږيدل	*puh-bāndé aur lagédal*	To catch fire.
پښ۔باند لوږه لږيدل	*puh-bāndé luaga lagédal*	To feel hungry.
پښ۔باند تنده لږيدل	*puh-bāndé tanda lagédal*	To feel thirsty.
پښ۔باند بد لږيدل	*puh-bāndé bad lagédal*	To take ill.
پښ۔باند باد لږيدل	*puh-bāndé bād lagédal*	To blow (wind.)
پښ۔باند خه لږيدل	*puh-bāndé khuh lagédal*	To like the sight of.

133. The following nouns take راتلل = *ratlal*
to come.

(ته) غُصه راتلل	*(ta) ghusa ratlal*	To feel angry.

پۀ بانډې) رحم راتلل (puh-bandé) raham ratlal	To feel comp-assion.
(ته) ژبه راتلل (ta) jhuba ratlal	To know (the language).
(پۀ) نظر راتلل (puh) nazar ratlal	To come into sight.
(پۀ) مخه راتلل (puh) makha ratlal	To meet.
(پۀ بانډې, تبه راتلل (puh bandé) taba ratlal	To catch fever.

134. The following nouns take خوړل= khwaral to eat as :—

قسم خوړل qasam khwaral	To take an oath.
دوکه خوړل dōka khwaral	To be deceived.
شکست خوړل shikast khwaral	To be defeated
تیندک خوړل tindak khwaral	To stumble.

135. څۀ = suh What, is sometimes put at the end of a sentence to form a question as :—

ما خپل کار نۀ دی *mā khpal kār*
څۀ کړی *nuh dáy karay* Have I not done
suh ?   my work ?

136. The following nouns are commonly met with as collective numerals :—

جوړه jōra	Pair, couple.
درزن darzan	Dozen.
کوړۍ kaurai	Score.
سيکړه saikára	Hundred (percent).

137. By adding ‏وارهٔ‎ = *wāra* all, to any numerals, with the exception of ‏یو‎ = *yau* one. totality is shown as :—

‏دوارهٔ‎ *dwāra*   Both.

‏درى وارهٔ‎ *dré wāra*   All three.

‏څلور وارهٔ‎ *salōr wāra*   All four.

‏پنځهٔ وارهٔ‎ *pinzuh wāra*   All five.

Similarly ‏پهٔ‎ = *puh* before and ‏ګونه‎ = *gūna*, after the numerals are used :—

‏پهٔ ساګونو‎ *puh sulgūmo*   Hundreds of.

‏پهٔ زرګونو‎ *puh zargūno*   Thousands of.

‏پهٔ لکونو‎ *puh lakūno*   Lakhs of.

*

138. The multiplicative numerals are formed by adding ‏چند‎—*chand*. after any numeral or by prefixing ‏یو پهٔ‎—*yau puh* to it as :—

‏دو چند‎ *dō chand*   twice more.

‏درى چند‎ *dré chand*   thrice more.

‏څلور چند‎ *salōr chand*   four times more.

‏پنځهٔ چند‎ *pinzuh chand* five times more.

or

‏یو پهٔ دوه‎ *yau puh dwa*   twice.

‏یو پهٔ درى‎ *yau puh dré*   thrice.

---

* NOTE.—On account of *puh* or *puh bānde*, they are put into the oblique plural.

يو پهٔ څلور   *yau puh salōr*   four times more.

يو پهٔ پنځهٔ   *yau puh pinzuh*   five times more.

139.   The adverbial numerals once, twice, thrice etc. are formed by adding څل—*zal* = time, in the singular. څله—*zala*, in the plural which is inflected to څلو—*zalō*, in the oblique plural as :—

يو څل	*yau zal*	once.
دوه څلَ	*dwa zala*	twice.
درى څلَ	*dré zala*	thrice.
څلور څلَ	*salōr zala*	four times.
لهٔ څلورو څلو	*luh salōro*	
څلو نه زيات	*zalō na ziāt*	More than four times.

140.   The fractional numerals are :—

نيم	*nim*	half.
پاو	*pāw*	quarter.
درى پاو	*dré pāwu*	three quarters.
پاو کم دوه	*pāw kam dwa*	one and three quarters 1¾.

141.   دٔ = *da* = is sometimes used instead of لهٔ = *luh*, the first half of the ablative case as :—

دٔ کور نه *da kōr na* or دٔ کوره *da kora* from the house, instead of :—

لهٔ کورنه *luh kōr na* or لهٔ کوره *luh kōra* from the house.

142. ليكن = *léken*   خو = *kho*   مگر = *magar*
ولى = *walé* all mean "But" مگر = *magar* and
ولى = *walé* are used in the case of expressing
exceptions and بلكه = *balké* means on the other
hand or instead of as :—

ما ورنه تپوس وکړو چه کور د   *mā war na taᵽōs wo*
چرته دى ليکن يا خو جواب يى   *krō chi kōr dé charta*
                                day lekén (or) *khō*
رانۀ کړ   *jawāb yé rā nuh kar.*

I asked him where his house was but he did not
answer.

ټول کليوال ښۀ دى مگر يو په   *tōl kali wāl khuh di*
                                magar (or *walé*) *yau*
کښ ښۀ نۀ دىَ   *pa ké khuh nuh day*

All the villagers are good except one who is not
good.

زۀ نۀ صرف دَ هغۀ. وروريم بلكه   *zuh nuh sirf da haghuh*
                                vrōr yam balké naukar
نوکر يى هم يم   *yé hum yam*

I am not only his brother but (or on the other
hand) I am his servant as well.

143. The past tense is used to express past
conjunctive as :—

چه کابل ته ورسيدم نو ستا دوست   *chi Kābal ta wo*
                                rasédam no stā dōst mé
م وليدلو يا ستا دوست راته ملاؤشو *wo lidalo* or *stā dōst rā*
                                ta milāo sho

Having arrived in Kabul I met your friend.

144. The simple present is idiomatically used to express desire of a person, wish and present continous as : —

زۀ ځم   *zuh zam.*
- I want to go.
- I like to go.
- I wish to go.
- I am going.
- I go.

145. ملاست = *mlāst* Lying is only used for animate objects acting of their own accord, while پروت = *prōt* prostrate or lying, is used for inanimate objects and an animate objects with any kind of disease or helplessness.

زۀ پۀ کټ باند ملاست یم   *zuh puh kat bandé mlāst yam*
I am lying on the bed.

زۀ درى ورځى ناجوړ پر پروت وم   *zuh dré vrazé nājora prōt wam*
I was lying ill for three days.

کتاب پۀ میز باند پروت دى   *kitāb puh méz bandé prōt day*
The book is lying on the table

146. حاضر = *hāzir* = Present or at the service of. while موجود = *maujūd* = present is used for superiors or in the case of inanimate objects denoting existing or available etc. as :—

ټول نوکران حاضر دي   *tōl naukarān hāzir di*
All the servants are present.

خاں په موقعه موجود وه   *khān puh mōqa maujūd woh*

The Khan was present at the spot.

دا حکایت پۀ کتاب کښ موجود دی   *dā hikāyat puh kitāb ké maujūd day*

This story is (present) in the book.

NOTE :— خدای حاضر دی = *khudāi hāzir day* = God is present.

147. It is not polite to address the following persons without using the word صاحب = *sāhib* =

مُنشی	*munshi*	Munshi, teacher, writer.
با بو	*bābu*	Clerk.
جمعدار	*jamādār*	Lieut. (Indian rank.)
صوبیدار	*subédār*	Captain (Indian rank.)
سردار	*sardār*	Indian officer in the Army.
حکیم	*hakim*	Physician.
ڈاکٹر	*dāngtar*	Doctor.
مولوی	*maulvi*	Priest, learned.
قاضی	*qāzi*	Judge.

148. بعضی = *bazé* = Some, implies some out of a certain number and څینی—*ziné*—Some. implies some out of a certain number. Also it is a substitute for سخه = *sakha* = (Post position) as :—

بعضی خلق ښۀ دی   *bazé khalq khuh di*

Some people are good.

پُه بعضو کتابونو کښ راغلي دی *puh bazo̱ kitabūno ké rāghali di*

It is written (lit : come) in some books.

ځيني پُه رساله کښ نوکري کوي *ziné puh résāla ké naukari kawi̱*

Some of them serve in the Cavalry.

تا ځيني چاقو شته *tā ziné chāqū shta* Have you a pen knife.

149. مه = *ma* = is the sign of prohibition and is used at the end of a sentence to express fear or force as :—

ته نن ځه مه = *tuh nan za ma* = You must not go today (or else you will get into trouble).

150. In the present conditional, the past tense is sometimes used in the first clause to express definite action as :—

کۀ دا کار دٖ وزِر نو مه بٖ دٖ کړم *kuh dā kār dé wo kro, no̱ mar ba dé kram*

I will kill you if you do this.

151. ماوٖ = *mā wé* or ماووٻل = *ma wo wayal* I said, spoke or told has a secondary idiomatic meaning "I meant" as :—

ما وٻل زۀ بٖ پُه رساله کښ نوکري کوم *mā wayal zuh ba puh resāla ké naukari kawam_*

I meant to serve in the Cavalry.

152. In the following examples it will be noticed that the use of different prepositions is highly idiomatic. Sometimes a change of preposition completely changes the meaning not only of the whole sentence but of the nouns and verbs used as :—

هغه پۀ سپين آس باند سوردي	*hagha puh spin āss bāndé sōr day*	He is riding on a white horse.
هغه پۀ سپين آس کښن سوردى	*hagha puh spin āss ké sōr day*	He is riding in a trap with a white horse in the shafts.
هغه مورنه تلَى دى	*hagha mōr ta talay day*	He takes after his mother.
هغه مور باند تلَى دى	*hagha mōr bāndé talay day*	Lit: He has gone back into his mother (term of abuse).
هغه موټر ته پريوتو	*hagha mōtar ta préwato*	He threw himself in front of a motor car.
هغه موټر باند پريوتو	*hagha mōtar bāndé préwato*	He bumped into a stationery motor car.
هغه کورته ننوتو	*hagha kōr ta nanawato*	He went into his house.
هغه پۀ کور باند ننوتو	*hagha puh kōr bāndé nanawato*	He went into someone else's house.
هغه باغ ته ننوت	*hagha bāgh ta nanawat*	He went into a Garden.

هغه پٔه باغ ورننوت *hagha puh bāgh war nanawat* — He went into someone else's garden (because of fear) or he was chased into a garden.

هغه پٔه پیښور کښ دَی *hagha puh pékhawar ké day* — He is in Peshawar.

هغه پٔه پیښور باند دَی *hagha puh pékhawar bāndé day* — He is in charge of Peshawar.

هغهٔ ته اواز وکړه *haghuh ta awāz wo kra* — Call him.

هغهٔ باند اواز وکړه *haghuh bāndé awāz wo kra* — Challenge him.

153. Use the word خان = *zān* = self, or خپلخان = *khapal zān* = oneself, with the Dative case before a compound transitive verb formed from an adjective to express "pretended to be", e.g :—

هغهٔ ورته خان مړ کړ *haghuh war ta zān mar kar* — He pretended to be dead.

هغهٔ ورته خپل خان اودهٔ کړ *haghuh war ta khpal zān ūduh kar* — He pretended to be asleep.

ما ورته خپل خان لیونَی کړ *mā war ta khpal zān léwanay kar* — I pretended to be mad.

154. Note the following idioms dealing with the use of څومره چه = *sōmra chi* = as much, before

the first clause and دومره = *dōmra* = so much, before the second clause, e. g. :—

خومره چه دَ وسَ م کیږ‌ری دومره
کوشش به کوم

sōmra chi dā wasā mé kégee, dōmra kōshish ba kawam

I will try my best.

خومره چه دَ وَس دِ کیږ‌ری دومره
زر هلته لاړشه

sōmra chi da wasa dé kégee, dōmra zar halta lārsha,

Go there as soon as you can.

خومره چه دَ وسَ م کیدل دومره
جوارم ورکړل

sōmra chi da wasa mé kédal, dōmra jowār mé war kral.

I gave him as much maize as I could afford.

خومره چه دَ وسَ م کیدلی دومرهٔ
روپئ م ورکوله

sōmra chi da wasa mé kédalé, dōmra rūpai mé war kralé

I gave him as much money as I could afford.

155.   When animals and birds are counted use سر = *sara* = Heads, before them as :—

شل سرهٔ مال   *shal sara māl*   twenty head of cattle

دیرش سر   *dérsh sarā*

مرغا بئ   *marghābai*   Thirty geese.

156.   In the following idiom "with" the English preposition is not translated as :—

تهٔ خپل طلب   *tuh khpal talab* What do you do

ساه کوې   *sāh kawé*   with your pay ?

157. تا لاش کول = *talāsh kawal* = to search for.
takes indirect object while اتول = *latawal* = to
search, takes direct object.

ما دَ کتاب تالاش و کړلو   *mā dā kitāb talāsh wo*
kralo

or

ما کتاب دَ پاره تالاش و کړلو   *mā kitāb da para talāsh*
wo kralo

I searched for the book.

ما کور و لتو لو   *mā kōr wo*
latawalō   I searched the house.

158. ډک = *dak* = Full, is always governed by
ablative case.

تلاؤ لۀ اوبو نه ډک   *talāw luh obo*   A   tank   full   of
na dak   water.

بیړۍ لۀ سړو نه ډکه   *bérai luh saro*
na daka   A boat full of men

کمرې لۀ کرسو نه   *kamré luh kursō*   Rooms   full   of
ډکی   *na daké*   chairs.

159. نه رشتیا = *na rishtiā* = Lit. what I said
is not right and the following is correct, is used
to express "As you were or "I mean."

دَ کور خاوند احمد خان نه رشتیا   *da kōr khāwand Ahmad*
محمد خان دَی   *Khan na rishtiā*
Mohmad Khan day

The owner of the house is Ahmed Khan-as
you were-it is Mohamad Khan.

160. Adjectives denoting "belonging to" or native of a place, country etc. are formed by adding ي = *ay* as :—

پنجاب *punjāb* Punjab.   پنجابي *punjābay* from Punjab.

كابل *kābal* Kabul.   كابلى *kābalay* from Kabul.

پيښور *pékha-war* Peshawar.   پيښورى *pékha-wray* from Peshawar

161. Note the following forms :—

سپينه ګيره	*spīna gira*	White beard.
سپين ګيرى	*spin giray*	White bearded.
سره لكئ	*sra lakai*	Red tail.
سۇر لكى	*sūr lakay*	Red tailed.
توره غاړه	*tōra ghāra*	Black neck.
تور غاړى	*tōr ghāray*	Black necked.
سرکوز	*sar kūz*	Head hanging.
سرکوزى	*sar kūzay*	Pig.
پي مخ	*pai makh*	Milk face.
پي مخى	*pai makhay*	Milk faced.

162. Note the force of repetition of tense in the following examples :—

كه لاړو لاړو   *kuh lāro lāro*

If he has gone by his own wish let him go ! I don't care !

كة كوي كوي كوي كة نة كوي نة كوي   *kuh kawī kawī kuh nuh*
kawī nuh kawī

If he means to do it let him do it, if he does not
mean to do it let him not do it, it makes no
difference to me.

163.   Note the following suffixes :—

زر *war*	زرور *zrawar*		Bold.
	ښكرور *khkarawar*		Horned (term of abuse).
	بختور *bakhtawar*		Lucky.
وان *wān*	باغوان *bāghwān*		Gardener, mali.
	جاله وان *jālawān*		Th: owner of the ra ..
	كاروان *kārwān*		Caravan.
چی *chī*	نشانچی *néshānchī*		Standard bearer.
	توپچی *tōpchī*		Marksman.
	ډنډورچی *dandōrchī*		Halerd, proclaimer.
دان *dān*	زندان *zandān*		Prison.
	خاندان *khānadān*		Family.
	نمكدان *namakdān*		Salt cellar.
دار *dār*	سردار *sardār*		Indian Officer, leader.
	دوكاندار *dūkāndār*		Shopkeeper.
	تانړيدار *tānrédār*		Sub-Inspector of Police.
	ديندار *dindār*		Pious.
	وفادار *wafādār*		Faithful.
	زميندار *zamīndār*		Farmer.

گار gār	خدمتگار	khidmatgār	Servant.
	مدد گار	madadgār	Helper.
	گناهگار	gunāhgār	Sinful, guilty.
داری dāri	خبرداری	khabardāri	Care.
	لمبرداری	lambardāri	Headman's job.
	څوکيداری	saukidāri	Watchman's job.
گر gar	زر گر	zargar	Goldsmith.
	جا دو گر	jādugar	Juggler.
	کيميا گر	kimiāgar	Gold aud silver maker
	کاريگر	kārigar	Blacksmith.
کار kār	زنا کار	zanā kār	Adulterer.
	بد کار	bad kār	Licentious.
	جفا کار	jafākār	Tyrannical.
گي gī	مهر بانگي	méhrabān gi	Kindness.
	روانگي	rawāngi	Departure.
	پيشگي	péshgi	An advance (of money).
گين gīn	غمگين	ghamgin	Sorrowful.
	مالگين	mālgin	Saltish or salt mine.
مند mand or من man	درد مند	dārdmand	Painful.
	شته مند	shtuhmand	Rich.
	فكر مند	fikarmand	Anxious,
	سود مند	sūdmand	Profitable.

ناک	nāk	حرصناک	harasnāk	Greedy.
		صبر ناک	sabar nāk	Patient.
		شرمناک	sharam nāk	Shameful.
ستان	stān	گلستان	gulistān	Place of flowers.
		و زیرستان	waziristān	Waziristan, Country of Waziris.
		کفر ستان	kufaristān	Country of unbelievers.
وار	wār	آمید وار	umaidwār	Hopeful, candidate.
		پیدا وار	paidāwār	Produce.
		سزا وار	sazāwār	Punished.
ژن	jhan	دروغژن	darōgh jhan	Liar.
		کبر ژن	kabar jhan	Proud.
		غمژن	ghamjhan	Full of grief.
زن	zan	تورزن	tūrzan	Brave.
		لاپزن	lāpzan	Boaster.
		لانبوزن	lānbōzan	Swimmer.
وال	wāl	هینډیوال	handiwāl	Mess mate.
		کلیوال	kaliwāl	Villager.
		بنیروال	bunérwāl	Man of Buner.
		تیراوال	tirawāl	Man of Tirah.

164. The following particles are used with adjectives to express quite, very, entirely, absolutely.

تک *tak*	سؤر تک *tak sūr*	Quite red.
	سپین تک *tak spin*	Quite white
	شین تک *tak shin*	Quite green
تپ *tap*	تور تپ *tap tōr*	Very decrepit.
	تپ رؤند *tap rūnd* or پہ ٹپر رؤند *puh tapo rūnd*	Quite blind / Stone blind
ګرب *grab*	زور ګرب *zōr grab*	Very old. (applied to a person)
پر *par*	خر پر *khar par*	Quite grey, full of dust.
	غور پر *ghwar par*	Very greasy
پشت *pusht*	خوشت پشت *khusht pusht*	Quite wet.
خوشت *khusht*	اؤند خوشت *lūnd khusht*	Very wet.
غوټ *ghut*	غوټ پریکاری *ghut prékari*	Clear or quite cut off
پہ *pat*	غہ پہ *ghat pat*	Very fat.
روغ *rōgh*	روغ جور *rōgh jōr*	Quite well.
تکنره *takanra*	تکنره غرمہ *takanra gharma*	Blazing noon.
تم *tam*	تورتم *tōr tam*	Quite dark.
لغر *laghar*	بربند لغر *barband laghar*	Stark naked
پخ *pakh*	یخ پخ *yakh pakh*	Very cold.
نوزی *nūzāy*	نوی نوزی *nāway nūzay*	Absolutely new.
پور *pōr*	زور پور *zōr pōr*	Very old. (applied to things worn out)

	شور پور shōr pōr	Very greasy
کپر kapar	کنډ کپر kand kapar	Destroyed
ووز wōg	کوږ ووز kōg wōg	Entirely crooked:
چوړ chūr	چپ چوړ chap chūr	Badly shuttered.
وډ wad	ګډ وډ gad wad	Mixed up.
سمخ samakh	سوړ سمخ sōr samakh	Very cold.
وړ wōr	خور وړ khōr wōr	Scattered.
پنګ pang	رنګ پنګ rang pang	Smeared (with blood etc.)
جک jak	جک جوړ jak jōr	Quite well
چنباق chun-bāq	چاق چنباق chāq chunbāq	Very energetic.
پنړ panr	چنړ پنړ chanr panr	Noise of birds.
پل pal	دل پل dal pal	Absolutely crushed.
ګوم gūm	ګم ګوم gūm gūm	Entirely last
تروش trush	تنګ تروش tang trush	Very Tight.
		,, small.
		,, narrow.

Section 11.

PARTS OF SPEECH.

ADVERBS.

زر zur	Soon.

زر زر	*zur zur*	Quickly.
ولی	*walé*	Why.
هسی	*hasé*	Thus.
ناصا په	*nāsāpa*	} By chance.
ناگها نه	*nāghāna*	
لا	*lā*	Yet.
خو	*kho*	But, at least.
سره	*sara*	Together.
لكه	*laka*	Like, as.
ورو ورو	*vrō vrō*	Slowly.
تل	*tal*	}
مُدام	*mūdām*	} Always.
همیشه	*hamésha*	}

ADVERBS OF PLACE.

بهر	*bahar*	Outside.
چرته	*charta*	Where.
دلته	*dalta* or	}
دلی	*dalé*	} Here.
هلته	*halta*	There.
بیرته	*biarta*	Back.
پورته	*pōrta*	Above.
هر چرته	*harcharta*	Everywhere.
دننه	*danana*	Inside.
نیزدی	*nizdé*	Near.
بل چرته	*bal charta*	Some where else.

هيچرته	*hicharta*	No where.
ښکته	*khkatā*	Below.
لاند	*lāndé*	
لاند باند	*lāndé bāndé*	Upside down.
چاپيره	*chāpéra* or	Around.
گير چاپيره	*gér chāpéra*	
لۀ لرى نه	*luh laré na*	From a distance.
دَ وراېه	*da vrāya*	
ورسته	*vrōsto*	Behind.
وراند	*vrāndé*	Before.

THE ADVERBS OF TIME.

آخر	*ākhér*	At last, in the end.
بيا	*biā*	Again.
پخوا	*pakhwā*	Formerly.
اوس	*ōss*	Now.
زر زر	*zar zar*	Quickly.
ورو ورو	*vro vro*	Slowly.
ورمبى	*vrumbay*	Firstly.
وار پۀ وار	*wār puh wār*	In time.
هاله	*hāla*	Then.
كله نه كله	*kala na kala*	Occasionally.
تر كله پورى	*tar kala pōré*	Until when.
كله	*kala*	When.
كله كله	*kala kala*	Sometimes.
پۀ دى شپو ورزو كى	*puh dé shpo vrazo ké*	Now a days.

چری۔چری	charé charé	Now and then.
تر اوسَ پوری	tar osa poré	Until now.
لا تر اوسَ	lā tar osa	Even until now.
بیگاه	bégāh	Last night.
پرون	parūn	Yesterday.
صبا یا صباله	sabā or sabāla	Tomorrow.
بل صبا	bal sabā	Day after tomorrow.
سحر	sahar	Morning.
ما خام	mākhām	Evening.
نن سحر	nan sahar	This morning.
لا بل صبا	lā bal sabā	The second day after tomorrow.
نن	nan	To-day.
سږ کال	sag kāl	This year.
مښی کال	makhé kāl	Next year.
پروسکال	parōsa kāl	Last year.
اوړم کال	oram kāl	Year before last.
پس	pas	After.
هرکله	har kala	Ever, at any time.
هرکله چه	har kala chi	Whenever.
مُدام	mudām	Always.
و ختی	wakhti	Early.
نا وَ خته	nāwakhta	Late.
یو ځل	yau zal	Once.
دوه ځلَ	dwa zala	Twice.
څو ځلَ	zala	How often ?
ډیرځلَ	dér zala	Many times.

THE ADVERBS OF QUANTITY.

ديٖر	dér	Much.
څو مره	sōmra	Howmuch, how many.
دومره	dōmra	This much.
هرڅومره	har sōmra	How ever much.
لٔ كؤ تٖی	lūkūti	A little.
زيات	ziāt	More.
هر	har	Every.
څه	suh	Some.
هر څو	har so	How ever many.
هر څه	har suh	Whatever.
هر يو	har yau	Everyone.
هر څوک	har sōk	Everyone.
تر حدَ پورٖی	tar hada pōré	To the utmost extent.
تر حدَ زيات	tar hada ziāt	Beyond degree.
له حدَ زيات	luh hada ziāt	,, ,,
بيحدَ	béhada	Unlimited.

CONJUNCTIONS.

او	aw	And.
چه	chi	That.
كه	kuh	If.
و لی چه	walé chi	Because.
بلكه	balké	More over.
خو	kho	But.
ځكه	zakā	Therefore.

خکه چه *zaka chi*	Because.
هم *hum*	Also.
یا *yā*	Or.
سره د دی *sara da dé*	Not withstanding.

PREPOSITIONS.

See Page No. 14.

INTERJECTIONS.

ای *ay*	Oh.
آفرین *āfrin*	Bravo.
وای وای *wāi wāi*	Oh dear.
توبه *tōba*	Fie.
واه واه *wāh wāh*	Bravo, Oh (To express extreme surprise).
اخ *akh*	Oh (To express extreme surprise).
چښَی *chakha*	} Get away, (to a dog).
کوری *kuré*	
رختیا *rikhtiā*	Indeed.
افسوس *afsōs*	
های های *hāi hāi*	
وای وای *wāi wāi*	} Alas.
ارمان ارمان *armān armān*	
امان *amān*	Mercy.
شتاباش *shābāsh*	Bravo.

PART II.

PROSE COMPOSITION.

Section 12.

This section of Part II contains sixty short English into Pushtu and Pushtu into English Exercises with Vocabularies, beginning with simple sentences and working upto the standard required for the Higher Standard Examination. The beginner who is taking the Lower Standard Examination is advised to learn the words first and do one or two exercises a day.

VOCABULARY I.

څوک	*sōk*	Who.
نوم	*nūm*	Name.
سړی	*saray*	A man.
ښځه	*khaza*	Woman or wife.
هلک	*halak*	Boy.
جينۍ	*jinai*	Girl.
ځوی	*zōi*	Son.
لور	*lūr*	Daughter.
ورور	*vrōr*	Brother.
خور	*khōr*	Sister.
چرته	*charta*	Where ?
دلته	*dalta*	Here.
هلته	*halta*	There.

کور	*kōr*	Home, House.
کلّی	*kalay*	Village.
څو یا څومرهٔ	*sō* or *sōmra*	How many or how much.
څو مرهٔ لری	*sōmra laré*	How far.
لری	*laré*	Far.
نیزدی	*nizdé*	Near.
چاونړۍ	*chāwnrai*	Station or Cantonment
نوکر	*naukar*	Servant.
نوکری	*naukari*	Service.
دُشمن یا دُښمن	*dushman* or *dukhman*	Enemy.
دوست	*dōst*	Friend.
چوټی	*chuti*	Leave.
ولی	*walé*	Why ?
حاضر	*hāzér*	Present.
غیر حاضر	*ghair hāzér*	Absent.
نن	*nan*	To day.
پرون	*parūn*	Yesterday.
صبا یا صبا له	*sabā* or *sabāla*	To-morrow.
بل صبا	*bal sabā*	Day after to-morrow
بیګاه	*bégah*	Last night.
بیګاله	*bégāla*	To-night.
ماښام	*mākhām*	Evening or p. m.
سحر	*sahar*	Morning or a. m.
غرمه	*gharma*	Noon.
نن سحر	*nan sahar*	This morning.

NOTES :— (a) In Pushtu the 2nd person singular is normally used in address i. e., ﺗﻪ = tuh = thou, instead of ﺗﺎﺳﻮ = tāso = you, and ﺳﺘﺎ = stā = they, instead of ﺳﺘﺎﺳﻮ = stāso = your.

The 2nd person plural is occasionally used for extreme politeness.

(b) The order of the sentence in Pushtu is usually subject, object, verb.

EXERCISE 1.

1. Who are you ? 2. What is your name ? 3. Who is that man ? 4. Where is your house ? 5. How far is it from the Cantonment ? 6. I am his servant. 7. My name is Ahmad. 8. He is my friend. 9. What is his name ? 10. How many men are on leave ? 11. Why were you absent ? 12. What time is it ?

EXERCISE 2.

1. ﺍﺩ ﺳﺮﻯ ﺧﻮﮎ ﺩﻯ = dā saray sōk day ? 2. ﺩ ﻫﻐﻪ ﻧﻮﻡ ﺳﻪ ﺩﻯ = da haghuh nūm suh day ? 3. ﮐﻮﺭﻭﻧﻪ ﺋﻰ ﭼﺮﺗﻪ ﺩﻯ = kōrūna yé charta di ? 4. ﺳﺘﺎﺳﻮ ﮐﻮﺭﻭﻧﻪ ﺧﻮ ﻣﺮﻩ ﻟﺮﻯ ﺩﻯ = stāso kōrūna sōmra laré di ? 5. ﭼﺎﻭﻧﺮﯼ ﺧﻮﻣﺮﻩ ﻟﺮﻯ ﺩﻩ = chāwnrai sōmra laré dah ? 6. ﺩ ﭼﺎ ﻧﻮﮐﺮ ﺋﻰ = da chā naukar yé ? 7. ﺗﻪ ﺫﻣﺎ ﻧﻮﮐﺮ ﻧﻪ ﺋﻰ = tuh zamā naukar nuh yé.

8. څومره سړی غير حاضر دی = *sōmra sari ghair hāzér di?* 9. پرون زه حاضر نۀ وم = *prūn zuh hāzér nuh wam.* 10. هغه ستا دوست دی کۀ نه = *hagha stā dōst day kuh na ?* 11. صاحب پۀ چوټۍ باند دی = *sāhib puh chūtai bānde day.* 12. څۀ وخت وو ؟ = *suh wakht woh ?.*

VOCABULARY II.

Common salutions and expressions used by Pathans.

Q. ستړی مۀ شی؟ *staray muh shé?* May you not get tired ?

A. خوار مۀ شی *khwār muh shé* or تۀ ستړی مۀ شی *tuh staray muh shé* } May you not become poor !

Q. پۀ خير راغلی ؟ *puh khér rāghlé ?* You are welcome ?

A. پۀ خير اوسی *puh khér osé* May you live happily ! (or in peace)

Q. هر کله راشه یا *har kala rāsha?* or راشه هر کله *rāsha har kala?* } You are always welcome ?

A. هر کله اوسی *har kala osé* May you live for ever !

Q. ښه چاری ؟ *kha chāré ?* Good luck to you ?

A. چار د ښه شه *chār dé kha sha* May your luck be good !

Q. پۀ مخه د ښه *puh makha dé kha ?* Good bye ?

A. آمین تا سره   *āmin tā sara*   Same to you.
    (*amin* = so be it).

A. خدای د مل   *khudāi dé mal*   May God be with
  شه   *sha*   you.

A. خدای د   *khudai dé wo*   May God forgive
  وبخینه   *bakha*   you.

Q. خدای ته   *khudāi ta spā-*   You are entrusted
  سپارلی یې   *ralay yé ?*   to God ?

A. خدای د اباد لره *khudāi dé abād*   May God keep you
          lara   prosperous.

Q. څه حال دی؟ *suh hāl day ?*   How are you ?

A. ښه حالدی د *khuh hāl day*   I am all right by
  خدای فضل دی   *da khudāi*   the grace of God.
          fazal day

حال	*hāl*	Condition.
جوړ	*jōr*	Well.
ناجوړ	*nā jōr*	Ill.
جک جوړ	*jak jōr*	Quite well. (جک = *jak* is only used with جوړ = *jōr*)
تکړه	*takra*	Strong.
خوشحال	*khushhāl*	Happy.
څنګه	*sunga*	How.
فصل	*fasal*	Grop.
فصلونه	*faslūna*	Crops,
غنم	*ghanam*	Wheat.
جوار	*jowār*	Maize.
اوربشی	*orbashé*	Barley.
پنبه	*punba*	Cotton.

شوتل	*shautal*	Clover.
شولی	*shōlé*	Rice (Crop).
نری جوار	*nari jowār*	Charri, cattle fodder.
کال	*kāl*	Year.
میاشت	*miāsht*	Month, Moon.
جمعه	*juma*	Week or Friday.
سږ کال	*sagkāl*	This year.
پروسکال	*parōsakāl*	Last year.
اورم کال	*oram kāl*	Year before last.
مخی کال	*makhé kāl*	Next year.
دولت	*daulat*	Wealth.
دولت مند	*daulatmand*	Wealthy.
غریب	*gharīb*	Poor.
ښه	*khuh*	Good.
خراب	*hharāp*	Bad.
مَلک	*malak*	Head man.
خان	*khan*	Chief.
فوځ	*fauz*	Troop, Army.
پلټن	*paltan*	Regiment.
رساله	*risāla*	Cavalry.
حوالدار	*havāldār*	Sergeant (infantry)
دفعدار	*dafédār*	Sergeant (Cavalry).
سپاهي	*spāhi*	Soldier.
لیس	*lais*	Corporal.
لیس نائک	*lais naik*	Lance Corporal.

EXERCISE 3

1. May you not get tired, Malak Sahib!
2. How are you? (lit, what condition is)
3. Are you well? 4. Yes, I am quite well.
5. Are you strong? 6. Yes, I am strong.
7. Are you happy? 8. Yes, I am happy.
9. Who is the Khan of this village? 10. Is
he a wealthy man? 11. What is the name of
this village? 12. The name of this village is
Mardan. 13. Are there any troops in Mardan?
14. Yes, there are two Infantry and three
Cavalry Regiments there.

NOTE :—The inflected form of دا = *dā* This
is :— دي = *dé* as :—

ذ دى كلى *da dé kali*   Of this village.

لۀ دى كلى نه *luh dé kali na* From this village.

VOCABULARY III.

ځکه *zaka*		Therefore.
ځکه چه *zaka chi*		Because.
خو - مـګر *kho, magar,*	} But.	
ليكن - ولى *lekan, walé*	}	
باران *bārān*		Rain.
لږ *lag*		Little.
ډير *dér*		Very, many, much, plenty.

مُلک یا وطن	*mulk* or *watan*	Country.
ښهر	*khahar*	City.
قحط	*qahat*	Famine.
خلق	*khalq*	People.
ټول	*tōl*	All.
دواړه	*dwāra*	Both.
معلوم	*mālūm*	Known.
ما ته یا را ته	*mā ta* or *rā ta*	
معلوم دی	*mālūm day*	I know it.
سور	*sōr*	Rider, Horseman.
عهده	*uhda*	Rank.
عهده دار	*uhda dār*	Non-Commissioned Officer.
پۀ کښې	*pa ké*	In it.
مزدوري	*mazdūri*	Labour, work, wages.
تنګ	*tang*	Oppressed, worried.
اوس	*oss*	Now.
کۀ	*kuh*	If or or
ځای	*zāi*	Place.
کله	*kala*	When ?
کله کله	*kala kala*	Sometimes.

EXERCISE 4.

۱ ـ دَ فصلونو د څۀ حال دی ؟   ۲ ـ سږ کال فصلونه ښۀ نۀ
دی ـ ځکه چه باران لږ وۀ   ۳ ـ کله کله پۀ باره کښې وی اوکله
نۀ وی   ۴ ـ تۀ عهده داری کۀ سپاهي ؟   زۀ دَ رسالی سورېم

٥ دَ دى كلى نؤم در ته معلوم دىَ؟ ٦ تول فوش اوس پهُ
چاونړيَ كښ دى ٧ تهُ پهُ نوكرِيَ كښ خوشحال يَ كهُ نه
٨ دَ كلو خلق دولتمند نهُ وى ٩ بارانو نه ابر وِ ښه پهُ وطن
كښ قحط دىَ ١٠ سنا پهُ پلتن كښ خومره سپاهيان دى
١١ دَ هغهُ دوا پو نوكرانِ پهُ نوكريَ كښ تدش دى ١٢ دَ هغهُ
ځايي نوم وړنه معلوم نهُ دىَ ١٣ پروسكال دَ غنمو او جزو فصلونه
خراب ؤو ١٤ چاونړيَ لويه ده خو په كښ مزدورِيَ ابرهوى -
دَ خان څلور خامس په پهُ فوش كښ دى -

1: See syntax rule No. 23.
2. Learn the numerals on Page 41.

VOCABULARY IV.

دَ چا	*da chā*	Whose ?
كتاب	*kitāb*	Book.
دا	*dā*	This or these.
كتاب چه	*kitab chı*	The book which.
ميز	*méz*	Table.
كُرسي	*kursai*	Chair.
صاحب چه	*sāhıb chı*	The sahib who.
جرنيل صاحب	*jarnail sāhib*	General.
د-پهُ مينځ كښ	*da-puh ṃianz ké*	Between, through.
هلك چدنؤم يي	*halaḳ chi nūm yé*	The boy whose name.
تربؤر	*tarbūr*	Cousin.
ترهُ	*truḥ*	Uncle.
لارچه	*lār chı*	The road which.

شی zee		Goes.
گرم garam		Hot, warm.
گرمي garmī		Heat.
یخ yakh		Cold. (adj.)
یخني yakhni		Cold (noun.)
اوری oray		Summer.
منی manay		Autumn.
ژمی jhamay		Winter.
سپرلی sparlay		Spring.
موسم mōsam		Season.
سیند sind		River.
خور khwar		Ravine.
غاړه ghāra		Bank (river)
بیړي bérai		Boat.
مانړگی mānrgay		Boat man.
ښکار khkār		Shooting, Hunting
کب kab		Fish.
کبان kabān		Fish (plural.)
یا yā		or
دَ کبانو ښکار da kabāno khkār		Fishing.
چغتی chaghaté	Snipe	(Sing. چغته chaghata)
هیلۍ hilai	Duck	(Sing. هیلۍ hilai)
بطی baté	Geeṡe	(Sing. بطه bata)
تنزری tanzari	Partridges	(Sing تنزری tanzary)
زرکی zarké	Chikor	(Sing زرکه zarka)
مرزی marzé	Quails	(Sing مرز maraz)

سوی‌ sawé   Hares   (Sing سوه sawa)
ارسئ osai   Deer   (Sing ارسئ osai)
اوچ och   Dry

EXERCISE 5.

1. [1] Have you a book ? 2. Yes, I have a book, 3. No, I have not a book. 4. Whose book is this ?. 5. It is not my book. 6 The books [2] which are on the table are not mine. 7. The sahib who was here this morning is the General's brother. 8. The country between Peshawar and Kabul is dry and bad. 9. The boy whose name is Ahmad, is my uncle's son. 10. The road which goes through Mardan is not a good one 11. I [3] like Peshawar, but my brother does not like it. 12. Why don't, you like Peshawar ?. 13. The heat is great in summer 14. There is little water in this country.

NOTES—1. شته = shta = Is there or are there ? Look up syntax rule No. 45. 2. چه = ché = that (conjunction) makes any interrogation relative i. e. څوک چه = sôk chi = He who. 3. خوښ khwakh = pleasant or liked See syntax rule No. 28.

VOCABULARY V.

تماكو tamāku   Tobacco.
چيلم chilam   Pipe.

تیلی	*tilay*	Match.
هم	*hum*	Also.
خایئسته	*khāista*	Beautiful or handsome
بدرنگ	*badrang*	Ugly.
هوښیار	*hukhyār*	Clever.
کم عقل	*kam aqal*	Foolish.
و رُوکی یا	*warūkay* or	Small.
ورکوتی	*warkōtay*	
لوی	*loi*	Big or Large.
هسپتال	*haspatāl*	Hospital.
په خوازمانهکښ	*puh khwā zamāna ké*	Formerly.
جبه	*jaba*	Marsh.
چینه	*china*	Spring (of water).
توپک	*tōpak*	Rifle.
کونیز توپک	*kūniz tōpak ?*	Snider Rifle.
گوریز توپک	*gōraiz tōpak*	A Martini Henry Rifle.
اوۀ دزی توپک	*owuh dazay tōpak*	Lee Metford Rifle.
درېوال توپک	*darewāl tōpak*	Pass-made Rifle.
بندری توپک	*bandari tōpak*	Persian Gulf made Rifle.
چقمقی توپک	*chaqmaṗi tōpak*	A flint lock gun.
باتیدار توپک	*bātᴈdar tōpak*	A match lock gun.
دَ چرو توپک یا	*da charo tōpak* or	A Shot gun.
چری دار توپک یا	*charidār tōpak.* or	
ښکاری توپک	*khkāri tōpak*	

چري *charé*	Shots.
گوليئ *gōlai*	Bullet.
دارؤ *dārū*	Gun Powder or Medicine.
اوس اوس *oss oss*	Presently, Recently.
اوسنيَ *osanay*	Recent.
كارتُوس *kārtūs*	Cartridge.
گټه *gata*	Packet of 10 Cartridges.
نښه *nakha*	Mark.
رنگ *rang*	Colour.
سپين *spin*	White.

EXERCISE 6.

۱ تا سخه تماكؤ شته ؟ ۲ ما سخه تماكؤ نشته او تيليَ شته
۳ هغه سخه څلور كتابونه دي مګر هغه نۀ دي ۴ تا سخه څومره
روپيِ دي . څما ترؤ سخه ډير دولت وه ۵ څما يو ورور دیَ هغه
هم په هسپتال كښ دیَ ۶ ستا څومره څامن دي ؟ ۷ څما
يو آس دیَ چه رنگ يی سپين دیَ ۸ څما دَ ورور پۀ ښهر
كښ پنځۀ كورونه وُو ۹ څما يو لس دیَ ۱۰ دا جنئی دَ
هلك خور دَه ۱۱ هغوی دواره خائيسته دي ۱۲ دَ هغوی
پلار هغه سړیَ وه او دَ هغوی مور هونيارَه بنڼه دَه ۱۳ په خوا
زمانه كښ په دی وطن كښ ښكار وه مګر اوس نيشته ۱۴ څموذبر
كلي ته نيژدی جبه شته خو ما سخه دَ ښكار ټوپك نشته

VOCABULARY VI.

| څوكيدار *saukidār* | Watchman, Chaukidar. |

څوکۍ	*saukai*	Post.
جماعت	*jumait*	Mosque.
حجرﮦ	*hūjra*	Guest house.
میلمﻪ	*mélma*	Guest.
میلما نﻪ	*mélmānuh*	Guests.
غریب	*gharib*	Poor.
دولتمند	*daulatmand*	Rich.
دَ۔طرف تﻪ	*da-taraf ta*	Towards.
طرف۔خوا۔دده۔پلو	*taraf, khwā, dada, palau*	Side or direction.
نور پریوانﻪ یا قبلﻪ	*nwar préwātuh* or *qablā*	West.
قبلﻪ	*qabḷa*	Polite word for west
نور خاتﻪ	*nwar khātuh*	East.
سُهیل	*suhail*	South.
قُطﺐ	*qutab*	North.
لاس	*lās*	Hand.
ښی لاس	*khay lās*	Right hand.
گس لاس یا	*gas lās* or	}Left hand.
کینرلاس	*kinr lās*	
غر	*ghar*	Hill.
اُوچﺖ	*ūchat*	High.
مندری	*mandray*	Short.
زوړ	*zōr*	Old (Thing or person.
سپین ګیری	*spin giray*	Old, grey bearded man.

نا ست	*nāst*	Sitting	
ر ولار	*walār*	Standing	Take the Verb "to be."
أوده	*ūduh*	Sleeping	
ملاست	*mlāst*	Lying	

EXERCISE 7.

1. This man's house is in the city. 2. This boy's father was my servant. 3. These girls' mother was in the house. 4. When I was in Kohat I had two chaukidars. 5. When I was at home (in the house) my horse was not ill. 6. The khan's house is this side of the Mosque. 7. The guest house is beyond the Malak's house. 8. My uncle had much wealth, but now he is poor. 9. What is your father's name ?. 10. There are many hills towards the west of Peshawar. 11. That is the Afridis' country. 12 Where is your Regiment ? 13. What is your Colonel's name ? 14. The old man was sitting on the chair.

VOCABULARY VII.

خاوند	*khāwand*	Owner.
ماليه	*mālia*	Land Tax.
آبيانه	*abiāna*	Water Tax.
محصول	*mahsool*	Tax on property.
زمکه	*zmaka*	Land or ground
أوي زمکه	*āvi zmaka*	Irrigated land.

للمه زمکه	*lalma zmaka*	Unirrigated land.
سا دین	*sādin*	Ploughed land.
و تره	*watra*	Land ready for sowing.
شاره زمکه	*shāra zmaka*	Barren land.
ویجاره زمکه	*wijāra zmaka*	Waste land.
شولگره	*shōlgara*	Rice land.
دَ ازغو تار	*da azgho tār*	Barbed wire.
تار	*tār*	Wire, telegram, thread.
څینی څینی	*ziné ziné*	Some.
نه.نه	*na-na*	Neither-nor.
ژونديَ	*jhwanday*	Alive.
گينټه	*gainta*	An hour.
پس	*pas*	After (time.)
پسی	*pasé*	After (person.) or business)
روان	*rawān*	Going on. (in the act of going.)
دروازه	*darwāza*	Gate.
ور	*war*	Door.

EXERCISE 8.

۱   دَ دی کور خاوند څوک دَی   ۲   دَ هغهٔ ملک نوم څهٔ دَی
۳   مالیهٔیی څوصره ده   ۴   کله چه زهٔ په دفتر کښی وم نو نوکرم یا هر
ناست وهٔ   ۵   ستا پلار ژونديَ دَی ؟—تهٔ کله هلته وی   ۶   دوه گينټی
پس زهٔ به په دفتر کښی یم   ۷   له چاونړیٔ نه گیر چاپیره دَ ازغو تار
دیَ   ۸   یو سړی خان پسی روان دیَ   ۹   قبلی طرف تهٔ دَننه

لویه دروازه ده ۱۰ اوس څمو َنر پۀ پلټن کښ دوه کر نیلان دی ۱۱
د اپریدو ملک ټول غرونه غرونه دی ۱۲ خیني خیني پۀ کښ
ډیر هوښیار دی ۱۳ پۀ دی کلی کښ نۀ حُجره شته نۀ جماعت
۱۴ زمکه یی تله اوی دۀ ——

SHORT SENTENCES

AND

VOCABULARY VIII.

پو ه شوی	*pōh shwé*	Did you understand ?
هو زۀ پو ه شم	*ho zuh pōh shwam*	Yes I understood.
پو هیږی	*pōhégé*	Do you understand ?
هو زۀ پو هیږم	*ho zuh pōhégam*	Yes I understand.
بیا و وایه	*biā wo wāya*	Say it again.
ورو ورو و وایه	*vro vro wo wāya*	Say it slowly.
زۀ خبر نۀ یم	*zuh hhabar nuh yam*	I don't know.
دا رښتیا خبره ده	*dā rikhtiā khabara dah*	This is true.
ډیره ښه ده	*déra kha dah*	That is all right.
هوښیار	*hukhyār*	Intelligent.
سر کار	*sarkār*	Government.
سر کاری	*sarkāri*	Belongs to Govt. (Adj.)
قلا	*qalā*	Fort.
تعلیم	*talim*	Education.

تعليم يا فته	*talim yāfta*	Educated.
بى تعليم	*be talim*	Uneducated.
رنگروٽ	*rangūt*	Recruit.
كمزورَى	*kamzōray*	Weak.
نوَى	*naway*	New.
خټه	*khata*	Mud or muddy.
گران	*garān*	Dear or difficult.
اسان	*asān*	Easy.
ارزان	*arzān*	Cheap.
ژبه	*jhuba*	Tongue or Language.
اور دي	*urdi*	Uniform.
خيرن	*khiran*	Dirty.
پاك	*pak*	Clean.
رڼى اوبۀ	*ranré obuh*	Clear water.
خړى اوبۀ	*kharé obuh*	Dirty water.
بندوبست	*bāndubast*	Arrangement.
عمر	*umar*	Age.
ژور	*jhawar*	Deep.
پاياؤ	*payāw*	Shallow.
گناه يا قصور	*gunāh* or *qasūr*	Fault.
غزان	*ghuzān* Walnuts. (غز *ghuz* S.)	
بادام	*bādām* Almonds. (S. and P. ١	
خټکى	*khatakay*	Melon.
ايندوانه	*indwāna*	Water Melon.
كيله	*kéla*	Banana.
سمتره	*samtara*	Sweet Orange

لۀ_نه دک	*luh-na dak*	Full of.
بیشکه	*béshaka*	Certainly.
گُند یا شاید	*gundé or shāyad*	Perhaps.
کار	*kār*	Work.
ذمه	*zema*	Responsibility.
ذمۀوار	*zema ẉār*	Responsible.
مشر	*mashar*	Older.
کشر	*kashar*	Younger.
پنسن	*pensan*	Pension.
دستوُر	*dastūr*	Custom.
مغرور	*maghrūr*	Proud.
پټکَی	*patkay*	Turban.
توپيي	*topai*	Topi.
کورته	*kōrta*	Shirt.
پر توُ.ز	*partūg*	Trousers.
پنړی	*panré*	Shoes (F. P.)
خپلی	*saplai*	Grass sandals.
کېږيي	*kérai*	Leather sandals.
خادر	*sādar*	Sheet.
سينه	*sina*	Chest.
پوُږه	*pūra*	Complete or up to the standard.
رووُند	*rūnd*	Blind.
گُی	*gud*	Lame.
گووُنګ	*gūng*	Dumb.
کونړ	*kūnr*	Deaf.
حمله	*hamla*	An attack.

نه خبره نۀ دَه	*kha khabara nuh dah*	It is not a good thing.
خبره	*khabara*	Word, speech, matter.

EXERCISE 9.

1. She is an intelligent woman. 2. Is he your son ? 3. It is a big station. 4. That is the Afridis' Fort and not a Government Post 5. Is it true ? 6. How many educated soldiers are there in your Regiment ? 7. He is ill today. 8. All these recruits are weak. 9. Owing to the rain all the roads are very muddy. 10 Pushtu is not a difficult language. 11. Your uniform is dirty. 12. Whose arrangement is this ? 13. How old are you (what is your age) ? 14. How deep is this river ? 15. Whose fault is this ? 16. How many years' service have you (Thou of how many years servant art) ?.

VOCABULARY IX.

ورځ	*vraz*	Day.
شپه	*shpa*	Night.
نیمه شپه	*nima shpa*	Midnight.
شومه قلاره	*shūma qalāra*	Still night.
قلاره قلاری	*qalāra qalāri*	Quiet.
بادشاه	*bādshāh*	King.
لږ	*laʐ*	Little.

باغ	*bāgh*	Garden.
ميوه	*méwa*	Fruit.
انار	*anār*	Pomegranates (M.S. & Plu.)
سيوان	*séwān*	Apples (Sing. سيو *séw*).
انگور	*angūr*	Grapes (M. Plu.)
شلتالان	*shaltālān*	Peaches (M.P.) (Sing. شلتالو *shaltālū*)
ناک یا ناشپاتي	*nāk or nāshpātai*	Pears.
نارنجان	*nāranjān*	Oranges. (*nāranj* S.)
بيهي	*behai*	Quinces. (F.S. & P.)
پوره	*pūra*	Complete.
خبرى	*khabaré*	Conversation (F.P.)
خبر	*khabar*	Message or news.
ترکارى	*tarkāri*	Vegetables.
تيپر	*taipar*	Turnips.
مولي	*mūlai*	Radish.
گازرى	*gāzaré*	Carrots.
مټر	*matar*	Peas.
الوگان	*alūgān*	Potatoes. (M. P.)
ساگ	*sāg*	Spinach.
زور ور باران	*zōrawar bārān*	Heavy rain.

EXERCISE 10.

۱ یوه ورځ چه زۀ پۀ دفتر کښې وم نو زورور باران وۀ ۲ پۀ
هندوستان کښې یو بادشاه وۀ چه نۇمی اکبر وۀ ۳ زۀ پۀ پښتو پوهیږم
مګر لږ، لږ ۴ څما نوکر په پښتو نۀ پو هیږي ۵ هغه دَ وني لاند
۰، کښي ملاست دیَ ۶ باغ دَ میوو له ونونه ډک دیَ ۷ بیشکه داستاکار

دَی تۀ ذمه واړيي ٨ ځما مشر وزور پۀ رساله کښی جمعدارؤه مۀر
اوس پۀ پنس باند دی ٩ دا دَ دی مُلک دستۀر دی ١٠ ستا
رټکی ولی خیرن دی ١١ دَ دی رنګونت سینه پۀره نۀ دۀ دا خو
رؤند نۀ دی هغه دوه کڼ دی او دا دری کمزوری دی ١٢ سیند زور
نۀ دی ١٣ پۀ دی حمله کښی یوه رسَاله او دری پلټن وی
١۴ کۀ دا دهغۀ قصۀ روی نو ته خبره نۀ دۀ.—

VOCABULARY X.

لۀ دی ځای نه	luh dĕ zāi na	From here
ځای	zāi	Place.
څومره مده کیږی	sōmra mūda kĕgee	How long ago.
څومره مُده پس	sōmra mūda pas	How long after.
څومره مُده راسی	sōmra mūda rāsĕ	Since how long.
چُټی	chūtī	Leave.
پلن	plan	Broad.
اوږد	ūgad	Long.
مورچه	mōrcha	Trench.
پټی	paṭay	Field.
سۀر	sūr	Red.
شین	shin	Green.
تۆر	tōr	Black.
زیېر	ziar	Yellow.
آبی	ābi	Blue.
دَ ننه	danana	Inside.

باهر *bāhar*   Outside.

خپل *khpal*   Own, relative.

خپلوان *khpalwān*   Relations.

کرائیی *karāyeé*   Rent, hire.

څومره لوي *somra loi ?*   How big ?

MISCELLANEOUS COLLOQUIAL SENTENCES I.

Is there anyone there ?	*sōk shta ?*
Who are you ?	*tuh sōk yé ?*
What is your name ?	*stā nūm suh day ?*
What is your father's name ?	*da plār nūm dé suh day ?*
Where is your houe ?	*kōr dé charta day ?*
How far is it from here?	*luh dé ᶻāi na sōmra laré day ?*
Is that your village ?	*dagha stā kallay day ?*
How wide is the trench?	*mōrcha sōmra plana dah ?*
How deep is the river ?	*sind sōmra jhawar day?*
Whose fields are these ?	*dā da chā pati dee ?*
Where is my gun ?	*tōpak mé charta day ?*
This colour is red	*dā sūr rang day.*
Is my servant inside ?	*zamā naukar danana day ?*
Is he a relation of yours ?	*hagha dé khpal day ?*
Are you the owner of this house ?	*tuh da dé kōr khāwand yé ?*
What is the rent of this house ?	*dā dé kōr karāyee sōmra dah ?*

How big is your house ?   *stā kōr sōmra loi day ?*

I don't know who is   *zuh khabar nuh yam*
your servant.   *chi stā naukar sōk day.*

VOCABULARY XI.

اسٹیشن	*istaishan*	Station.
مور پلار	*mōr plār*	Parents.
مړ	*mar*	Dead.
ژوندی	*jhwanday*	Alive.
څنګه	*sunga*	How.
سپاهی توب	*spāhi tōb.*	Soldiering.
فوځ	*fauz*	Troops, Army.
اباد	*abād*	Populated, cultivated.
ابادي	*abādi*	Population, cultivation.
کمپنۍ	*kapnai*	Company.
پښتون	*pukhtūn*	Pathan.
طلب	*talab*,	
تنخواه	*tankhwāh*	Pay.
تغمه	*taghma*	Medal.
لنډه لار	*landa lār*	Short road.
ناجوړتیا	*nājōrtiā*	Sickness.
چرې	*charé*	Ever.
هیچرې	*hicharé*	Never.

EXERCISE 11.

1. What is the name of your village ?   2. In
what direction is it ?   3. · How far is your
village from the Railway Station ?   4. What

is the Railway fare? 5. How many brothers
have you? 6. Are your parents alive? 7.
No, they are both dead. 8. How much land
have you? 9. How are the crops in your
country? 10. Do you like soldiering? 11.
Have you any relations in the Army? 12. Is
there a river near your village? 13. What is
the population of your village? 14. Are you
a private or N.C.O.? 15. How many Pathan
companies are there in your Regiment? 16.
What Regiment are you in? 17. Where is
your Regiment? 18. Who is the Officer
Commanding of your Regiment? 19. What
is your pay? 20. Have you a medal? 21.
Which is the shortest way? 22. Whose
horses are these? 23. I don't like him.

VOCABULARY XII.

چرته	*charta*	Anywhere or where?
څه	*suh*	Any, some, what?
څه قسم	*suh qisam*	What kind of?
تا واده کړی دی	*tā wāduh karay day*	Are you married?
تږی	*tagay*	Thirsty.
تنده	*tanda*	Thirst.
اوږی	*ogay*	Hungry.
لوږه	*lwaga*	Hunger.
کوم	*kum*	Which?

كوم ځاى	*kum zāi*	Where, in which place ?	
په دى شپو ورځو كښى	*pa dé shpo vrazo ké*	Now-a-days.	
مُوندلى شي	*múndalay shee*	Can be had, can be obtained, can be received.	

بيعه	*baya*	Price	ځنګل	*zangal*	Forest
په كښى	*pa ké*	In it	راسى	*rāsé*	Since
چه په كښى	*chi pa ké*	In which	لوى	*lõi*	Great big, large
لرګى	*largay*	Wood, stick	خداى	*khudāi*	God
			خبر	*khabar*	news
لرګي	*largi*	Wood (Plural)	اكثر	*aksar*	Generally
سكارهٔ	*skāruh*	Charcoal (M. P.)	قسمت	*qismat*	Luck
دَ كانرى سكارهٔ	*da kānri skāruh*	Coal	نصيب	*nasīb*	Fate
خشاك	*khashāk*	Firewood	غله	*ghala*	Grain
كانرى	*kānray*	Stone	دومرهٔ	*dōmra*	this much or as much so much
			داسى	*dāsé*	thus, such.

EXERCISE 12.

۱ په كلي كښى د ډبرو ناجوړ تيا دهٔ ؟ ۲ ستا كلي ته نيژدى چرته ښكار موندلى شي ؟ ۳ ځهٔ قسم ښكاردى ؟ ۴ تا وادهٔ كړى دى ؟ ۵ دَ دى سكارو بيعه ځهٔ دَه ۶ ځما اس تربرى دى اوبهٔ

كوم ځايي دى ٧ په دى شپو ورځو كښ په بازار كښ څۀ قسم
ميوه موندلى شى ٨ دلته غله ارزانه ده كۀ گرانه ٩ افغانستان
ۀ وطن دى مۀر په كښ يخنى ډيره وى ١٠ دنمر خلق
ۀ دى ١١ ۀر ته نيز دى د لرگو يو لوى ځنګل دى ١٢
هغه لوى سړى دى ولى هوښيار نۀ دى ١٣ پښتو اسانه ژبه
ده ١٤ څومره مده راسى تۀ په فوځ كښ يى ١٥ عهده
داران قبول په دفتر كښ دى ١٦ ولى د نن رنگ زبردى ١٧
خداى خبر چه ولى دلته تر كارى دومره ارزانه ده ١٨ د دولتمند
سړى دوستان ډير وى ١٩ زۀ غريب يم څكه دوست م نشته ٢٠
اكثر د هوښيار سړى قسمت خراب وى—

VOCABULARY XIII.

راشه	*rāsha*	Come !
لارشه	*lārsha*	Go !
كينه	*kéna*	Sit !
څمله	*samla*	Lie down !
(تۀ) و وايه	*(ta) wo wāya*	Say, speak, tell !
راوړه	*rāwra*	Bring ! (inanimate)
راوله	*rāwala*	Lead ! (animate)
يوسه	*yausa*	Take away ! (animate)
بوزه	*bōza*	Lead away ! (animate)
وبله	*wo bala*	Call !
وليكه	*wō lika*	Write !
ايسار شه	*isār sha*	Wait !
لرى كړه	*laré kar*	Open !
پورى كړه	*pōré kra*	Shut !

كيږده	*kégda*	Place, put !
كړه	*kra*	Do !
شه	*sha*	Become, be !
راوغواړه	*rā wo ghwāra*	Send for ! (thing)
راوبله	*rā wo bala*	Call for ! (person)
گوزه	*gōrā*	Look !
مه ويښوه	*muh wikhawa*	Don't wake up !
بل	*bal*	Next or other.
نور	*nōr*	More. or others.
چتنى	*chitai*	Letter.
خوراك	*khurāk*	Food.
ډوډئ	*dōdai*	Bread.
دفتر	*daftar*	Office or landed property.
سايس	*sāis*	Syce.
كلف	*kalaf*	Club.
جواب	*jawāb*	An auswer.
موټر	*mōtar*	Motor.
بائيسكل	*bāisekal*	Bicycle.
لينر	*lainr*	Lines.
بيرته	*biarta*	Back.
بيا	*biā*	Again.
دَ سكلو اوبهَ	*da skalo obuh*	Drinking water.
كاغذ	*kāghaz*	Paper.
قلم	*qalam*	Pen.
مشوانرئ	*mashwānrai*	Ink pot.
سياهى	*syāhi*	Ink.

اخبار	akhbār	Newspaper.
سمدستی	samdasti	At once.
صاف صاف	sāf sāf	Distinctly.
ورو ورو	vro vro	Slowly.
مرمت	muramat	Repair.
سم یا نیغ	sam or négh	Straight.
گل زیرئ	gul ziarai	Target.
مهربانی ده	mehrabāni dah	Thank you.
ډیره مهربانی ده	déra mehrabāni dah	Thank you very much.
لوکوتي	lūkūti	Little or just.

EXERCISE 13.

1. Come inside, sit on the chair and tell me some thing about your regiment. 2. Call my servant. 3. Tell him to come to the office. 4. Tell the syce to take my horse to the Club and wait for me there. 5. Shut the door. 6. Take this letter to the Adjutant and bring an answer. 7. Take the Sahib's motor to the lines. 8. Bring the bicycle back. 9. Tell my bearer to bring me some water. 10. Is this water fit to drink? 11. Take these papers at once to the office and then tell the mali to bring water for this field. 12. Speak distinctly and slowly. 13. Send for the jemadar; Why is he not here? 14. Take my boots for repair.

15. Look straight towards the target. 16. Don't wake me up before 9 o'clock. 17. Please write him another letter. 18. Just call the head man of this village. 19. Bring food for the dogs. 20. Is there any letter for me ?

NOTE :—Wheeled vehicles and irrigation water are treated as moveable objects and take the verbs *"biwal"* and *"rāwastal"*.

VOCABULARY XIV.

راكو *rā kra*	Give me or give us.
وركو *war kra*	Give him, them, her it.
يا ليږه و *wo légā* or واستوه *wāstawa*	} Send.
واچوه *wāchawa*	Put.
مه ايسا ريږه *muh isāréga*	Don't wait.
اسپه *aspa*	Mare.
ميدان *maidān*	Plain.
يو خوا بل خوا *yaw khwā bal hhwā*	Hither and thither.
مه ګوره *ma gōra*	Don't look.
لمـنه اول يا *luh-na awal*	} Before in time.
لمـنه وړمبى *luh na vrumbay*	
بالكل *bilkul*	Quite, absolutely.
پنځهنيمه بجى *pinzanimé bajé*	Half past five.

پاؤ باند پنځهٔ بجی	*pāw bāadé pinzuh bajé*	Quarter past five.
پاؤ کم پنځهٔ بجی	*pāw kam pinzuh bajé*	Quarter to five.
لس ملټ باند	*las mélata bāndé*	10 minutes past.
لس ملټ کم	*las mélata kam*	10 minutes to.
درۊند	*drūnd*	Heavy.
سپک	*spak*	Light.

NOTE :—For خهٔ دی = *suh di*, look up Syntax rule No. 52. For ورته ووایه چه دَ ننه راشی یا راشه = *warta wo wāya chi danana rāshee* or *rāsha* look up syntax rule No. 16.

EXERCISE 14.

۱ ټول کتا بۉنه راوړه او په میز باند ئی کیږده ۲ یوه بله کُرسۍ راوړه او په برنځهٔ کښ ئی واچوه ۳ ټولو سپاهیا نو ته و وایه چه دَننه راشی ۴ ور ته و وایه چه زر جواب راوړه ۵ نوکرانو ته و وایه چه په کُرسو باند نهٔ کیني ۶ مالی ته و وایه چه صبا خما دَ باغ دَ پاره اوبهٔ راولی ۷ میز پوری دوه کرسۍ هم کیږ ده ۸ خما موټر د لته راوله او بائیسکل م کور ته بوزه ۹ پهٔ پاؤ باند شپږ بجی را ته نوکر راواستوه ۱۰ دا چټي دفتر ته یو سه خو جواب دَ پاره مهٔ ایسا ریږوه ۱۱ ټول اسۊنه او سپی هسپتال ته بوزه ۱۲ ما ته سم ګوره یو خوا بل خوا مهٔ ګوره ۱۳ له دریۉ بجو نه اول راشه او ما وینس کوه ۱۴ لهٔ دفتر نه یو بل داسی کتاب هم راوړه ۱۵ مهر بانی وکوه دا خبره بیا وکوه ۲۶ دَ اوبهٔ دَ سکلو دَ پاره خی دی کهٔ نه ۱۷ خپل کار وکوه نو دفتر ته راشه ۱۸

ملک ته سلام ورکه او ورته و وایه چه صاحب په حجره کښی ناست
دی ۱۹ داخۀ دی او دغه څوک دی ۲۰ دَ دی کلي مالیه
درنه ده ـ ـ

VOCABULARY XV-

اول	awal	First, at first.
بیشکه	béshaka	Certainly.
ما و ویل	mā wo wayal	I said spoke or told.
هیڅ	hiss	Nothing (takes tense in negative.)
داسی	dāsé	So, such or thus.
څۀ	suh	Any thing.
څنګه	sanga	How.
خپل	khpal	Own, (used for reflexive pro.)
جوار	jowār	Maize, Indian Corn.
تخم	tukhum	Seed.
تا نڼی	tānté	Stalks.
مال	māl	Cattle, property.
حکم	hukum	Order.
ګلډانګ سپی	guldāng spay	Bull dog.
شراب	sharāp	Wine.

EXERCIE 15.

1. I beat him, because he beat me first. 2. Certainly he beat me yesterday, but I said nothing. 3. You beat me yesterday and you are beating me again to day. 4. I struck the owner of the house because he had struck all my

dogs. 5. The dog is so ill that he does not eat food. 6. Will you drink any thing ?. 7. I will write a letter to his father, 8. Please write another letter for me. 9. How can I write ?. 10. Tell my servant to keep this dog in his house. 11. We have sown some maize, the grain is very good, but the stalks are so hard that the cattle will not eat them. 12. This man does not obey my orders. 13. We used to keep a bulldog in our house. 14. I wrote a letter to his Colonel at Cherat. 15. The dog bit the man therefore the man beat the dog. 16. I will also send him a message. 17. Can you call my servant ?. 18. I was so ill that I could not drink water. 19. This Darzi cannot sew well so call the Jemadar to arrange for a better one. 20. Don't drink wine.

VOCABULARY XVI.

واښه	wākhuh	Grass.
خاي خائبٯی یا پته	zāi zaigay or pata	Address.
خاوند	khāwand	Owner.
کله	kala	When.
کله کله	kala kala	Some times.
سر	sar	Head.
پری یا رسۍ	paray or rasai	Rope.
ونه	wana	Tree.

رو تَي	*rōtai*	Bread, food.
مه ورکوه	*muh warkawa*	Don't give him !
گنډل	*gandal*	To sew, sewing.
خپل ځان	*khpal zān*	Oneself.
په لیکلو کښ	*puh likalō ké*	In writing.
زر	*zar*	Soon.
زر زر	*zar zar*	Quickly.
پخپله	*pakhpala*	Myself, yourself, herself, itself etc.
و یل	*wayal*	To say, speak, tell.
میاشت	*miāsht*	Month, moon.
دَ دی میاشتی	*da dé miāshté*	On the 20th of this
په شلم تاریخ	*puh shalam tārikh*	month.
ما جب	*mājeb*	Pay.
تپین	*tepan*	Lunch.
غوښه	*ghwakha*	Meat.
پرَدی مال	*praday māl*	Others' property.
گناه	*gunāh*	Sin.
گنهگار	*gunahgār*	Sinner, guilty.
بی گناه	*bé gunah*	Not guilty.
موقعه	*moqa*	Chance, spot, opportunity.
موجُود	*maujūd*	Present.
غل	*ghal*	Thief (غله *ghluh* Plu.)
ځان	*zān*	self.

EXERCISE 16.

اس م ناجوَر دی ځکه نه واښه خوري او نه اوبه سکي ۲ په ,

دی کاغذ باند خپله نامه او دَ پلار نامه او خای خائوهی ولیکه ۳ هغه
هغهٔ نوکر نه وی چه دَ مالک خبره نهٔ منی ۴ کله کله راته چټي
راليږره ۵ اوس ټول فصلونه کرلیَ شوی دی ۶ ما په نایی باند
سړ خرئیلو پهٔ موقعه موجود نه وم خکه راته معلومه نه دَه چه چا
وهلیَ دیَ ۷ ما غل په پوی باند ونی پوری وټرلو او خپل نوکر تنم
روویل چه روتیي او اوبهٔ مهٔ ورکوه ۸ کوټ کنئول داسی اسان
کار نهٔ دی هغه خپل خان لوی کنپي مهر دانهَ خبره نهٔ دَه و
ما درته چټي لیکله چه ستا خبر راورسیدلو ۱۰ که ما ورته چټي
لیکیَ نهٔ ویَنو هغهٔ به زهٔ بللیَنه وم ۱۱ ما ورته تار ولیږلو او په کینم
و لیکل چه پلار د نا جوړ دی زر راشه ۱۲ هغهٔ راته خبر راولیږلو
چه زهٔ پخپله هم ناجوړ یم او کرنیل صاحب پهٔ چوټي دیَ خکه اوس
هیڅ ویلیَ نه شم ۱۳ دَ دی میاشتی په شلم تاریخ ماورته یوه چټي
ولیکله ۱۴ که خوری خوره که نهٔ خوری مهٔ خوره ۱۵ هغه لهٔ
سر کار نه دوه سو روپیي ماجب خوری ۱۶ ډیره مهر بانی دَه هیڅ
نهٔ خورم خکه چه ما اوس ټپین خوړلیَ دیَ ۱۷ خینی خینی
هندوان بالکل غوښه نهٔ خوری ۱۸ پرَ دیَ مال خوړل ګناه دَه ۱۹
دا ورزکیَ هلک ماله راکړه زهٔ پهٔ خپل کور کینس به یی ساتم ۹۰
ما ورته ولیکل چه څما دَ کلي مال ټول ناجوړ دی—

VOCABULARY XVII.

دَ پهٔ مینځ کینس	*da-puh mianz ké*	Through.
دیوال	*déwāl*	Wall.
غیر علاقه	*ghair alāqa*	Independent. territory.
رعیت	*rait*	British territory, subject.

دَ اور ګاډيَ	*da aur gāday*	Train.
كتل	*katal*	To look, examine.
ګورم	*gōram*	I examine (present)
زخم يا پرهر	*zakham or parhar*	Wound.
زخمى يا ژوبل	*zakhmi or jhōbal*	Wounded.
پۀ وخت	*puh wakht*	In time
اسمان غوریږي	*asmān ghurégee*	It is thundering.
غالب ګمان	*ghālib gumān day*	Probably.
باران وریدل	*bārān warédal*	To rain.
واورۀ وریدل	*wāwra warédal*	To snow.
واورۀ	*wāwra*	Snow, ice.
داړه	*dāṛa*	Raid, Raiding party.
داړه مار	*dāṛa mār*	Raider.
لۀ ټولونه نیزدي	*luh tōlo na nizde*	The nearest.
تور	*tōr*	Black.
دوكان	*dukān*	Shop.
دوكاندار	*dukāndār*	Shop keeper.
زۀ ځم	*zuh zam*	I go.
زۀ راځم	*znh rāzam*	I come.
كۀ تۀ لاړشى	*kuh tuh lārshé*	If you go.
لواړګی	*lwārgay*	Landi Kotal.
جم	*jam*	Jamrud.

داسى dāse	Like this, so, such or thus.
هم پۀ هغه شپه hum puh hagha shpa	On the same night.
هم پۀ هغه ورځ يا امروزه hum puh hagha vraz or amrōza	On the same day.
لښکر lakhkar	Party of tribesmen.
گرزيدل garzédal	To walk or wander.
بيرته biarta	Back.
پراؤ parāw	Camp.
رسد يا راسن rasad or rāsan	Supplies, rations.
كله چه kala chi	When (Relative).
وختى wakhti	Early or earlier.
نا وخته nā wakhta	Late.
كليوال kaliwāl	Villagers (S & P).
(ته) نقصان رسيدل (ta) nuqsān rasédal	To suffer loss.
اوسنى osanay	Recent.
جنگ jang	War or battle.

EXERCISE 17.

1. Where do you live ? I am not living in the village. 2. I am living in Peshawar City, my brother lives in Kohat and after two months we shall live in Cherat. 3. The water of the river flows through my garden. 4. As we reached the wall of the village, the villagers fled towards the mosque. 5. This boy can run

faster than this girl. 6. All the thieves fled towards independent territory. 7. The train arrives at the Station at 2-30 p. m. 8. Don't move, I am going to examine your wound. 9. If you had arrived earlier, you would have seen the king of this country. 10. It is thundering now, it will probably rain tonight. 11. As we saw the raiding party we ran to the nearest village. 12. In the recent war we have suffered a great loss. 13. If you go now you will reach Landi Kotal at 4 p.m. 15. Has your brother arrived from Lahore ? 16. Yes, he arrived before 5 a. m. 17. All my servants cannot live in a small house like this. 18. We arrived there the same night, but the lashkar had run away to the hills. 19. I [1] must go to the office now. 20. When did your regiment arrive in this station ? 21. Has your Colonel arrived back from the camp ?.

VOCABULARY XVIII.

خالی *khali*	Empty, only, Saturday.
پروت *prōt*	Lying.
هڅوک *hisōk*	Nobody (takes tense in negative.)

NOTE:—1. For " must " or " should ", see syntax rules Nos. 21 & 22.

كُوڅه *kūsa*	Street.
وينى *winé*	Blood (Feminine plural.)
سَره د *sara da*	With.
څه داسى يا *suh dāsé* or	
داسى *dāsé*	So.
هر *har*	Every.
وار پۀ وار *wār puh wār*	Turn by turn.
كثرت *kasrat*	Bodily exercise.
فقير *faqir*	Beggar.
شپه او ورځ *shpa aw vraz*	Day and night.
شهزاده *shāhzāda*	Prince.
شهزادګۍ *shāhzādgāi*	Princes.
خلاص *khlās*	Free, finished.
اسمان پړ كيږي *asmān ṭarkégee*	It is lightning.
باران به وشي *bārān ba wo shee*	It will rain (lit the rain will become.)
وخت پۀ وخت *wakht ṗuh wakht*	Time to time.
پياده *ṗyāda*	On foot.
خط *khat*	Letter,
ګيده يا خيټه *géda* or *khéta*	Stomach.
درد *dard*	Pain,
څرب *surb*	Fat.
اتوار *itwār*	Sunday.
پير يا ګل *ṗir*	Monday.
نهى *nahé*	Tuesday.
چار شنبه *chārshanba*	Wednesday,

پانشنبه	pānshạnba	
یا	or	Thursday.
دَ زيارت ورځ	da ziārat vraz	
جمعه	jūmạ	Friday.
خالی	khāli	Saturday.
دَ اتوار پۀ ورځ	da itwār pūh vraz	On Sunday.
ځوان	zwān	Youngman or soldier.
مورچه	mọrcha	Breastwork.

EXERCISE 18.

۱   نۀ هغه را ورسید او نۀ د هغۀ نوکر   ۲   چه مؤذن ور ورسيدُو
نو كلیَ خالی پروت وه قبل خلق تر تښتیدلی وُو   ۳   نۀ زۀ په خپل
وطن كښ اوسم او نۀ ښما ورور   ۴   داسی جذت وه چه د كلی
په كوڅو كښ وينی بهيدلی   ۵   پو لقيلل صاحب ته خبر ور كړه چه
ښما نو كر سره دَ سلو روپو تښتیدلیَ دی   ۶   دَ هغۀ. كور ته رسيدل
څۀ داسی 'سان كار نۀ وه   ۷   چه وخزَ زبدلو نو زۀ پوه شوم چه
ژوندیَ دیَ   ۷   دَ كمان افسر صاحب حکم دی چه سپاهيان د هر
سهر وار په وارِ دَ كثرت دَ پاره زغلی   ۹   فقير شپه او ورځ په دی غم
كښ كړيدلو چه پس لۀ مانه به ښما دَ ښای مانک څوک وی   ۱۰
يوه ورځ زۀ خپل نوكرسره وكړيدلم   ۱۱   نۀ زۀ زار رسيدلیَ نۀ وی نو
غل به تښتیدلیَ نۀ وُه   ۱۲   اسمان غورېږي او پرکيږي باران به وشی
۱۳   چه پلټنی ته ور ورسيدېرۍ نو صوبيدار صاحب ته ښما سلام ورۍوه
۱۴   چه ښما چقنُی در ورسيدېرۍ نو جواب اكړه   ۱۵   كوټ ماسټر
صاحب ته و وايه چه واخنه او نور دَ خوراک ښيزونه پۀ وخت راورسی
۱۶   زۀ پوه شوم چه په يوه ګينټه كښ پياده رسيدلیَ نۀ شم
۱۷   يېره مهربانۍ دَه ستا خط راته په تيراه كښ را رسيدلیَ وُه   ۱۸

زۀ زغلیدلیَ نۀ شم څکه چه پۀ ګیلیه کښں م درد دیَ ۱۹ دَ جیڼن

صاحب پۀ حکم باند ټول څوانان څپلو څپلو مورچوته بیرته وتښتیدل

۲۰ جمعدار صاحبَ ویر څورب دیَکڅه سپاهیانو پسی نۀ شو رسیدلیَ

VOCABULARY XIX.

کټ	kat	Bed.
دا هغه سړیَ دیَ	dā hagha saray day	This is the man.
سپین	sp̣in	White.
صُندق	sunduq	Box.
څیل	khayāl	To show, direct.
قالین	qālin	Rug.
دری	darai	Carpet.
ترپوری	tar-poré	Till, upto.
دوره	daura	Tour.
چای	chāi	Tea.
پۀ یو ملټ کښں	puh yaw melat ké	In a minute.
سرشته دار	sarishtadar	Reader (of the court)
کمره یا کوټه	kamra or kōta	Room.
ڈاګي	dāgi	Postman.
آئنده دَ پاره	ainda da p̣āra	In future.
دـپه مخ کښں	da-p̣a makh ké	In the presence of, infront of.
بیعه	baya	Price.
مدام.تل.همیشه	mudām, tal, haméshā	Always.
څوک نه څوک	sōk na sōk	Someone or other.
ځان سره	zān sarā	With me, with him etc.

پكار دى چه اصلى پښتون وى	pakạr di chi asli pukhtūn wi	He must be a real Pathan.
اصلى پښتون	asli pukhtūn	Real Pathan.
ضلع	zela	District.
کم ذات	kam zāt	Low class, menial.
أستكار	ustakār	Village workman.
برنده	baranda	Vranda.

EXERCISE 19.

1. Bring a bed and put it in the vranda. 2. This is the man who brings horses from Afghanistan. 3. I brought a letter from your Colonel. 4. Tell the syce to bring my white horse to the Club and wait for me if I am not there. 5. Where did you put my gun? I put it under the box. 6. The servants used to bring our food from the city. 7. I will take you to the city and will show you all kinds of carpets. 8. Take away the dogs and don't bring them till the day after tomorrow as I shall be on tour. 9. Bring tea for four men who are coming in a minute. 10. Take my servant to the city and show him my reader's house. 11. [1] He said his name was Ahmad and he said he was a good man. 12. Yesterday my father told me I was a good man. 13. He said his room was smaller than my office. 14. Tell the Postman to bring my letters to the office

in future 15. He brought 20 rupees and put them before the owner of the house saying that it was the price of his food. 16. He always brings someone or other with him. 17. How can I bring the head-man with me ? 18. All whom you bring in [2] must be real Pathans of the Peshawar District. 19. Menials and the village workmen will not do. 20. Can you take my servant's son with you.?

VOCABULARY XX.

له نن تاريخ نه	*luh nan tārikh na*	From this day.
يو ځل	*yaw zal*	Once.
دوه ځلَ	*dwa zala*	Twice.
درى ځلَ	*dré zalā*	Thrice.
داځل	*dā zal*	This time.
ويل	*wayal*	To say, speak, tell.
ضروري	*zarūri*	Important, necessary, urgent.
ضروري ضروري	*zarūri zarūri*	Very important ones.
معمولى	*māmūli*	Ordinary.
عرضى	*arzi*	Petition.
عرضي	*arzai*	Petitions.
درخواست	*darkhwāst*	Ordinary petition, request.

NOTE :—1. Direct speech.
2. In syntax rule No. 22.

کچوړی	*kacharai*	Court.
جمع کول	*jama kawal*	To collect.
ښۀ غوندی	*khuh ghundé*	Somewhat good.
خرڅ دَ پاره	*khars da pāra*	For sale.
لۀ بَدَ نصیب	*luh bada nasiba*	Unfortunately.
لۀ ښۀ نصیب	*luh khuh nasiba*	Fortunately.
هره ورځ	*hara vraz*	Every day.
وزګار	*wōzgār*	At leisure.
نا وزګار	*nā wōzgār*	Busy.
مفرور	*mafrūr*	An outlaw.
إنعام	*ināam*	Reward.
مؤندل	*mūndal*	To get, obtain, receive, find.
زۀ مؤمم	*zuh mūmam*	I get, etc. (present).
ٹګی	*tagi*	Deceit.
اسان	*asān*	Easy.
ربړ	*rabar*	Trouble.
لرګی	*largay*	Stick, wood.
لاله	*lāla*	To me or for me.
را بَند ډیر کار دی	*rā bāndé dér kā: day*	I have plenty to do.
پۀ دی شپو ورځو کښی	*pa dé shpo vrazo ké*	New a days.
یوا ځی	*yawāzé*	Alone.
باران کوټ	*bārān kōt*	Overcoat, water proof coat.
بونګه	*bōnga*	Ransom.

Exercise 20.

۱ يو سړی يی لۀ څنګل نه راوست او ورته يی وو چه لۀ نن
تاريخ نه تۀ ځمونږ بادشاه يی ۲ بۀ مرزا صاحب څۀ دَ راوړي دي؟
ما در ته ويلي دي چه ضروري ضروري كاغذونه راوړه او معمولي
عرضي او درخواستونه په كڅوري كښ جمع كوه ۳ زۀ به د دَ ملک
حجري له بوزم ۴ نن څويم تاريخ دی . پرون دَ څۀ ورځ وه ـ بل
صبا دَ پير ورځ ده ۵ ما له يو غۀ غوندی نوكر راوله ۲ دَ دی
وطن خلق لۀ څنګل نه واچه او لرګي راوړي او په ښهر كښ يې
خرڅوي ۷ مؤنږ خرځ دَ پاره سكارۀ هم راوړ ۸ كۀ تا مفرور ځما
بذهلی ته راوستی وی نو ما به ډير لوی انعام دركړی وه ۹ نوكر ته
م و وايه چه ځما ټپن هرۀ ورځ دفتر ته راوړي ځكه چه را باند ډير
كار دی ۱۰ بی لۀ ټمي نه دَ مفرورانو راوستل اسان كار نۀ دی
۱۱ بيا هيڅري ځما چاي په دی ميز كينه زدی ۱۲ ځما آس
غلو بيولی وه دَ اپريد و يو ملک لا له پۀ بوذكه راوست ۱۳ ما ته يی
وو چه ستا آس م په ډير رلږ سره راوستی دی ۱۴ لږ ی نوری اوبۀ
په ګلاس كښ راوړه ۱۵ پرون مالي دَ دی پقي دَ پاره اوبۀ
راوستی وی ۱۶ رايی وله چه انعام وركړم ۱۷ زۀ ځۀ وكړم په
دی ښپو ورڅو كښ زۀ ډير ناوزګاريم ۱۸ دا كار ما يواځي كولی نۀ
شو ۱۹ ځما نوكر ته و وايه چه دفتر ته را پسي باران كوټ م راوړي
۲۰ ټول ټوپكونه راوړه او دَ صاحب پۀ مخ كښ يې و شماره ـ

VOCABULARY XXI.

ګرځه و ۔ **garza**   Turn !

كس لس	*gas lās*	Left hand.
خى لس	*khay lās*	Right hand.
پيش كړه	*pésh kra*	Bring before or produce.
قدم	*qadam*	Pace.
پونده	*pūnda*	Heel.
سمدستى	*samdāsti*	At once.
لږول	*lagawāl*	To fix, apply, and arrange (Flowers etc.)
سنگين	*sangin*	Bayonet.
مه ځه	*muh za*	Do not go.
مه را ځه	*muh rāza*	Do not come.
شور	*shōr*	Noise.
چپ	*chup*	Silent.
وبستل	*wistal*	To take out, take off.
وباسم	*wō bāsam*	I take off (present.)
جامى	*jāmé*	Clothes.
أدريدل	*odrédal*	To stand.
نيغ	*négh*	Straight.
كوږ	*kōg*	Crooked.
لږ يا لوكوتى	*lag* or *lūkūti*	Little or please
گرمى	*garmi*	Heat.
يخنى	*yakni*	Cold.
ناراست	*nārāst, sust*	Lazy.

MISCELLANEOUS COLLOQUIAL SENTENCES II.

Why did you strike him ?	*walé dé hagha wo wahalo*

Turn to the right.	*khi lās ta wō garza.*
Bring him before the C. O.	*kamān afsar ta yé pésh kṛa.*
Turn to the left.	*gus lās ta wo garza.*
Where do you live ?	*charta osé ?*
When did you arrive here ?	*ḍalé kala rā wo rasédé ?*
Keep in step.	*qadam melāo kra.*
Heels together	*pundé yaū zāi kra.*
Bring him at once	*zar yé rāwala.*
Fix bayonet	*sangin wo lagawa.*
Pull vigorously	*puh zōr sara yé rā wobāsa*
Come here	*ḍalé rasha* or *dalta rāsha.*
Do not go there	*halta muh za.*
Hurry up	*zar sha.*
Tell the sepoys not to make a noise	*spāhyāno ta wo wāya chi shōr nuh kawee.*
Keep quiet.	*chup sha.*
Take the horse to the house	*ass kōr ta bōza.*
Take off your clothes	*jāmé dé wo bāsa.*
Stand up straight	*négh wodréga.*
Lie down	*sumla.*
Wait a little	*lūkūti sabar wo kra,* or *wār wo kra.*
Take this letter to the Adjutant	*dā chitaī jitan sāhib ta yāusa.*

Bring an answer quickly	*zar jawāb rāwra.*
It is very hot today	*nan déra garmi dah*
Owing to the rain it is cold	*da bārān puh sabab yakhni dah.*
You are very lazy	*tuh dér nārāst yé.*
Do not bring all the papers	*tōl kāgazūna muh rāwra.*
Put them in the office	*puh daftar ké yé kégda.*

VOCABULARY XXII.

قصه	*qisa*	Story.
اخستل	*akhistal*	To take or buy. آخلم = *akhlam* I take (present).
خرچ	*khars kawal*	To sell, spend.
مجرم	*mujrem*	Accused or offender
جرم	*juram*	Crime.
قتل يا خون	*qatal* or *khūn*	Murder.
قاتل يا خونى	*qātél* or *khūni*	Murderer.
وژلے شوے	*wajhalay shaway saray* or *maray*	
سړے يا مړے		Murdered man.
ما خبر کړه	*mā khabar kra*	Let me know
مدرسه	*madrasa*	School.
تيار شه	*tayār sha*	Get ready.
ضرورى	*zarūri*	Necessary, urgent.
کار	*kār*	Work.

ناوختہ *nā wakhta*	Late.
وختی *wakhti*	Early.
خما پہ فکر کښ *zamā puh fikar ké*	I think, I am afraid, In my opinion.
قریب *qarib*	About, nearly.
لیدل *lidal*	To see.
بیرتہ *biarta*	Back.
بیا *bia*	Again.
تړ را تړ *tag rā tag*	Coming and Going.

EXERCISE 21.

1. When will you go back ? 2. He came inside, sat on the chair and told me to tell him my father's story. 3. When did your brother come from Lahore ? 4. We went to the City but did not see Mahabat Khan's Mosque. 5. The people of the city come to my garden to buy fruit. 6. When you first saw the accused, was he coming to his house or had he arrived there ? 7. Where did you come from ? 8. Let me know when my servant arrives. 9. I will sit on this chair, you can lie down on that carpet and the village people will come to us. 10. I go at 10 in the morning and come back at 4 p. m. 11. Get ready! We will go to the cantonment at 2-30 p. m. 12. Come to my house every day and do the necessary work. 13. It is very late now, I think you had better

go tomorrow. 14. My servant has gone to
the bazar and will be back in about an hour.
15. Yes, the Khan had come, but I did not see
him. 16. My regiment was in Pindi but it
has now come to Peshawar. 17. Ahmad went
to his house and did not come back again.
18. If he had come, you would have seen him.
19. We used to sit on the bank of that river.
20. I went to the hill without seeing anyone
coming or going.

VOCABULARY XXIII.

راځه چه	*rāza chi*	Let us.
(ته) نقُصان رسَوَل	*(ta) nuqsān rasawal*	To cause damage.
ناراستی	*nārāsti*	Idleness.
نیستی	*nésti*	Poverty.
تُخم	*tukhum*	Seed.
(ته) نقُصان رسیدل	*(ta) nuqsān rasédal*	To suffer loss,
پریټ	*parait*	Parade
اخبار	*akhbār*	Newspaper.
دَ پهٔ ځای کښ	*da puh zāi ké*	Instead of
وینځل	*winzal*	To wash.
بندول	*bandawal*	To close.
کنجی	*kunji*	Key.
ناظِر	*nāzer*	Manager.
کار	*kār*	Work.

ملاحظه کول	*mulāheza kawal*	To inspect.
ورته به معلومه شي	*warta ba malūma shi*	He will find.
ضرور	*zarūr*	Certainly.
معافول (معاف کول)	*muāfawal (muāf kawal)*	To remit, forgive.
په یو مخ	*puh yau makh*	All in one time.
هله یا حمله	*hala* or *hamla*	Attack.
نۀ صرف...بلکه	*nuh serf..balké*	Not only...but
سیزل یا سوزول	*sézal* or *swazawal*	To burn.
سوزیدل	*swazédal*	To be burnt.
ته شکست ورکول	*(ta) shikast warkawal*	To defeat.
شکست خوړل	*shikast khwaral*	To be defeated.
بدرګه	*badraga*	Escort.
قام	*qām*	Tribe.
(سـ.) شپه کول	*(sara) shpa kawal*	To stay the night with.
وخت راته نۀ وه	*wakht rā ta nuh woh*	I had no time.
خرڅ دَ پاره	*khars da pāra*	For sale.
تر اوسَ پورې	*tar osa pōre*	Up to the present, till now.
تیر کول	*tér kawal*	To pass (time).
هیلۍ	*hilai*	Duck.
جبه	*jaba*	Marsh.

گشت	*gasht*	Rounds, patrol
دَ چرو توپک	*da charō tōpak*	Shot gun.
څوکئ کول	*saukai kawal*	To guard.
ملا بانگ مالى	*mulā bāng mālé*	At dawn.
نښه	*nakha*	Sign, mark.
نوَی	*naway*	New.
زوړ	*zōr*	Old.

EXERCISE 22.

۱ راغله چه هغه کلی ته لاړشؤ او دَ کلی ملک سره دَ رسد بندوبست وکړؤ ۲ صاحب یو خان راغلی دیَ او تا سره لیدل غواړی ۳ یو کم عقل سړی خپل دښمن ته دومره نقصان نۀ شی رسولی لکه چه خپل ځان ته ئي رسوی ۴ دا رښتیا خبره ده چه ناراستی دَ نیستی تخم دیَ ۵ نن درۀ ځله ځه. ته لاړم او راغلم مګر ستا ورور م و نۀ لید ۶ ما هغه دفتر ته رَغوښتلو او ورنه م تپوس وکړ چه پرون چه ته تۀ پۀ پریښ باند وی نو چا پوری دَ خندلی ژو ۷ صبا سحر پۀ پنځهٔ بجی زۀ به ښکار له ځم ته به راسره ځی که نه ۸ پرون م پۀ اخبار کښں ولوستل چه ستا سو پلتن به ستا ښۀ ته ځی او بیرته به نۀ راځی ۹ که تۀ تۀ پخپله نۀ شی راتلی نو ورور د پۀ خپل ځای کښں راواستوه ۱۰ قلمونه وینښل او دَ دی کمری تولی کُرسئ او میزؤنه صافول او پنځهٔ بجی دفتر بندول او بیا کڼسی ناظر ته ورکول ستا کار دیَ ۱۱ که تحصیلدار دَ فصلونو ملاحظی دَ پاره راشی نو ورته به معلومه شی چه فصلونه ښۀ نۀ دی او ضرور به دَ مالیی معافولو دَ پاره رپوټ و کوی ۱۲ که نول برګیږ پۀ یو مخ پۀ دښمن باند همله کوی زوی نو نۀ صرف

ورته شکست به ئی ورکوے ؤ بلکه د هغو کلی به ئی هم سیزلي ؤو

۱۳ که زۀ راتلیَ شوَی نو پخپله به راغلی وم اوَدقام بدرﻛﻰ سره به م

د وطن دوره کړی ؤه اوشپه به م تاسره کوله مهر وخت راته نه ؤه

۱۴ اسؤنه لۀ افغانستان نه راوستلیَ کیږي او پۀ پیښورکښں پۀ

ﻛﺮاﻧﻪ بیعه خرڅیږي کله کله دا اسؤنه پنجاب ته هم د خرڅ د پاره

بیولیَ کیږي   ۱۵ هغه پاڅیدو روان شو وېی و چه صبا به بیا راشم

مهر تراوس پوری را نۀ غیَ   ۱۶ مؤنږ دوه د چرو ﻠﭙﻮﻠﮕﻮﻨﻪ خان

سره واخستل او د ښکار د پاره روان شو خلقو راته و چه پۀ جبوکښں

ډیری هیلي راغلی دی مؤنږ ټوله ورځ تیره کړه مهر یوه هم ونۀ لیدلیَ

شوه   ۱۷ زۀ خبر درکولو د پاره راغلیَ یم چه که نں ستاسو ﮔﺸﺖ

د لاری ﺧﻮﯾﻲ ﻛﻮﻟﻮ د پاره لا نۀ ﺭﻭ نو پۀ قلا باند به د قطب له ډوی

نه حمله وشي   ۱۸ خلوبمنت ترں خوانان خان سره واخله او لس

لس ﻛﺴَ ﺧﺎﯼ په ﺧﺎﯼ په لر کینوه تر ملا بازﮔﺶ مالی د پۀ ﺧﭙﻠﻮ

ﺧﭙﻠﻮ ﺧﺎﯾﻮﻨﻮ ناست وي   ۱۹ که تر ﺧﻠﻮﺭﻭ بجوَد دشمں ننہ نه وي

نورﺍﺧﻲ د   ۲۰ ته د لکه ﻧﻮﻛﺮ خما ئی او ﻛﺎﺭ د د بل ﻛﻮﯼ—

NOTE :—1. For *rāza chi* look up syntax
rule No. 30.

2. For the infinitive of purpose see syntax
rule No. 12.

VOCABULARY XXIV.

روان کیدل	*rawān kédal*	To start.
پوری کول	*pōré kawal*	To shut.
ما ورنه تپوس	*mā war na tapōs*	
وکړو	*wo kro*	I asked him.
کوم	*kum*	Which.

پس لۀ هغه	*pas luh hagha*	After that, later on, afterwards.
هم پۀ هغه ورځ	*hum puh hagha vraz*	On the very day.
لام	*lām*	Expedition.
جنگ	*jang*	Fight, war, battle.
تیره میاشت	*téra miāsht*	Last month.
تیندک خورل	*tindak khwaral*	To stumble.
خوږ کیدل	*khūg kédal*	To hurt.
ښپه	*khpa*	Foot, leg.
لالتین	*lāltain*	Lamp.
پۀ غلا تلل	*puh ghlā tlal*	To be stolen.
غلا	*ghlā*	Theft.
غل	*ghal*	Thief.
غله	*ghluh*	Thieves
غلا کول	*ghlā kawal*	To Steal.
توره	*tūra*	Sword.
پیشقوزه	*peshqauza*	Killing knife.
توره پۀ لس	*tūra puh lās*	With a sword in hand.
لختی	*lakhtay*	Water cut.
برتی کول	*barti kawal*	To enlist.
قافیله	*qāfela*	Caravan.
ماشی	*māshay*	A mosquito.
کتمل	*kātmal*	Bug.
وروږه	*vraga*	A flea.
میزری	*mézaray*	Dwarf palm.
بوڼر	*būnr*	String made of dworf pa'm.

منجور	*manjawar*	Shrine keeper.
اهام	*imām*	Leader in prayer.
سيّد	*sayad*	Descendent of prophet.
ميان	*miān*	Descendent of any religious person.
سپږه	*spaga*	Louce.
پاتی كيدل	*paté kédal*	To remain.
تير	*tér*	Last.
ميله	*maila*	Fair.
زيارت	*ziārat*	Shrine.
بل كول	*bal kawal*	To light.
مړ كول	*mar kawal*	To put out.

EXERCISE 23.

1. I gave him an order to go to that village in the plain. 2. He started but an hour later sent me a message that he could not go. 3 Please shut the door. 4. I asked him what village he came from (Thou of which village art?) 5. He said his name was Ahmad but afterwards said it was Mohammad. 6. He died on the same night. 7. All the crops have been harvested. 8. Two of my sons had been wounded in the Tirah expedition. 9. He became a Jamadar on the 15th of last month. 10. The Colonel's horse stumbled this morning but the Sahib was not hurt. 11. We fell off the

motor and I broke my leg (my leg was broken).
12.   Light the lamp and do not put it out till
11 o'clock.   13.   My house was burgled and all
my clothes were stolen.   14.   As we opened the
door of the house I saw a man standing near the
tree with a sword in his hand.   15.   The land of
the village is irrigated from this river by a small
water cut.   16.   I am glad that the Adjutant
enlisted me on the very day.   17.   I cannot shut
the door as I am ill.   18.   In the winter and
spring the caravans go on Tuesdays and Fridays ; in the hot weather and rains they only go
on Fridays.   19.   The jirga came to the Political
Agent on Sunday last, but as the Sahib was out
on tour, they had to stay in the city for the
night.   20.   A fair is held every year at the
shrine of Kaka Sahib at Nowshera.

VOCABULARY XXV.

أوښ	*ūkh*	Camel.
ساروان	*sārwān*	Camelman.
ګنی	*ganay*	Sugar cane.
هيڅ فائده نشته	*hiss faida nishta*	There is no use.
شولی	*shōlé*	Rice (Crop)
زميندار	*zamindār*	Land owner, farmer.
چای کار	*chalé kār*	Cultivator.
ماليه	*māliya*	Land revenue.
زيات	*ziāt*	Excessive.

ګوړه	*gura*	Brown sugar (gurh)
خرڅول یا خرڅ کول	*kharsawal* or *khars kawal*	To sell, spend.
خرڅیدل یا خرڅ کیدل	*kharsédal* or *khars kédal*	To be sold, to be spent.
پنبه	*punba*	Cotton.
علاج	*ilāj*	Remedy, Cure.
روژه	*rōjha*	Fast or fasting.
ور	*war*	Door.
د روپو تیلی	*da rūpo télai*	Bag of money
پاتی کیدل	*pāté kédal*	To remain.
نیمه لار	*nima lār*	Half way.
کوز کول	*kūz kawal*	To take down, take off.
کوز کیدل	*kūz kédal*	To get down, dismount.
حجره	*hujra*	Guest house.
سلام اچول	*salām achawal*	To say salam to.
پۀ بانډ خوړول	*puh-bāndé khurawal*	To cause to eat.
پۀ بانډ سکول	*puh-bāndé skawal*	To cause to drink or smoke.
خذمت	*khizmāt*	Service.
غرق اوده	*gharq ūduh*	Fast asleep.
هینرهار	*henrahār*	Neighing of horses.
خبر	*khabar*	Message or news.
کم	*kam*	Less, deficient.
دارو	*dārū*	Medicine.

پیشنمَیٰ یا	*péshnamay*	The time of first
or		meal before dawn in
پیشمنَیٰ	*péshmany*	month of Ramzan.
گاډیٰ	*gáday*	Cart, car.
دُعا	*dūaā*	Prayer.
مُونځ کول	*mūnz kawal*	To pray.
اغوستل	*aghustal*	To wear etc.
اغوندم	*aghundam*	I wear (present.)
پیغمبر	*péghambar*	Prophet.
کوچ کول	*kōch kawal*	To march.
افسوس کول	*afsōs kawal*	To be sorry.
سینتری	*séntri*	Sentry.
پهره	*pehra*	Sentry-go.
ناگهانه	*nāgahāna*	By chance.
ناصاپه	*nāsāpuh*	Suddenly.
چپاؤ	*chapāo*	Surprise attack.
پۀ‌باند ورختل	*puh-bāndé warkhatal*	To invade.
(سره) مقابله کول	*(sara) muqā-bela kawal*	To withstand.
هم هغَسی	*hum haghasé*	Still, in the same manner.
تخت	*takht*	Throne.
فقیر	*faqir*	Beggar.
عبادت	*ibādat*	Worship.
پۀ‌باند لاس پوری کول	*puh bāndé lās pōré kawal*	To start, commence.
سار فصلونه	*sār faslūna*	Withering crops.

مينه	*maina*	House.
سترگه	*starga*	An eye.
سر	*sar*	Head.
مخ	*makh*	Face.
خوله	*khuluh*	Mouth.
مرئ	*marai*	Throat.
څټ	*sat*	Back of neck.
تندی	*tanday*	Forehead.
غوږ	*ghwag*	Ear.
وېښتهٔ	*wékhtuh*	Hair (M. S. and P.)
لاس	*lās*	Hand.
ښپه	*khpa*	Foot or leg.
گوته	*gōta*	Finger.
پوزه	*pōza*	Nose.
زړه	*zruh*	Heart.
تېز	*téz*	Fast, sharp.
پهٔ۔باند اواز کول	*puh-bandé awāz kawal*	To challenge.
(تهٔ) اواز کول	*(ta) awāz kawal*	To call out to.
پهٔ۔باند دز کول	*puh-bandé daz kawal*	To fire at.
پهٔ تکی	*puh taki*	Instantly.
گير کول	*gér kawal*	To surround.
مدت راغوښتل	*madat rāghukhtal*	To call for help (re-inforcements).
تار	*tār*	Wire, telegram.
شيشه	*shisha*	Helio.

جنډۍ	*jandai*	Flag, signalling.
مخبر	*mukhber*	Informer, spy.
ضمانت	*zamānat*	Security.
ضامن	*zāman*	Surety.
منظور کول	*manzūr kawal*	To sanction.

EXERCISE 24.

۱ ساروان نا جوړ شو قافلي پسي وَنه رسیدلی شو ۲ اوس
دَ گنو په فصل کښ هیڅ فائیده نشته ځکه چه مالیه یی ډیره زیاته دَه
اوکوره ډیره ارزانه دَه ۳ موږ له پکاردی چه هغه فصلونه وکرُو چه گران
گران خرڅیږی پکار ړو چه موږ سکال پنبه کرلی وی ۴ موږ یی
ډیر علاج وکړ مګر دَ روژی دَ میاشتی په دریمه ورځ مړ شو ۵ دَ
دوکان ور یی پوری کړ چه تلو نو دَ روپو ټیلئی ورنه هم په هغه ځای
پاتی شوه ۶ چه نیمی لاری ته ورسیدم نو له گاډی نه ئی کوز
کړم ځکه چه ځما ټکس خالی تر پیو پوری وُو هلته یوی حجری ته
ورغلم سلام مې وا چاوُه کینا ستم دَ حجری خاوند را باند ډوډیئ وخوړوله
چلم ئی را باند وسکولو نو راته ئی ویل چه که ما ته نور ځه خدمت
وی نو هم زَه ورته تیاریم ۷ که دَ کلی ځلق غرق اوده نَه وی نو
ځمُوږ دَ اسونو هیڼهار به ئی اوریدلی وُه ۸ صاحب که دا انعام
د پَه ما پیروز وی نو راته به د دَ داری دَ راتلو خبر راکوی وُه
۹ بادشاه لَه تخت نه کوز شو او فقیر ته ئی وو چه راخه ځما په ځای
اوس تَه کینه پخپله یی دَ فقیرانو جامی واغوستی په جماعت کښ
کیناست دَ ځدای پک په عبادت ئی لس پوری کړ ۱۰ زَه نوَدرِئ
پسی له وطن نه راغلی یم مګر اوس ځمُوږ دَ علاقی برتی بنده دَه
۱۱ کله چه ډوډیئ وخورم نو ستا چپئ به ولولم ۱۲ که ډیڅی
نمشتر صاحب دَ فصلونه ملاحظی کولو دَ پاره راتلی نو تر اوس بد

راغلی وۀ ارمان دیَ چه یوهل خو ئی ځمونږ دا سار فصلونه لیدلیَ
وی ۱۳ کار را باند دومره زیات دیَ چه کم ناکم م دوۀ چلی
کاران وسائل او خوا سنحوا به ورله مینی هم دَ اوسیدلو دَ پاره ورکوم
۱۴ ملک سخه یوۀ اسپه دَ چه یو ستړکۀ یِي دَه (یا پۀ یوۀ ستړکۀ ژنده
دَه) ولی داسی تیزه دَه چه په دری سزَ ئی هم نۀ ورکوی ما خپل
آس پۀ ملک باند پۀ سل روپیِي ځرخ کړ ۱۵ اۀل سنتری پۀ غل
باند اواز وکړ او بیائي وویشت پۀ ټکی ئی م کړ ۱۶ ستا خو
خامن دی لۀ ټولونه مشر ځوی د دَ ځوَ کالو دیَ او تۀ دَ ځوَ کالو
نوکر ئی ۱۷ ناګهانه دَ سرکار فوځ پۀ قلا باند حمله وکړه او دَ جرمن
فوځ ئي په کښں ګیر کړ فوځ مدت راغوښتلو دَ پاره ټیلیفون ورکړ مګر
دَ سرکار فوځ ټول تارونه پری کړی ؤو بیائي زر شیشه ورکړه او جنډیِي
یِي هم ورته ووهله ۱۸ مؤنږ خپل مخبر ته ویل چه مخکښں مخکښں
ځه مګر هغه پۀ یوۀ ستړکۀ مغذور ؤه نۀ شو تلیَ ۱۹ کرنیل صاحب یو
پښتُون سړیَ دیَ مُدام پۀ خپلو سپاهیانو ولاړ وبِ ۲۰ که ورشی
او وګوری نو صاحب به راغلیَ وبِ ِ او ستا ضمانت به یِي منظور
کړی وبِ ِ

VOCABULARY XXVI.

بی لۀ طلب نه	bé luh talab na	Without pay.
دَ شفارس کول	da-shafāras kawal	To recommend.
کمان افسر	kamān afsar	Officer Commanding
(سره) اتفاق کول	(sara) ittefāq kawal or manal	To agree.

هغۀ ولیدل	*haghuh wo lidal*	He saw.
ما تہ معلومہ شوه	*mā ta malūma shwa*	I found out.
ختل	*khatal*	To climb.
پوُرہ کول	*pūra kawal*	To complete.
سر	*sar*	Head, top, end.
گټل	*gatal*	To win.
بیلل	*bélal*	To lose.
ها کی	*hāki*	Hockey.
لوبی کول	*lōbé kawal*	To play.
لوبه	*lōba*	Game.
کوټ گارت	*kōt gārat*	Quarter Guard.
تماچه	*tamācha*	Pistol or revolver.
بدی	*badi*	Feud.
اوړم کال	*ōram kāl*	Year before last.
پۀ ښۀ شان سره	*puh khuh shān sara*	Well, satisfactorily.
پوری غاړه	*pōré ghāra*	Far bank.
راپوری غاړه	*rā pōré ghāra*	Near bank.
ساتل	*sātal*	To engage, (servant) keep.
نیول	*niwal*	To engage (barrister).
کیږی	*kégee*	Ago, becomes (present of *kédal*
غوږ ددی	*ghwag dé day*	Are you listening ?
تیریدل	*térédal*	To pass by.
اغوستلی وه	*aghustalay woh*	Was wearing (lit : had worn.)

خاکی یا خر	*khāki* or *khar*	Khaki, grey.
خان پټ کول	*zān pat kawal*	To take cover.
تر بلَ حکمپوری	*tar bala hukma pōré*	Till next order.
واده	*wāduh*	Marriage.
وعده کول	*wada kawal*	To promise.
مال	*māl*	Cattle.
څرول	*sarawal*	To graze (transitive.)
ورشو	*warsho*	Grazing ground.
ګوره	*gora !*	Look here !
یو څو	*yau so*	A few,
دامان	*dāmān*	Summer pasture ground.
منډۍ	*mandai*	Market.
ګانړۍ	*gānrai*	Sugar cane press.

EXERCISE 25.

1. What do you want? 2. I want ten days leave, without pay. 3. I will recommend you to the Commanding Officer and will send for you if he agrees. 4. The boy fell into the well and saw that he could not climb up. 5. Can you go across the river? 6. There is no boat, the river is deep so how can I cross? 7. Can you recognise this man? Yes he is the man whom I saw in the bazar yesterday. 8. Sultan Mahmud went to Ghazni and left his sardars to complete the necessary work, 9. We found

that the enemy were on the top of the hill. 10.
Every one of the boys got 50/- rupees as a
reward for winning the hockey match. 11. A
thief was running towards the Guard Room and
the sentry shot him dead with a revolver. 12
He had a feud with Mohmands, because they
killed his father the year before last. 13. Can
you read and write ? 14. I cannot read but in
two months I shall be able to read well. 15. Do
you see that big tree on the near bank of the
river ? That is our camp. 16. Look here,
young man I engaged you as Mali on 15/-
rupees a month, a few months ago. 17. Do
you hear ? 18. I saw a man passing by here
wearing a khaki coat. 19. The sepoys will
have to dig trenches and take cover till next
order. 20. I have heard that the King of
Afghanistan is coming to Peshawar.

VOCABULARY XXVII.

خه ټوپک ويشتل	*khuh tōpak wishtal*	To shoot (well.)
ذنخه	*nakha*	Mark.
دزکول	*daz kawal*	To fire.
سيلاب	*sélab*	Flood.
نُقصان	*nuqsān*	Loss.
(نه) بد بد کتل *(ta) bad bad katal*		To stare at.

بی خودَ	bé khuda	Senseless.
پهٔ خود	puh khud	In senses
سترزی غرول	stargé gharawal	To open eyes.
سترزی پټی کړه	stargé paté kra	Shut your eyes !
خولهٔ وازه کړه	khuluh wāza kra	Open your mouth !
خولهٔ پیچی کړه	khuluh piché kra	Shut your mouth !
غوږ کیږده	ghwag kégda	Lit. place ear. } Listen !
پروت	prōt	Lying.
خپل خپلوان	khpal khpalwān	Relations.
گیر چاپیره	gérchāpéra	All round.
پیشکی	péshki	Advance (of money)
پټکی پهٔ سرکول	patkay puh sar kawal	To wear a pagri.
پنړی پهٔ خپو کول	panré puh khpo kawal	To wear shoes.
دستانی پهٔ لاس کول	dastāné puh lās kawal	To wear gloves.
سور کیدل	sōr kédal	To mount.
خیر خیریت	khér kheriat	All well.
بالکل	bélkul	Absolutely, entirely
تباه کول یا برباد کول	tabāh kawal or barbād kawal	To ruin.

پۀ-باند اعتبار کول	*puh-bāndé ittebār kawal*	
پۀ-باند یقین کول	*puh-bāndé yaqin kawal*	To trust.
پۀ-باند باور کول	*puh-bāndé bāwar kawal*	
رشتیا	*rishtiā*	Truth.
دروغ	*darōgh*	Lie.
غلط فهمی	*ghalat fahmi*	Misunderstanding.
پۀ کلی باند داره پریوتله	*puh kali bāndé dāra préwatala*	The village was raided.
پۀ کلی باند جُرم پریوت	*puh kali bāndé jurm préwat*	The village was fined.
چغه	*chagha*	Pursuit party.
مازدیګر	*māzdigar*	Early evening (between 3 o'clock and sunset).
ماښپښین	*māspakhin*	Afternoon.
ما ښِتن	*māskhutan*	Night prayer time (between 8 o'clock and midnight.
پۀ لاس راتلل	*puh lās rātlal*	To come in hand, procure.
تحقیقات کول	*tahqiqāt kawal*	To enquire.
تفتیش	*taftish*	Police enquiries.
معلومه شوه	*malūma shwa*	It turned out.
کلیوال	*kaliwāl*	Villager.
غفلت	*ghaflat*	Negligence.

لار نيول (ته)	*ta lār niwal*	To ambush.
خرا په خبره ده	*kharāpa khabara dah*	It is a bad bussiness.
ډير ځل	*dér zal*	Many times.
د-پرواه كول	*da-parwāh kawal*	To take notice of.
هيڅ پروا نشته	*hés parawāh nishta*	Never mind.
هيڅ باك نشته	*hés bāk nishta*	Never mind.
پهم كول	*paham kawal*	To take care.
سپين سرى ښځه	*spin saré khaza*	White headed woman, old woman.
خندل (پورى)	*pōré khandal*	To laugh at.
لهـنه-روان كيدل	*luh-na rawān kédal*	To start, leave, set out from.

EXERCISE 26.

۱ ما دَكلى ملک گواهي دپاره ډير ځل راوغوښت مګر
نۀ غى ۲ افريديان ډير تورك ولي هغوى هره ورځ په خپل خپل
كلي كښى پۀ نښو باند ډزى كوى ۳ پۀ جنگ كښى همونږو
څلور تنَ سپاهيان ووژلَ شول ۴ دكور خاوند ور چه ما درى تنَ
ډارۀ ماران پيژندلي دى ۵ پۀ سيند كښى سيلاب دى ښكه ورنه
پوزيوتل گران كاردىَ ۶ ددى كتاب پۀ لوستلو كښى ستا څۀ
نقصان دىَ ۷ ولي بدبد گورى ۸ لۀ اس نه پريوتم بيه م ماته
شوه بى خودَ شوم چه پۀ خود شوم اوستنرګى م وغـړَى نوبه هسپيتال
كښى پۀ يو كټ باند پروتوم اوخپل خپلوان رانه ګير چاپيره ناست ؤو
اوبى ژړل ۱۰ داڅاس روپيي پيشكى واخله اونورى بۀ بيادركوم

١١ أُوردى ئي واغوسته پټكَي ئي په سر کړو بوټونه ئي په ـبیوکړل
دستانى يى په لاس کړى اوپه اس سورشه لو ١٢ تؤوائى چه فصلونه
موسم.رکال غٹۀ دى په باره کښ اوبه کمى دى ـدَسکلو دپاره هم
نه راخي مهر پرون خان راغلىَ وه هغۀ خو ويل چه ټول خیرخیریت دىَ
فصلونه بالکل غنۀ دى اوبۀ ډیرى دى ١٣ صاحب مؤن.رغۀ ووایؤ
چه نایى مو مړوى نوتول کلىَ مو مړوى نو ١٤ په کلى دا ړه پریوته
دوه کور وفنىىى لوټ کړل چغۀ ورپسى روته خو مازدیمر بیرته راغله
څکه چه دا روۀ-اران په لاس ورنه رغلل ١٥ پولس تحقيقات وکړ
معلومه شوه چه دا د کلیوالو غفلت دىَ څکه ور باند دوه زر روپيي جرم
پریوت ١٦ هغه په ډیر ربړ سره لۀ کور نه راووتلو ١٧ څلورو وتنو اپریدو
ورته لار نيولىَ وه ټولى جامى ئي تر واخستى ١٨ صوبيدار صاحب
دا د دى دا روۀ ډیره خراپه خبره ده . ما تۀ ډیر ځل پوه کړىَ ئي چه
هره شپه د خپلى کپنيَ سره په وطن کښ ګشت کوه ـ مهر تۀ څما دَ
خبرى هیڅ پرواه نۀ کوى ١٩ سپین سرى غنْڅى تانړه ډار پورى
وخندل او تر روانه شوه ٢٠ صاحب کۀ تۀ راغلىَ نه وىَ نو زۀ به ئي
وژلىَ و م -

VOCABULARY XXVIII.

لیونیَ	*léwanay*	Mad.
لیونیَ سپیَ	*léwanay spay*	Mad dog.
اوچ کول	*ūch kawal*	To dry.
لوَند	*lūnd*	Wet.
نور	*nwar*	Sun, sunshine.
سپو.رزميَ	*spōgmai*	Moon
تور.رزميَ	*tarōgmai*	Moonless.

سِتوری	*stōray*	A star.
دير ساعت	*dér sāat*	Much longer, for a long time.
دومره ساعت	*dōmra sāat*	So much longer.
نِيول يا گرفتار كول	*niwal* or *géréftār kawal*	To arrest.
پۀ موقعه باند	*puh mōqa bāndé*	On the spot.
پاڅيدل	*pāsédal*	To get up.
هسى تازهيږوي	*hasé tā zāhirawee*	They are only pulling your leg !
ټوقى كول	*tōqé kawal*	To joke.
مږه	*maga*	Rat.
ټکړه	*tukra*	Piece.
پريږده چه لارشى	*prégda chi lārshee*	Let him go !
چمن	*chaman*	Grass lawn.
كله چه	*kala chi*	As soon as.
اواز	*awāz*	Sound, voice.
بيګل	*bigal*	Bugle.
فوځ	*fauz*	Troops, Army.
(تۀ) چوټی وركول يا شړل	*ta chuti war-hawal* or *sharal*	To dismiss.
جوارى كول	*jawāri kawal*	To gamble.
جوارګر	*jawārgar*	Gambler.
لۀ نه قرض اخستل	*luh-na qarz akhistal*	To borrow.
تۀ قرض وركول	*ta qarz war-kawal*	To lend.

ژما پۀ هغۀ باند لس روپئی دی	*zamā puh haghuh bāndé las rupai di*	He owes me ten rupees.
دَ هغۀ پۀ ما باند لس روپئی دی	*da haghuh puh mā bāndé las rupai di*	I owe him ten rupees.
بنیا	*bania*	Bunia.
أمید دی	*omaid day*	I hope.
دَ کټ جامی	*da kat jāmé*	Sleeping suit.
فرش	*farsh*	Floor.
شړل	*sharal*	To drive out, turn out.
جرمانه کول	*jarmāna kawal*	To fine.
ویښ کول	*wikh kawal*	To wake up (transitive.)
تر هغه وختَ پوری	*tar hagha wakhta pōré*	Then, till that time
اودۀ کیدل	*úduh kédal*	To sleep.
خوب	*khōb*	Sleep.
خوب لیدل	*khōb lidal*	To dream.
غسل	*ghusal*	Bath.
وینځل	*winzal*	To wash.
ټوله رښتیا خبره	*tōla rikhtia khabara*	The whole truth.

EXERCISE 27.

1. He came out of the door and ordered me to shoot the mad dog 2. Take all the

tables and chairs out of this room and dry them in the sun. 3. The jamadar went into the room and did not stay any longer. 4. Do not laugh at him 5. A boy was sitting on the roadside crying, a man came up on him and asked him why was he weeping. 6. The Police arrested him on the spot ond produced him before the Magistrate. 7. He got up and went out, saying that he would come again tomorrow 8. The old man wrapped the rat in the piece of cloth and took it to the house. 9. Untie the horse and let it go to that grass field. 10. As soon as the horse heard the sound of the bugle he ran towards our troops. 11, I dismissed my servant, because he had lost 200/- rupees in gambling, which he had borrowed from the regimental Bania. 12. I hope you did not mind seeing me in my sleeping suit. 13. The Colonel found a sentry sleeping on guard, and shot him dead with his revolver. 14. Jemadar! tell these people that if any one spits on the floor I shall certainly turn him out and fine him five rupees. 15. Wake me at 7 o'clock if I am still asleep. 16. I could not sleep the whole night, because the old man was coughing all the time. 17. The sepoys used to bathe in the spring near the fort. 18. If you had sent for the bearer, he would have told you the whole

truth. 19. Turn to the left. 20. What a
fool you are !

VOCABULARY XXIX

خپنی ziné	From, some.
ورو vro	Slow.
داک dag	Post, mail.
هوائي جهاز hawāi jehāz	Airship, aeroplane.
پښتو pukhtu	Modesty, Pushtu.
پښتون pukhtūn	Modest, Pathan.
پۀ.باند اودریدل puh-bandé odrédal	To take the side of.
مدام پۀ خپلو سپاهیانو باند والروي mudām puh khpalo spa hiyāno bandé wlār wi	He always takes the side of his soldiers.
تیښته tékhta	Flight.
خلاصیدل khlasédal	To escape.
معلومیدل malümédal	To be seen.
پۀ پهم سره puh paham sara	Carefully.
کتل katal	To look, examine.
ملاحظه کول mulāhéza kawal	To inspect.
ما تۀ یاد دي mā ta yād dee	I remember.
بهانه bahana	Pretence.
(تۀ) تندی تریو کول (ta) tanday triw kawal	To frown at.
لرل laral	To have.

دنيا	*dunia*	World. wealth.
آخِرت	*ākherat*	The day of judgement.
بدله	*badala*	Revenge.
غضب	*ghazab*	Rage.
په توقو توقو کښ	*puh tōqo tōqo ké*	Jokingly.
قربان دِ شم	*qurbān dé sham*	May I be sacrificed !
بار	*bār*	Load.
قچره	*qachara*	Mule.
په دى حساب سره	*pa dé hisab sara*	At this rate.
نور پريواته	*nwar prewātuh*	Sunset, west.
نور خاته	*nwar khātuh*	Sunrise, East.
دره	*dara*	Valley (over mountain).
غاښى	*ghākhay*	Pass.
په باندِ گمان کول	*puh-bāndé gumān kawal*	To suspect.

EXERCISE 28.

۱ یو مارغۀ دَ بل مارغۀ څېنى لوُر غوارِي ولى هغه ترِ دَ مرغانو
دستوُر غوارِي ۲ دا سړى و پېژنه کله چه زۀ پۀ جذبُ کښ
اپرېدو و بيولىَ وم نو څما یی ډېر خذمت کوىَ وه ۳ صاحبَ تا ته
څو معلومه ده چه زۀ پۀ لیکلو لوستلو نۀ پوهیږم نو ستا چقِي راته یو
بل سړى ولوسته ۴ کۀ تا څوخلىَ نۀ وى نو نور مرغان به د هم
ویشتلى ژو م؟ر بیا هم تۀ ډیر هغۀ توریک ولى ۵ کۀ رښتیا وایم دَ

هر چا بدي شم که دروغ وايم نو دَ ملکَ م شړي ٦ زۀ لرکوټي پۀ
غوږرو درۆند يم ورو خبره نه اورم ٧ اوس ﯨاﯨ پۀ هوائي جهاز
کښ ځې راځي ٨ زۀ پۀ رساله کښ برټي کيدل غواړم دَ رنگوټ
افسر دفتر راته وښيه ٩ زۀ پوه شوم چه پۀ تيښته نۀ خلاصيږم
١٠ دا آس م پۀ شکل خوښ دیَ خو کۀ ښکارﯨبﯨری ١١ جرنيل
صاحب راغلو ټول ځيزونه يې پۀ پهم سره وکتل دير خوشحال شۀ چه
تلو وئ ليکل چه هر شیَ دير نۀ اوصاف دیَ پۀ درﯨمه مياشت
بۀ ﯨيا ملاحظه کوم ١٢ ولی چرتي اخلی؟ مدام ستا پلار مړ وي
ستا هير دی ولی ما ته نۀ ياد دی چه دَ تير اکتوبر پۀ پنځلسم
تاريخ د هم پۀ دی بهانه چرتي اخستی رَوَ ١٣ غوږرونه بۀ
د وباسم ١٤ پښتون له شاباشیَ ورکوۀ نو کار به درله پۀ نۀ شان
سره کوی ١٥ او کۀ تندیَ د ورته تريوۆ کړ نو دَ نۀکار آميد ترمۀ کوه
١٦ کله سړیَ خاندي او کله ژاړي ١٧ بادشاه دَ غضب جامی
واغوستی په تخت کيناست ١٨ وزير پۀ ټوکو ټوکو کښ بادشاه ته
وو چه قربان د شم نن يغلی وايي چه بيۀاله به دَ فوځ داسی
خذمت وکړم چه صبا له به بادشاه او وزيران دَ خپلو خپلو اسونو
خذمتونه پيغيله کوي ١٩ نو اوس زرشه دا بارونه له اوهانو نۀ
کوزکړه پۀ قچرو یی واچوه نو دی حساب به تر نۆر پرﯨواتۀ پوری
له دری نه و نۀ خوۆ ٢٠ تانۀدار دَ کور لۀ خاوند نه تپوس وکړ چه
چاړوبل کوﯨ ئی او په چا باند ستا گمان دیَ ۔

VOCABULARY XXX.

پۀ يو کلي کښ *puh yau kali ké* In a certain village.

تر اوس پوری *tar osa ṗoré* Up to the present, so far.

خما ښکار خوښ دی	zamā khkār khwakh day	I am fond of shooting
په خطا	puh khatā	Accidentally.
لۀ قصدَ	luh qasda	On purpose.
قسم خورل	qasam khwaral	To take oath.
سوګند خورل	saugand khwaral	To take oath.
ایران	Irān	Persia.
سیلاب	sélāb	Flood.
تناؤ	tanāw	Boat rope.
بيړۍ پۀ تناؤ دۀ	bérai puh tanāw dah	The boat is pulled by a rope.
چا ﻱ	chāi	Tea.
پۍ	pai	Milk.
چينﻯ	chini, misri	Sugar.
هګﻯ یا ها	hagai or hā	Egg, Eggs.
ها سپينوَل	hā spinawal	To shell an egg.
ختل	khatal	To climb.
داړه مار	dāra mār	Raider, dacoit.
شوکه کول	shūka kawal	To loot, rob.
شوکمار	shūkmār	Rcbber.
خوا و شا	khwā-o-shā	Neighbourhood, vicinity.
ګنډ خنځهل	ganr zangal	Dense jungle.
رنګﻯ واښۀ	rangay wākhuh	Thin grass.
ويريدل	veyarédal	To fear.

كه ستا نصيب به	*kuh sta nasib*	
وي	*khuh wi*	If you are lucky.
رنگى باران	*rangay baran*	Slight rain.
را گرزيدل	*ra garzédal*	To return.
بيرته راتلل	*biarta ratlal*	To come back.
ساده	*sada*	Simple.
غلطى كول	*ghalati kawal*	To make a mistake.
رسيد	*rasid*	Receipt.

EXERCISE 29.

1. In a certain village there was a clever boy, who was so clever that his father said that up to the present such a clever boy had never been. 2. He used to read books and newspapers and never played with bad boys. 3. In the city of Peshawar there was a king who had two sons and three daughters. 4. The younger son was fond of shooting. 5. One day he went out shooting to Adam Khel pass and was accidently shot by his own gun. 6. His father took an oath that he would kill all the servants who came with him from Persia. 7. The Kabul river was in flood (in the river of Kabul flood was) and people crossed in a boat which was pulled across by a rope. 8. On the 15th of June of that year I was enlisted as a Jemadar and three years afterwards I became a Subadar. 9. Will you drink tea? 10. I will eat some

eggs, shell one for me. 11. Put very little
sugar in the tea. 12. No, do not put in any
milk, I do not like it. 13. Subadar Sahib!
take your company and climb the hill. 14. The
dacoits appeared to be in great fear of the
Indian troops and whenever they heard of any
in the vicinity, they at-once moved away to
dense jungle or jowar crops. 15. His father
died when he was only three years old.
16. When he was very young, he used to drive
birds from the field. 17. If you are lucky the
raiding gang will probably return on that road
this morning. 18. The people of this country
are very simple. 19. They are ruined by their
Khans and Maliks. 20. You made a great
mistake in that you did not take any receipt
from him.

VOCABULARY XXXI.

دربار	*darbār*	Darbar.
دَ بادشاه پۀ ښپو	*da badshah*	Fell at the king's
پرېوت	*puh khpo prewat*	feet.
پۀ ژړا شو	*puh jhara sho*	Began to weep.
موسم	*mōsam*	Season.
اکثر	*aksar*	Generally.
حوالات	*hawalāt*	Custody.

لږ ډير	*lag dér*	Somewhat.
ټول کول	*tōl kawal*	To collect.
جمع کول	*jama kawal*	To collect.
حاجت	*hājat*	Need.
حاجتمند	*hājatmand*	Needy.
ځنګل ويستل	*zangal wéstal*	To take out weeds.
وړوکی	*wrūkay*	Small.
واړۀ	*wāruh*	Small (M. Plu).
زيات	*ziāt*	More (in comparison)
بی سبب	*bé sababa*	Without reason.
مواجب	*mājéb*	Pay, allowance.
ذمه وار	*zémā wār*	Responsible.
ذمه	*zéma*	Responsibility.
پۀ خوا زمانه کښی	*puh khwā zamāna ké*	Formerly.
مشر	*mashar*	Elder.
سپين ګيری	*spin giray*	Grey beard, elder.
پۀ	*pa:*	Loser.
وړ	*war*	Winner.
فريق	*fariq*	Party.
سوره	*swara*	A girl in exchange.
رواج	*rewāj*	Custom.
شاباش	*shābāsh*	Well done.
نمک حلال	*namak halāl*	Loyal.
نمک حرام	*namak harām*	Disloyal.
بال بچ	*bāl bach*	Children, family.
ماشوم	*māshūm*	Child.

زۀ دَ هغۀ دَ لاسَ	zuh da haghuh	
تنګ یم	da lāsa tang yam	I am worried by him.
څمالاس تنګ دیَ	zamā lās tang day	I have no money.
دَ هغۀ کارجوړ دیَ	da haghuh kār jōr day	He is flourishing.
اورول	aurawal	To announce, to cause to hear,
سپکوالَی	spakwālay	An insult, disgrace.
سپک کول	spak kawal	To insult.
مرګ	marg	Death.
سزا	sazā	Punishment.
خپیمانَ کیدل	khpémāna kédal	To repent.
رعیت	rait	Subject (to Govt.)
ارام	arām	Rest.
کوشش	kōshash	Try.
زلزله	zalzala	Earth quake.
لوټی لوټی کول یا	luté luté kawal or	To destroy.
بر باد کول	barbād kawal	
لوټه یا غونده یا	lūta or ghunda,	
تیګه	tiga	Clod of earth.
بهادر	bahādar	Brave.
عمر	umar	Age.
نیت	niat	Intention.
مسافر	musāfar	Traveller.
منت کول	menat kawal	To entreat.

دلی	*walé*	But, why.
هيڅ فائده ونۀ شوه	*hiss faida wo nuh shwa*	No use.
خيال	*khyāl*	Thought.
خير خو دیٗ؟	*khér kho day*	Is all well ? Can I do anything for you ?
نظر	*nazar*	Sight.
پۀ باند نظر لږيدل	*puh-bāndé nazar lagédal*	To see.
پۀ باند مين كيدل	*puh-bāndé main kédal*	To fall in love.
مسكیٗ كيدل	*maskay kédal*	To smile.
فائده	*fāida*	Use, benefit.
پۀ نظر راتلل	*puh nazar rātlal*	To come into sight.
و فادار	*wafādār*	Faithful.
بی وفا	*béwafā*	Faithless.
ديوريا	*wéryā*	Free, gratis.
تنګول	*tangawal*	To worry.
سوال	*swāl*	Question.
كانړیٗ مات كول	*kānray māt kawal*	To declare war, (lit to break stone.)
كانړیٗ كينودل	*kānray kékhodal*	To make a truce.

EXERCISE 30.

۱ يوه ورځ يو فقير پۀ دربار راننوت دَ بادشاه پۀ مخو پريوت او پۀ

ژړا شو ۲ غلو دروازه ما ته كړه او ټول مال ئی بوت ۳ دَ كلو

ملکان اکثر په دی موسم کښ په حوالات کښ وی نه دی
سبب دا دی چه فصلونه هنۀ نۀ کیږی ځکه خلق مالیه نۀ شی
ورکولی او که څۀ لږه ډیره ټوله کړی نو ملک پخپله ورته حاجتمند
وی دئی خوری ۴ مالی ته م و چه دَ څنګل ویستو دَ پاره دری
واړۀ واړۀ هلکان وساته ولی چه طلب ئی دَ پنځو پنځو روپو نه زیاتنۀ
وی ۵ جرګی پوليټکل صاحب ته ووو چه کۀ تۀ بی سبب څنۀ زمور
مواجب بند وی نو آئینده دَ پاره دا امید مۀ لره چه مۀ زمور به ستا خدمت
وکړه که په لارو شوکی کیږی یا په کلو دارو پیریښی نو مونږ ذمه وار
نۀ یوؤ او هر رنګ مال چه څمونږ علاقی ته راوستلی شی نو په
بونه به ئی در نۀ کړؤ ۶ په څوا زمانه کښ به چه دَ ننګو په
سر بدی وشوه نو دَ قام مشرانو به جرګه وکړه او کوم فریق به چه
پوشو نو دَ ور فریق دَ پاره به ئی ور باند سوره کینوه مګر دا رواج
اوس کم دی ځکه چه په دی خبره بدی زیاتیږی ۷ چه دا ئی
واوریدل نو نوکر ئی راوبللو او ورته ئی وو چه شاباش تۀ ډیر نمک
حلال سړی ئی که تۀ مهشی نو ستا بال بچ له به زۀ روټی جامه او
دیرش روپی میاشت پنسن ورکوم ۷ افریدیان چه په بدی کښ تنګ
شی او یا دَ فصل وخت راشی نو کانړی کیږ دی ۹ اورنګزیب
دَ هندوانو دَ لاس تنګ شو نو حکم ئی واور اوؤ چه کۀ هر هندوؤ دَ
اسلام سپکوالی وکړ نو دَ مرګ سزا به ورکوی کیږی ۱۰ بادشاه هغه
دی چه دَ خپل رعیت دَ ارام دَ پاره کوشش کوی ۱۱ دا دا سی زلزله
وه چه په یو ملت کښ ئی ښهر لوټی لوټی کړ سړی ښځی ما شومان
سپی چرګان ټول دَ خاورو لاند شول ۱۲ هوښیار سړی هیچری
بهادر نۀ وی ۱۳ مۀ زمور دعا کوؤ چه نوی بادشاه له خدای لوی
عمر درکوی او غریب هندوستان ته یی نیت په خیر شی ۱۴ چه دَ

ﻫﺮ ﺩﺭﻭﺍﺯی ﺗﻪ ﻭﺭﺳﯿﺪ ﻧﻮ ﺩﺭﻭﺍﻧﭽﯽ ﺩَ ﻧﻨﻪ ﭘﺮی ﻧﻪ ﻫﻮﺩ ﻣﺴﺎﭘﺮ ﻫﯿﺮ ﻣﻨﺖ

ﻭﮐﺮﺧﻮ ﻫﯿﺦ ﻓﺎﺋﯿﺪﻩ ﻭ ﻧﻪ ﺷﻮﻩ ﺧﮑﻪ ﻻﺭ ﺩَ ﺳﺮک ﺧﻮﺍ ﺗﻪ ﮐﯿﻨﺎﺳﺖ

۱۵ ﺩﺭﻭﺍﺯﻩ ﻟﺮی ﺷﻮﻩ ﺍﻭ ﯾﻮﻩ ﺑﺨﻪ ﺭﺍﻭﻭﺗﻪ ﺍﻭ ﻓﻘﯿﺮ ﺗﻪ ﯾﯽ ﻭ ﺑﺎ ﻧﻦ ﻭﻟﯽ

ﻭﺳﯽ ﻭﺧﺘﯽ ﺭﺍﻏﻠﯽ ۱۶ ﭼﻪ ﺧﻤﺎ ﻧﻈﺮ ﻭﺭ ﺑﺎﻧﺪ ﻭﻟﺒﺮﯾﺪ ﻧﻮ ﻭﺭﺑﺎﻧﺪ ﻣﯿﻦ

ﺷﻢ ۱۷ ﻓﻘﯿﺮ ﺭﺍﺗﻪ ﻭﮐﺘﻞ ﺍﻭ ﻣﺴﮑﯽَ ﺷﻮ ۱۸ ﺻﺎﺣﺐَ ﺩﺍ ﻭﻓﺎﺩﺍﺭ

ﺳﭙیَ ﮐﻪ ﻻﻧﺪ ﺍﻭﺩﻩ ﺩﻩ ۱۹ ﮔﺎﺩیَ ﭘﻪ ﻟﺲ ﻧﯿﻤی ﺑﺠﯽ ﺭﻭﺍﻧﯿﺒﺮﯾﯽ

۲۰ ﻣﺎﻣﻪَ ﺗﮑﮑﻮﻩ ﺩﻭﻣﺮﻩ ﻭﺧﺖ ﺭﺍﺗﻪ ﻧﺸﺘﻪ ﭼﻪ ﺳﺘﺎ ﺩَ ﺳﻮﺍﻝ ﺟﻮﺍﺏ ﺩﺭﮐﺮﻡ-

Miscellaneous Colloquial Sentences III.

Can you recognize this man ?	*Dā saray péjhandalay shé ?*
Why cannot you recognize him ?	*Walé yé nuh pejhané ?*
Do you not know his father ?	*Tuh da haghuh plār nuh péjhané ?*
What is the latest news to-day ?	*Nan suh tāza khabar day ?*
How old are you ?	*Tuh da so kālo yé ?*
Are you married ?	*Wāduh dé karay day ?*
How long have you been in the service.	*Da so kālo naukar yĕ ?*
Take this recruit to the hospital and tell the doctor to let me know what is wrong with him.	*Dā rangūt haspatāl ta bōza aw dāktar ta wō wāya chi mā khabar kra chi pa duh suh chal shaway day.*
That hill is not within the range of our guns.	*Dagha ghar zamūng da tōpo da gōlo lāndé nuh rāzee.*

Let him write another petition and put it on the Sahib's table.	*War ta wō wāya chi bala arzi wo likee, aw da sāhib puh méz bāndé yé kégdee.*
We did not notice, but there was a big forest on our rear.	*Mūng wo nuh lidalo kho zamūng shā tā yau lōi zangal woh.*
Are the roads good? are supplies obtainable?	*Lāré khé dee? rasad múndalay shi?*
I will dine out to-night.	*Bégāla zamā rōtai bāhar dah.*
Why did you kill this man?	*Walé dé dā saray wō wajhalo.*
Who told you to kill him?	*Chā darta wayali woo chi wō yé wajhna?*
Why did you not take revenge on him?	*Walé dé war na badal wā nuh khistalo.*
Can you shoot well?	*Tuh khuh tōpak wōlé; kuh na?*
I did not see him.	*Mā hagha wō nuh lidalo.*
Did you not see me in the motor yesterday afternoon?	*Parūn māspakhin dé puh mōtar ké wō nuh lidalam?*
I greeted you but you did not answer.	*Mā darta salām wo kro kho tā jawab rā nuh kar.*
Have you heard that the Aka Khel are going to attack the fort?	*Aurédali dé di chi Aka khél puh qalā bāndé hala kawee.*
Go out of my house.	*Zamā da kōra wōza.*

You go and find out somewhere else.	*Lārsha aw bal charta yé malūm kra* or *wo mūma.*
Do not laugh at him.	*War p̄ōré muh khānda.*
The dog barked but when I threw a stone at him, he ran towards the lane.	*Sp̄i woghap̄al, kho chi p̄uh kānri mé wo wishtalo no da kūsé taraf ta wozghalédalo.*
The thief jumped into the street and got up by the ladder	*Ghal kūsé ta wo dangal aw p̄uh andrap̄āya bāndé wokhatalo.*
Have you seen him ?	*Tā hagha lidalay day ?*
Why cannot you cross ?	*Walé p̄ōré watalay nuh shé ?*
The Colonel fell off his horse and broke his arm	*Karnail sahib luh ass na p̄réwato aw lās yé māt sho.*
I cannot climb the hill.	*Zuh p̄uh ghar khatalay nuh sham.*
I left the book on the table	*Kitab ra na p̄uh méz p̄āté sho,*
I left Peshawar on the 20th	*Puh shalam tārikh zuh luh p̄ékhawar na rawān shwam.*
Pull this motor car to that village.	*Dā mōtar dagha kali ta rākāga.*
Whose round was it last night ?	*Bégā da chā gusht woh ?*
I shall stop this custom	*Dā dastūr ba zuh band kram.*
What will the people say ?	*Khalq ba suh wāyee ?*

Why do you not tell me the whole truth ?	*Tōla rishtiā khabara walé nuh kawé ?*
Give me a clean hand-kerchief.	*Yau pāk rūmāl rākra.*
Thank you for your trouble.	*Zuh stā da rabar da pāra déra shukria adā kawam.*
Every thing is very dear.	*Har shay dér grān day.*
We are paying famine rates.	*Puh mūng bāndé da qahat narkhūna dee.*
Keep it in your house ; I will take it when I come back from the camp.	*Puh khpal kōr ké yé wo sāta chi luh parāw na biarta rāsham, no ba yé wākhlam.*
There will be a big parade tomorrow.	*Sabāla ba yau lōi parait wee.*
The General will inspect the Regt.	*Jarnail sāhib ba da paltané mulāhiza kawee.*
It is very cold today, snow will fall on the hills.	*Nan déra yakhnī dah puh ghrūno ba wāwra préwozee.*
Try once more ! I am sure you will do it this time.	*Yau zal biā kōshash wo kra, zamā yaqin day chi dā zal khuh shan sara ba yé wo kré,.*
You mind your business! Who has brought this letter ?	*Tuh khpal kār kawa ! Chā dā chitai rāworé dah ?*
To whom did you take the letter.	*Chā ta dé chitai yaura.*
Can you show me the way to Shahi Bagh ?	*Da shāhi bāgh lār rā ta khayalay shé ?*

I cannot understand what you say.	*Zuh stā puh khabara nuh pōhégam.*
Is there any drinking water near the camp?	*Parāw ta nizdé da skalō obuh shta?*
How do you do?	*Suh hāl day?*
Does this road lead to Pabbi.	*Dā lār pabo ta talé dah?*

VOCABULARY XXXII.

زری	*zaray*	Guide.
خطا كول	*khatā kawal*	To miss.
ورك كول	*vrak kawal*	To lose.
پۀ وخت	*puh wakht*	In time.
منل	*manal*	To obey.
الؤندول	*alūzawal*	To blow up to make to fly.
چاودل	*chāudal*	To split, burst.
چوم	*chwam*	(Present.)
فتح مؤندل	*fatah mūndal*	To gain victory.
برى مؤندل	*baray mūndal*	To gain victory.
شكست وركول	*shikast warkawal*	To defeat.
شكست خوَرل	*shikast khwaral*	To be defeated.
شكايت كول	*shekāyat kawal*	To complain.
برابر	*barābar*	Proper, reasonable.
پۀ بيعه اخستل	*puh baya akhistal*	To buy.
شفارس كول	*shafāras kawal*	To recommend.
بار كول	*bār kawal*	To load. (animal).

سپک spak	Light.
درزند drūnd	Heavy.
پایه pāya	Wheel.
جرم jurum	Crime.
سزا ورکول sazā warkawal	To punish.
سزا موندل sazā mūndal	To be punished.
غوښتل ghukhtal	To ask for.
بیان کول biān kawal	To explain.
ټوله قصه tōla qisa	The whole story.
بد ګنزل bad ganral	To feel offended.
همیشه دَ پاره hamésha da pāra	For good, for always, for ever.
کُه نه وی kuh nuh wi	Otherwise.
هسی نه وی hasé nuh wi	Lest.

EXERCISE 31.

1. If he had come, I would have seen him.
2. If you had sent me a letter, I would have answered it. 3. If you had worked hard, you would have passed the examination. 4. Had they been loyal, the Government would have rewarded them. 5. If our guide had not lost his way, we should have reached the hill in time. 6. Had you accepted it, it would have been all right. 7. If the sentry had fired at the outlaw, he would have certainly killed him 8. If we had not blown up the fort, we could

not have gained the victory. 9. If the enemy had crossed the river we would have defeated them. 10. If I had not enlisted in the Army, I should not have become a Subadar. 11. If you had not struck him, he would not have complained to the police. 12. If you had charged (asked for) a reasonable price, I should have bought it from you. 13. If you had done well, I would have recommended you to the Colonel 14. If you had loaded it lightly the wheel would not have broken. 15. If you had not committed this crime, I would not have punished you 16. If you had asked for ten days leave I would have certainly given it to you. 17. Had I seen you in the bazar I would have told you the whole story. 18. If you had not come he would have killed me. 19. If the old man had not laughed, I should not have felt so offended. 20. If I had not felt so offended, I should not have run away, but I did not mean to run away for good, otherwise I should not have come back.

VOCABULARY XXXIII.

عدالت	*adālat*	Court.
وختى	*wakhti*	Early.
ناوخته	*nāwakhta*	Late.
سستى	*susti*	Laziness.
لۇكۇتى	*lŭkŭti*	Little.

اسانئ سره	asānai sara	Easily.
بی له ربړنه	bé lūh rabar na	Without trouble.
راویښ کیدل	rāwïkh kédal	To wake up (Intransitive.)
کنډر کول	kandar kawal	To burgle.
ارت	art	Broad, wide.
لۀ-نه پۀ لانبو	luh-na puh	
پوریوتل	lānbo pōré-watal	To swim across.
دولت	daulat	Riches.
متل	matal	Proverb.
دوکان کول	dūkān kawal	To be a shopkeeper.
دَ باد شاه لؤر به مې کړی وه	da bādshāh lūr ba mé karé wah	I would have married the king's daughter.
مُتیازی کول	mutyāzé kawal	To make water, urinate.
معامله	māméla	Affair.

EXERCISE 32.

۱ کۀ دَ کوز خاوند ور باندی را غلی وی وی نو غل به ئی نیولی
وه ۲ کۀ کومی زیاته نۀ وی نو زۀ به کشمیر ته تللی نۀ وم ۳ کۀ زۀ
ناجوړ شوی نۀ وی نو زۀ به پۀ عدالت کښ حاضر شوی وم
۴ کۀ لار خرابه نۀ وی نو مؤنږ به وختی رسیدلی ؤو ۵ کۀ دَ کلی
خلقو سُستی کړی نۀ وی نو داړه ما ران بهئی قول نیولی ؤو
۶ کۀ تۀ !ؤ کوټی وختی راغلی وی نو قول انتظام به پۀ وخت
شوی وه ۷ کۀ اوبۀ ډیری وی نو فصلونه به نۀ شوی ؤو او مؤنږ به

ما ليه اسانئى سره ورکولى شوه ٨ زۀ درنه دومره لوى يم چه كۀ
زۀ اوس وى نو تۀ به خروى ٩ كۀ پۀ نيمه شپه كښ راويښس شوى
نۀ وى نو غلو به م پۀ كور كښ كنډر كوى۫وۀ ١٠ كه سيند ارت
نۀ وى نو مۇنۢر به ورنه پۀ لانبو پوريوتى ۇو ١١ كۀ يو نۀ مركيدى
نو بل به ښۀ خورل كۀ دولت راسخه نۀ وى نو يو دوست به م هم نۀ وۀ
١٢ كۀ باران شوى نه وى نو دَ سكلو اوبۀ به هم نۀ وى ١٣ كۀ
ښمۇنۢر بيۍۋنه پۀ غرۀ باند ابريدلى نۀ وى نو دشمن به پۀ پراۇ باند
حمله كوى۫وۀ ١٤ كۀ زۀ پښتون نۀ وى نو به م دوكان كوى۫وۀ ١٥ كۀ
دولت راسخه وى نو به م دَ بادشاه لوۇر كوى۫وۀ ١٦ كۀ زۀ متيازو دَ پاره
باهر وتى نۀ وى نو دا معامله به م ليدلى نۀ وۀ ١٧ كۀ ابريدى م
نيكۀ قتل كوى۫ نۀ وى نو ورسره به م داسى سخته بدى نۀ وۀ
١٨ كۀ انگريزى م زده كولى نو اوس به لوى بابۇ وم ١٩ كۀ زۀ
لارنۀ شم نوتول مال به م بر بادشى ٢٠ كۀ زۀ پخپله راتلى شوى
نو ډيره ښه به وۀ مگر نۀ شم راتلى—

VOCABULARY XXXIV.

مرکيدل	mar kédal	To die.
لوږه	lwaga	Hunger.
هم پۀ هغه معامله كښ	hum puh hagha máméla ké	In the same case.
قسم خورل	qasam khwaral	To swear.
له ټولو نه لنډه لار	la tōlō na landa lār	The shortest road.
پۀ باند ورختل	puh-bāndé warkhatal	To invade.
نوى	naway	New.

خرڅ کول	khars kawal	To sell, spend.
بائسکل	baiskal	Bicycle.
زۀ تبی نیولی یم	zuh tabé niwalay yam	I have caught fever
زۀ یخنئی وهلی یم	zuh yakhnai wahalay yam	I have caught cold.
څما سر خوږ یږی	zamā sar khūgégee	I have a headache.
پۀ هغۀ باند ننکي ختلی دی	puh haghuh bāndé nanakai khatalé di	He has small pox.
ملګری	malgaray	Companion.
بله میاشت	bala miāsht	Next month.
تیره میاشت	téra miāsht	Last month.
سر	sar	Head
سترګه	starga	An eye.
پوزه	pōza	Nose.
غاښ	ghākh	Tooth.
خولۀ	khuluh	Mouth.
ژبه	jhuba	Tongue, language.
مخ	makh	Face.
غوږ	ghwag	Ear.
مرۍ	marai	Throat.
څټ	sat	Back of neck.
شا	shā	Back.
زړۀ	zruh	Heart.
پړپوس	parpus	Lung.
کناټی	kunātay	Buttock.

پتون *patūn*	Thigh.
دودۍ *dūday*	Hip.
تشى *tashay*	Loin.
خپه *khpa*	Foot, leg.
زنګون *zangūn*	Knee.
ګوته *gōta*	Finger.
تلى *talāy*	Sole of foot, palm of hand.

EXERCISE 33.

1. He said he was going to Persia.
2. They said that they were dying of (from)
hunger. 3. The Magistrate answered that he
was still enquiring into the same case. 4. He
asked me what had become of my dog. 5. I
asked him if he was prepared to come with me
(to go with me) to the city. 6. He swore that
he did not see this man with his own eyes.
7. He asked me which was the shortest way to
the city. 8. I asked him why was he staying
in the hotel. 9. He thought that he also came
to the office on the same day. 10. The general
concluded that it was difficult for him to invade
the country during the winter. 11. He said
his son was cleverer than his daughter. 12. The
Major himself said that he would take me with
him to Afghanistan. 13. He said his son
could not ride my black mare. 14. They

replied that they wanted 10 days leave. 15. Did he say he was new to the country and that he did not know the custom of the village? 16. Did you say you were thirsty and that you wanted to drink some water? 17. He said he would sell his bicycle. 18. Tell my reader to bring all the papers. 19. The next day I caught fever, I therefore told my companion that I could not go before the 1st, of next month. 20. Every body seems to have a cold, it is bad weather. 21. You must have written this letter, do you not remember?

VOCABULARY XXXV.

تيارهٔ	*tyāruh*	Darkness.
رنرا	*ranrā*	Light (day.)
رنرا ورځ	*ranrā vraz*	Broad daylight.
دومره لري	*dōmra laré*	So far.
بادشاهي	*badshāhi*	Kingdom.
زمونږ فصلونه پ	*zāmūng*	Our crops are de-
باران كيږي	*faslūna puh baran kégee*	pendent on the rain fall.
ظلم	*zulum*	Tyranny.
ظالم	*zālém*	Tyrant.
هيرول	*hérawal*	To forget.
باور كول	*bāwar kawal*	To believe.
فيصله كول	*faisala kawal*	To decide, settle.
ماښهٔ پوهٔ کړ	*mā khuh poh kar*	I made him under- stand well.

يوهَ پيسه *yawa paisa*   Single pice.

كوټه روپۍ *kōta ruṭi*   Bad rupee.

EXERCISE 34.

۱   اِر دلې جواب راکو چه زۀ ستا نوکر خو نۀ يم زۀ دَ سرکار
نوکرېم   ۲   بيائي وو چه پۀ تياره كښ ماسري ليدلې نۀ شو   ۳   دَ دې
علاقې خلق وائي چه مؤنږ جوار كرلي ووَ مګر چه اوبۀ كمي وي نو ونۀ
شوَ   ۴   كليوالو وو چه تر صبا پورې به مؤنږ دَ ماليئي معافولو دَ پاره
ډيرقى كمشنر صاحب ته درخواست وركوو   ۵   صاحبروو چه زۀ به
څلور ورځې پس له دورى نه بيرته راشم   ۶   دَ كلو هلكانو وو چه
دومره لرى مدرسي ته تلل مؤنږ دپاره ګران كار دىَ   ۷   سليم وو چه زۀ
دَ بادشاهئ هيڅ پروا نۀ كوم   ۸   دَ دې وطن ټول فصلو نه پۀ باران
كيږي   ۹   ما ته ئي وو چۀ بيشكه تۀ څما وروړئ مګر ستا ظُلم
نۀ شم هيرولىَ   ۱۰   څوىم راته وو چه څما بائسكل ستا له موټر نه
ګرندىَ دىَ   ۱۱   ملك وو څما دَ كلي خلق داسي هوښيار نۀ دي
چه تا ويرژني چه تۀ څمونږ تحصيلدار ئي   ۱۲   څما لۀ رسيدو نه
اول ئي را ته خبر ليدولىَ وَه چه پلار د مړشوي دىَ   ۱۳   ماورته وو
چه زۀ ستا پۀ خبره باور نۀ شم كولىَ   ۱۴   خان سلام راليدولىَ دىَ
او وائي چه صبا به زۀ پنځيله ستا ليدلو دَ پاره راشم   ۵،   ګل جان
پاڅيد او وئي و چه زۀ پۀ جرګه فيصله نۀ كوم   ۱۶   آستاذ وويل چه
ما ټولو هلكانو ته وويل چه خپل خپل نوم پۀ بورډ بلند وليكئيَ
۱۷   رحمت وو چه څما كلىَ له دې څائي نه سل ميلَ لرى دىَ
۱۸   پۀ كُرسۍ باند كيناست او را ته ئي وو چه دپلقن دَ څۀ حال دىَ
۱۹   ورتهم وو چه زۀ به ستا پۀ څايي كار كوم   ۲۰   ما هنۀ پوه كړ چه
كۀ بياد داسي كار وكړ نو يوه پيسه طلب به در نۀ كړم ——

VOCABULARY XXXVI.

پۀ غلا تلل	*puh ghalā tlal*	To be stolen.
برنډه	*baranda*	Verandah.
مشکل سره	*mushkil sara*	With difficulty.
نيول	*niwal*	To catch, arrest
راضى	*rāzi*	Willing, satisfied.
نوکرى کول	*naukari kawal*	To serve.
هيثوک	*hésōk*	No one.
تاريخ	*tārikh*	Date.
دا	*dā*	The following, this.ı
بيان	*bayān*	Explanation, statement.
دانه	*dāna*	Grain.
وسله	*wasla*	Arms.
وسله دار سرى	*wasla dār saray*	Armed man.
ما خبر کړه	*mā khabar kra*	Let me know.
تلاؤ	*talāw*	Tank.
ډنډ	*dand*	Pond of water.
لۀ ـنه دک	*luh-na dak*	Full of.
رڼى اوبۀ	*ranré obūh*	Clear water.
خړى اوبۀ	*kharé obuh*	Muddy water.
دَ هغۀ مطلب دا وۀ	*da haghuh matlab dā woh*	He meant.
هوار کول	*howār kawal*	To level
واښۀ مشين کول	*wākhuh mashin kawal*	To cut grass with a mower.

کوډ کول *gōd kawal*   To weed.

خذعل ویستل *zangal wistal* To weed.

وسله کیښودل *wasla*
         kékhōdal   To surrender.

EXERCISE 35.

1. My bicycle has been stolen from the veranda, please inform the Police. 2. 10 days leave was granted to him with great difficulty. 3. The letter was written and sent at once. 4. The doctor was sent for, but we could not understand what he was talking about, as he could not speak Pushtu. 5. The father was killed and the son was arrested. 6. Ask him if he is willing to serve in the Cavalry. 7. No one was seen on the spot. 8. I cannot shoot birds and animals flying and running besides I cannot afford to buy a shot gun. 9. Yesterday the Adjutant called me to the office and I made the following statement. 10. At what time do you feed the horses? 11. If you see any armed man let us know. 12. It is all very well for you to bring up recruits of this type, but they will certainly not be passed by me. 13. Tell all the non-commissioned Officers that the Officer Commanding wants to see them at 10 o'clock outside the office. 14. I saw him running

towards the cantonment. 15. This tank is always full of clear water. 16. The doctor asked me if I had bitten his dog. 17. I laughed when he said this, because he really meant to ask whether his dog had bitten me. 18. When a murder is committed in Lahore, do you make all the Nawabs and Sardars responsible? 19. Tell the mali that while I am away he must cut the grass and take out all weeds. 20. Tell him to make tea and put it on the table at 3-30.

VOCABULARY XXXVII

بُوڼر	*būnr*	Dwarf-palm string for making beds.
ميزری	*mézaray*	Dwarf palm.
گذران یا گذاره	*guzrān* or *guzāra*	Living.
(سره) بدنام کیدل	*(sara) badnām kédal*	To get bad name (with).
تبر	*tabar*	Family.
هاله	*halā*	Then.
بدی	*badi*	Feud.
خلاص کول	*khlās kawal*	To finish, settle.
لۀ یو بل نه	*la yāu bal na*	From one another.
یو بل سره	*yau bal sara*	With one another.
خشاک	*khashāk*	Firewood.

جرنده	*jranda*	Water mill.
میچن	*méchan*	Hand mill.
کار روزگار	*kār rōzgār*	Work etc.
برج	*braj*	Tower.
یو بل باند	*yau bal bāndé*	On one another.
(پۀ باند) بزکول	*(puh-bāndé) daz kawal*	To fire at.
طرف	*taraf*	Side. party.
برابر	*barābar*	Equal.
قام یا قوم	*qām*	Tribe.
مشر	*mashar*	Elder.
جوړه یا روغه یا صلح	*jōra, rōgha, sula*	Peace.
کاڼی	*kanray*	Stone.
برخلاف	*barkhélāf*	Against.
(پۀ باند) دعوی کول	*(puh-bāndé) dāwa kawal*	To claim, to charge, (against).
مدعی	*mudāi*	Plaintiff.
مدعالیه	*mudālay*	Defendant.
سیزل یا سوزول	*sézal* or *swazawal*	To burn.
سوزیدل	*swazédal*	To be burnt.
مقدمه	*muqadéma*	Case.
ثبوت	*sabūt*	Proof.
ثابت کول	*sābet kawal*	To prove.
منکر کیدل	*munkar kédal*	To deny.
(لۀ نه) انکا رکول	*(luh-na) inkār kawal*	To refuse.

په کانړی باندې ویشتل	*puh kānri bāndé wishtal*	To throw a stone at
جګړه کول	*jagara kawal*	To quarrel.
قاضی	*qāzi*	Judge.
ګانړه کول	*gānra kawal*	To mortgage.
څومره چه دَ وس م کیږی دمره کوشش به کوم	*sōmra chi da wasa mé kégee dōmra kōshash ba kawam*	I will try my best.
حق	*haq*	Right.
اسمان شین دی	*asmān shin day*	It is clear (to-day.)
کۀ دَ خوښه وی	*kuh dé khwakha wi*	If you like.
جوپه	*jōpa*	Trading party.
سختی	*sakhti*	Hardship, Evil day.
په کار راتلل	*puh kār rātlal*	To be useful to
طبیب	*tabib*	Doctor, a physician
بیماری یا ناجوړتیا	*bimāri* or *nājōrtia*	Disease.
رنځ	*ranz*	
رنځور	*ranzūr*	Patient (in hospital)
پوزی	*puzay*	Matting.

EXERCISE 36.

۱ په ژمی نیس دَ غیر علاقی خلق لرګی اومیزری او پوزی دَ
پیښور په ښهر کښی خرڅ دَ پاره راوړی او په دی باند ګزران کوی
۲ څوکیدار وائی چه په دی طلب باند ښما ګزاره نه کیږی یا م

طلب زيات كړه او يا چوټي راكړه   ٣   دَ اپريدو دا دستور دىَ چه
يوه بنتهه چا سره بدنامه شي نو خښتن دا بنتهه هم هغه سړي ته
ورو شړي او تر هغه به ئي ورسره بدي وي چه دوه سړي ورنه
ونه وژني   ٤   كله كله دا بدي تر پيړو پيړي چليدري او دَ يو بل
نه سړي وژني   ٥   بنتهي ئي دَ خذمل واهنهَ او خشاك راوړي
جرنده كوي دَ كور ټول كار روزگار كوي او سړي ئي پۀ برجونو كښ
نا ست وي او پۀ يو بل سره يزي كوي   ٦   پۀ بدي كښ بنتهي
نۀ ولي   ٧   چه دواړه طرف پۀ قتلونو كښ برابر شي نو دَ
قام سپين گيري را جمع شي جوړه ئي وكړي   ٨   كۀ يو طرف پرويَ
او بل و پرويَ نو دَ لبري مُدي دَ پاره كانړيَ كيږدي چه كارتوسونه
او غله خان ته واچوي نو پۀ مقرر وخت كانړيَ ئي مات شي
٩   كۀ پۀ روغه كښ چا پۀ يو بل يز وكړو نو ټول قام ور باند را جمع
شي كلَي ئي وسيزي   ١٠   پۀ دي مقدمه كښ ثبوت نۀ. وه خكه
تانوه دار هيڅ نۀ شوَ كولَي   ١١   مدعي وو چه خلور كالَ كيږي چه
ما ورته خلولبنست روپَي وزكړي دي   ١٢   مدعا عليه منكر شۀ
او وئي و چه زۀ تا نۀ پيژنم تۀ خوك ئي   ١٣   يیري جهړي كولو
پس موَنبر قاضي ته لاړو   ١٤   قاضي ورته و چه تا دَ دي سړي
مال ولي پنه كړيَ دىَ   ١٥   زمكه م كانړه كړه او خوي لۀ م پروادۀ
وكړ   ١٦   خوصره چه دَ وس م قيبري دومره كوشش به وكړم چه ستا
حق ثابت شي   ١٧   اسمان شين دىَ ورځ نه ته جوبي به راشي
١٨   دوست هغه دىَ چه پۀ سختي كښ پكار راشي   ١٩   چه
غلائي وشوه نو خوكيداړئي وساتلو   ٢٠   طبيب دَ هغي بيمارۍ علاج
پۀ بنۀ شان سره كولَيَ شي چه ور باند پخپله تيره شوي وي ‐

VOCABULARY XXXVIII.

پایاز	*payāw*	Shallow.
پۀ مخ کښ	*puh makh ké*	Further on, in front.
(سره) خبری کول	*(sara) khabaré kawal*	To converse with. to talk to.
نو	*no*	So, then.
لواړه ژبه کول	*lwāra jhuba kawal*	To speak indistinctly.
ژور	*jhawar*	Deep..
کنډه	*kunda*	Widow.
کنډاو	*kandāw*	A gap (in wall etc).
کنډو	*kandū*	Corn bin.
کنډه	*kanda*	Abyss.
کنډه	*kand* .	A small scale.
کنډۍ	*kundai*	Wooden cup
(ته) طلاق ور کول	*(ta) talāq warkāwal*	To divorce.
زنا	*zanā*	Adultery.
تربور	*tarbūr*	Cousin.
رضا	*razā*	Furlough.
وبا گیه ده	*wabā gada dah*	Cholera is prevalent.
إجازت	*ijāzat*	Permission.
مينځ	*mianz*	Middle.
سفر	*safar*	Journey.
پۀ مخه راتلل	*puh makha rātlal*	To meet.
لۀ لس نه	*luh lās na*	By the hand,

گواه یا شاهد	*gawāh* or *shāhad*	Witness.
گواهی یا شاهدی	*gawāhi* or *shāhdi*	Evidence
سپينه سپو.ز.ـمئ	*spina spōgmai*	Bright moonlight.
لۀ كمرى نه وتل	*luh kamré na watal*	To leave the room.
كوته	*kōta*	Room.
زورور باران	*zōrawar bārān*	Heavy rain.
سيند ختلى دىَ	*sind khatalay day*	The river rose, has risen.
و ړل	*vral*	To carry.
پُل	*pul*	Bridge.
ګوذر	*gūdar*	Ferry.
زورور باد	*zōrawar bād*	Strong wind.
(سره) واقف	*sara wāqif*	Acquainted (person.)
(لۀ-نه) واقف	*(luh-na) wāqif*	Acquainted (language.)
(پۀ-كښ) واقف	*(puh-ké) wāqif*	Acquainted (country.)
پۀ يهم سرۀ	*puh paham sara*	Carefully.
زرۀ	*zruh*	Heart.
پۀ زرۀ سره	*puh zruh sara*	Attentively.
محاوره	*muhāwera*	Idiom.
دَ خبرو سړى	*da khabaro saray*	Converser.
كمىَ	*kamay*	Scarcity.

ضلع	*zela*	District.
ويستلى تُوْره	*wistalé tūra*	Drawn sword.
ستړى	*staray*	Tired.
اوده کيدل	*ūduh ḳédal*	To sleep.
ويشل	*wéshal*	To divide.

EXERCISE 37.

1. The water is shallow here, but further on it is very deep. 2. How many sepoys are there who wish to speak to me? 3. You speak so fast and indistinctly that I can not understand a word you say. 4. Her husband is dead she is now a widow. 5. I have heard that he has divorced her. 6. Subadar, how many men of your company are on furlough? Have them all recalled at once. 7. Owing to the prevalence of cholera in the city, the people of the city are not allowed to come into the cantonment. 8. In the middle of our journey we met an old man, whom a little boy was leading by the hand. 9. One witness has stated that the night was dark and another that it was bright moonlight. 10. Ahmad Khan left the room where the Deputy Commissioner was sitting. 11. Owing to the heavy rain in Swat, the Kabul river rose and carried away the bridge. 12. I have come to make a report that at 2-30 last night Jan Mohammad killed his own father. 13. How long

before that were you acquainted with him?
14. How long have you been learning Pushtu?
15. If you study the Pushtu idioms attentive-
ly and carefully listen to your converser, you
will soon be able to speak the language and
understand others. 16. Why did you tell me
that my father had arrived? 17. On account
of scarcity of rain there is little grass in the
District. 18. I saw a man running with a
drawn sword in his hand. 19. I am tired, I did
not sleep last night. 20. Divide the money
among these people.

VOCABULARY XXXIX

لوټ کول	lūt kawal	To loot.
ماشوم	māshūm	Little child.
بهانه	bahāna	Pretence.
پۀ چغه تلل	puh chagha tlal	To pursue.
دَ پاره دَ دی	da pāra da dé	In order to, for this purpose.
را خلاص کول	rā khlās kawal	To release.
بونګه	bōnga	Ransom.
دَ دروغو ګواهی	da darōghō gawāhi	False evidence.
نرخ	narkh	Rate.
څرول	sarawal	To graze.
اګر کہ	agar kuh	Although.
همسایه	hamsāya	Tenant.

همسایه ګان	*hamsāyagān*	Tenants.
میلمستیا	*mélmastiā*	Hospitality.
میلمه دوست	*melma dost*	Hospitable.
حج	*haj*	Pilgrimage.
حاجی	*hāji*	Pilgrim.
ورته حاجی صاحب وائی	*warta hāji sāhib wāyee*	He is called pilgrim.
جوریدل	*jōrédal*	To be made.
معلومیدل	*mālūmédal*	To look like, to seem
کارتوس	*kārtūs*	Cartridge.
پا له اسانه	*pā la asāna*	Easily.
دَ غره لمن	*da ghruh laman*	Skirt of the hill.
زرکه	*zarka*	Chikor.
تنزری	*tanzaray*	Partridge
کرونده	*kurwanda*	Newly sown crops.
ښه ویشتونکی	*khuh wishtūnkay*	A good shot.
پۀ لږ ساعت کښی	*puh lag sāat ké*	In a short time.
یوی کول	*yawé kawal*	To plough.
تیریدل	*térédal*	To pass by.
ناګهانه	*nāgahāna*	By chance.
خطا کیدل	*khatā kédal*	To be missed.
عن	*an*	Right-up to, right down to.
لګیدل	*lagédal*	To be hit, to be struck against.
چرګ بانګ مالی	*charg bāng mālé*	At dawn.

ملا بانگ مالی	*mulā bāng mālé*	At·the time of early call to prayer.
ګنره يا کنی	*ganra* or *kani*	Otherwise.

EXERCISE 38.

۱ پۀ کلی دارۀ پريو تۀ دَيو هندوْ کورئ لوْټ کم او يو ماشوم
خوږئ ئی بوت ۲ دَ کلی خلقو هسی بها نه وَکړه چه داړی پسی
پۀ چغه تلی يوْ دپاره د دی چه پۀ کلی جرم پری نۀ وخی ۳ کۀ
دا څۀ مسلمان خوږي وَی نو کليوالوَ بۀ ضرور راخلاص کړی وۀ
مګر اوس دَ دی هلک راخلاصولو دَ پاره يوه لو يه بوزغه بۀ پکار وی
۵ زۀ بۀ ور باند پۀ عدالت کښ دعوی وَکړم او وکيل بۀ وَرله وَنيسم
۶ کۀ ګواهان پکارشی نو پۀ ښهر کښ ډير دی ۷ دَ دروغو ګواهی
ور کولو دپاره پنځۀ روپئ نرخ دی ۸ صاحب مؤثر پۀ خپلو غرونوکښ
مال څرولو او دَ دوی دَ قام لس سپی رابانِد راغلل ټول مال ئی
رانه بوتلو ۹ اګر کۀ موندر هلکان يوْ خو کۀ توپکونه راسَخه وی نو
مالئ را نه نۀ شو بيولی ۱۰ هغه مشهوْر سپی دَی او ډير همسايه
ګان لری او ډير ميلمه دوست سپی دَی ۱۱ دوه ځلۀ ئی حج کړی دَی
ښکه ورته خلق حاجی صاحب وائی ۱۲ دروغ خو بالکل نۀ وائی
۱۳ سپی غاپی ګوره چه غل خو نشته ۱۴ دَ کوهاټ پۀ درۀ کښ
ډير ښۀ ټور پکونه جوړيږی ۱۵ چه ماښام شی نو دَغرۀ نه زرکی
او تنزری راکوْز شی او پۀ کروندوکښ غنم او اوربشی خوری کۀ
سپی ښۀ ويشتونکی وی نو پۀ لږو ساعت کښ بۀ ديرش څلويښت
مرغان ولی ۱۶ ما يوی کوله او دی پۀ لار تيريدو ناګهانه يئی
رابانِد ديز وَکړ زۀ خطا شوم ولی غوايم وَلريدو ۱۷ چه ما پرِ ديز
وَکړ نو عن پۀ سر وَلريدو را پريوتۀ او مړ شو ۱۸ کۀ هغۀ رابانِد اول

یز کری نۀ وی َ نوزۀ خو لیونیَ نۀ وم چه ما بۀ ور باند یز کاوۀ

۱۹ چرګ بانګ مالی روانیدل پکار دی کنړه ګاڼی تۀ بۀ وَنۀ رسی

۲۰ لۀ دی خاپی نۀ تر لوارګی پوری خومره کرائی لروی—

VOCABULARY XL.

جاهل	*jāhel*	Ignorant.
پرہ جنبہ	*para junba*	Faction feeling.
پۀ خپلو کښ	*pūh khpalo ké*	Among themselves.
وران کیدل	*vrān kédal*	To be ruined, to go wrong.
مسافر	*musāfar*	Traveller.
سلامت	*salāmat*	Safe.
سلامتی	*salāmáti*	Safety.
ویرہ	*vyara*	Fear, danger.
ویرہناک	*vyara nāk*	Dangerous.
لۀ قچری نۀ بار کوز کول	*luh qacharé na bār kūz kawal*	To unload mule.
ګاڼی تش کول	*gāday tash kawal*	To unload cart.
غوا	*ghwa*	Cow.
غوایۀ	*ghwāyuh*	Bullock (Plural *ghwāyān*.)
پۀ څو د اخستیَ دیَ	*puh so dé akhistay day?*	How much did you pay for it?
خیمه یا تنبو	*khéma* or *tanbū*	Tent.
تنبو لګَوَل	*tambū lagawal*	To pitch a tent.

دَ اوبو څوکۍ	*da obo saukai*	Picquet on the water supply.
سخت جُرم	*sakht juram*	Serious crime.
مقيزه كول	*matiza kawal*	To elope.
كوشش كول	*kōshash kawal*	To try.
پۀ روپو باند فيصله كول	*puh rūpo bānde faisala kawal*	To make a money settlement.
ونۀ شو	*wo nuh sho*	Did not become, failed.
بدرګه	*badraga*	Escort.
تاوان ور كول	*tāwān war kawal*	To compensate.
څۀ وشو؟	*suh wo shoo ?*	What happened ?
ژبه د وباسه	*jhuba dé wo bāsa*	Put out your tongue.
دارُو	*dārū*	Medicine or gun powder.
كۀ نۀ وی	*kuh nuh wi*	Otherwise.
تبه به درباند بيا راشي	*taba ba dar bānde biā rāshee*	You will catch fever again.
چلى كار	*chalé kār*	Cultivator.
دَ زمكى خاوند	*da zmaké khāwand*	Land owner.
شپږمه حصه	*shpagama hisa*	1/6th part.
پيداوار	*paidā wār*	Produce.
لر لاند	*lag lānde*	Lower down.

كه زرکړی	*kuh zar kré*	If you make haste.
ګړئ	*garai*	Watch.
ګړی ساز	*gari sāz*	Watch maker.
ځما ګړی ورانه ده	*zamā garai vrāna dah*	My watch has gone wrong.
پۀ چا باند مرمت کول	*puh chā bāndé muramat kawal*	To have repaired.
پۀ صبانۍ ورځ	*puh sabānai vraz*	Tomorrow week.
پۀ نننۍ ورځ	*puh nananai vraz*	This day week.
پۀ پرونۍ ورځ	*puh parūnai vraz*	Yesterday week.
لس تړلی	*lās taralay*	Hands tied.
رسۍ پۀ غاړه	*rasai puh ghāra*	With a rope round one's neck.
واښه پۀ خولۍ	*wākhuh puh khulé*	Grass in one's mouth.
مریی	*mrayay*	Slave.
وینځه	*winza*	Slave girl
کړکۍ	*karkai*	Window.
جمع کیدل	*jama kédal*	To be collected, assemble.
انتظار کول	*intézār kawal*	To wait.
چاندماري	*chāndmārai*	Musketry, range.
د ګولو کار توسونه	*da gōlō kārtūsūna*	Ball cartridges.
شلخی کار توسونه	*shalkhi kārtūsūna*	Blank cartridges.

یا دِ پاره یِ سری هر   *har sari da*
‫د هر سری ﻧ‬   *para* or *da har*
‫سر ﭘﻪ سری هر ﻧ‬   *sari puh sar*   For each man.

EXERCISE 39.

1. They are ignorant people and owing to faction feeling and their fighting among themselves, the country is being ruined. 2. Travellers do not go that way now, all the roads being unsafe. 3. Unload tne mules first and then unload the carts. 4. Is this cow for sale, how much do you want for it and how much did you pay for it? 5. if the General pitches his camp on that spot, there is danger that the picquet on the water supply will be attacked from the pass. 6. My brother's son has committed a serious crime. 7. He eloped with a malak's wife and ran away to the hills. 8. We tried to make a money settlement, but failed. 9. If these villagers send their cattle to graze without a proper escort and refuse to send out a pursuit party after them when they are stolen, the Govt. will certainly refuse them compensation. 10. What has happened to the old man who killed Sarfaraz? 11. Put out your tongue; you must take this medicine at once otherwise the fever will recur. 12. The cultivator gets 1/6th of the produce from the land owner. 13. The boatman has gone away but there is a ford lower down and if

you make haste you can cross the river before
sunset. 14. My watch has gone wrong, tell the
bearer to have it repaired. 15. Come tomorrow
week, the office will then be open. 16. He came
in with his hands tied, with rope round his neck
and grass in his mouth and fell at the Deputy
Commissioner's feet and said "I am your slave."
17. Open all the windows while I am sitting
here. 18. At midnight the troops assembled
on the bridge and waited for the next order.
19. Take the recruits to the range tomorrow
and have every thing ready there before the
Adjutant arrives. 20. Take 10 rounds of ball
and 10 rounds of blank for each man.

VOCABULARY XLI.

بلوه	*balwa*	Riot.
زوبل کیدل	*jhōbal kédal*	To be wounded.
په آخرکښ	*puh akhér ké*	In the end.
په شروع'ښ	*puh shurū ké*	At the beginning.
عمرى قید کیدل	*ūmri qéd kédal*	To be sentenced to transportation for life.
په۔باند دپانسۍ	*puh-bandé da*	
حکم کیدل	*pansai hukam kédal*	To be sentenced to death.
اعتبار نۀ دی پکار	*itebār nuh day pakār*	One must not be trusted.
اعتبار	*itébār*	Trust.

ملګرى	malgaray	Companion.
محصول	mahsūl	Toll, custom duty.
سوداګر	saudāgar	Merchant.
ګته	gata	Profit.
فائده	fāida	Benefit.
مزدور	mazdūr	Labourer.
مزدورى	mazdūri	Labour, wages.
ګذاره کول	guzāra kawal	To make a living.
زخم یا پرهر	zakhām or parhar	Wound.
نو یا زوه	naw or zawa	Pus.
خوار	khwār	Poor fellow.
اوږه	uga	Shoulder.
چپ چوړ	chap chúr	Shattered.
اودس ماتى له تلل	audas māti la tlal	To go to make water.
اودس کول	audas kawal	To wash for prayer.
چينه	china	Spring of water.
مونځ کول	munz kawal	To pray,
مانځه دپاره	mānzuh da pāra	For prayer (Oblique.)
ډاکۍ	saṇkai	Post.
تار	tār	Wire, telegram.
بارانى زمکه	bārāni zmaka	Unirrigated land.
قید	qaid	Locked up, imprisonment.
بدن وجود	badan, wajūd	Body.

دَ.دَخاطَر نَهْ تِيردل	da-da khātera nuh téredal	To displease.
لَنگِيدل	langédal	To give birth to a child.
دَ يو بل نَهْ ويل	dā yau bal khuh wayal	To say good of each other.
خَير خَيريت	khér khériat	Welfare, all well.
معلوم کِيدل	mālūm kédal	To be found out.
خِيرن	khiran	Dirty.
کنزل کول	kanzal kawal	To abuse.
لَهْنَه بدل اخستل	luh-na badal akhistal	To take revenge.
شرم	sharam	Shame.
ښکاريدل	khkārédal	To appear.
پرَدَي ژبه	pradai jhuba	Foreign language.
زده کول	zda kawal	To learn.
ګڼل	ganral	To consider.
يو بل وژل	yau bal wajhal	To kill each other
ژوندون	jhwandūn	Life.
پيسې اخستل	paisé akhistal	To take bribe.
بډي اخستل	badé akhistal	To take bribe.

EXERCISE 40.

١ په دی بلوه کښ دوه سړی قتل شول او پنځه سخت ژوبل شول ٢ په آخرکښ يو سړی عمری شو او په دوهٔ دَ پانسي حکم وشو ٣ پهٔ ښهٔ پهٔ آس او پهٔ تورهٔ ښهٔ اعتبار دی؟ ٤ دلاری ماهري دَ مور مبرهٔ وی ٥ په دی موسم کښ ډير اسونه لهٔ افغانستان

دہ راوستلَے کیدوی اګر چه په لار کښے ورباند ډیر معصول لرِی
مهر بیا هم سودا ګر په کښے ډیره ګټه کوي ٦ غریب خلق په چاونړئ
کښے مزدوري کوي او ورباند ګذاره کوي ٧ داننهتر ورته ور چه مَه
ویریږه زخم د ګورم بیها ور نه ښه زوه راوتی وَه که نه ٨ یو سړے
رانه په موټر ولوبید خوار به موشی څکه چه اوزرنئی ماته ده
٩ زَه ودس ماتی دَ پاره له ښوکيٖ نه راووتم اودس م ماتکم او په
چینهم اودس وکم مانهئهَ ته اودریدم چه ستا تار راورسید ١٠ زمکهم
ټوله بارانی دَه ځکه مدام په مالیه کښے قید یم ١١ داسی ووریدم
چه ټول م ښولی خولی شه ١٢ څلور ورځی شوی دی
چه غوا م لذهه شوی نه څلور سیر پیٙ کوي ١٣، پښتانه هیڅری
دَ یو بل نهَ نه وائی ١٤، زَه ستا خیر خیریت معلومولوَ دَ پاره
راغلی یم ١٥ پښتوّن نه دوست دی او خطر ناک دشمن دی
په شاباش ډیر خوشحالیږی پښتوّن که ډیر غریب وی خو په وهلو
او کنزلو ورباند ښوک کا نه شی کولَے ١٦ پښتوّن خپل بدل
هیڅری نه پریږ دی ١٧ دَ پښتنو تعلیم خوښ نه وی او دوکان
کول ور ته شرم ښکاري ١٩ پښتوّن پردنئ ژه زر زده کولَے شی
٢٠ په ښکو او په زمکه مدام پښتانه سره پوبل وژنی او بیا مفروران
شی مهر په غیر علاقه کښے هم دَ مفرور ژوندوّن ګران وی ځکه چه
اپریدیان پریپسی واخلي او وئ وژنی—

Does this road go to the city ?	*Da lar khahar ta talé dah ?*
He always tells lies.	*Hagha mudam darogh wayee.*

There will be no parade this evening.	*Nan māzdigar ba parét nuh wee,*
Why do you not come in time?	*Walé puh wakht nuh rāzé?*
It is very cold here in the winter.	*Puh jami ké dalé déra yakhni wee.*
These boys are playing the whole day.	*Dā halakān tōla vraz lōbé kawee.*
If your gun is loaded, unload it.	*Kuh tōpak dé dak wi no khāli or tash yé kra.*
Please forgive me this time I shall never do it again.	*Méhrabāni wōkra dā zal mé māf kra, biā ba dāsé kār hicharé wo nuh kram.*
We had five hundred women to cook our food.	*Mūng sara pinzuh sawa khazé wé chi zamūng dōdai ba yé pakhawala.*
How long will it take you to reach there?	*Puh sōmra sāat ké ba hal ta wo rasé?*
We arrived there a little after midday.	*Mūng halta luh gharmé na lūkūti vrōsto wōrasédaloo.*
He is quite innocent.	*Hagha bilkul bégunāh day.*
What time will the guard change?	*Gārat ba suh wakht badlégee?*
Show me some other samples.	*Suh nōré namuné rā ta wo khaya.*
Keep your accounts always clear.	*Mudām khpal hésāb sāf sāta.*
Is he a relation of the headman?	*Haghada malak khpal day?*

You are young and strong, why do you not enlist in the army.

Tuh zwān yé aw takra hum ye, walé puh fauz ké nuh barti kégé.

Are the pass made rifles any good ?

Daréwal tōpakūna suh khuh wee ?

I have forgotten your name.

Sta nūm rā na her sho

Have you ever been on active service ?

Tuh charé puh lām talay yé ?

Tell all Indian Officers that I want to see them tomorrow at 4-30 p.m.

Tōlo sardārāno ta wo wāya chi saba puh salōr nimé bajé yé lidal ghwāram.

The ration arrangements were not very good.

Da rāsan intézām bilkul khuh nuh woh.

Have you finished your annual musketry ?

Tā da kāl chāndmārai khlāsa karé dak ?

I get up at five and after a bath and having had my breakfast I go to the office.

Zuh puh pinzuh bajé pāsam aw da ghusal aw hāzérai na pas daftar ta zam.

When did you last go on leave ?

Tér zala tuh kala puh chūtai bāndé talay wé.

I do not remember exactly what clothes the man was wearing.

Mā ta bilkul yād nuh di chi hagha sari sanga jāmé aghustalé wé.

I walked in from Shabkadar this morning.

Nan sahar zuh luh Shabkadar na pyāda rāghlam.

Show me your certificates.

Chitaɩ dé wō khaya.

Take this parcel to the post office and bring a receipt.	*Dā pārsal dākkhāné ta yausa aw rasid rāwra.*
Our ration is free but we can't save any money.	*Zamūng rāsan muft day lékin hiss paisa na shoo bach kawalay.*
Whom do you want to see ?	*Tuh sōk lidal ghwāré ?*
The village has two quarters, the upper and the lower ones Sarfarāz is the head man of the upper quarter.	*Puh kalī ké dwa kandi di, bar aw kūz. Sarfarāz da bar kandı malak day.*
The knife and fork are both dirty.	*Chāruh aw kānta dwāra khirané di.*
Take this cheque to the treasury and cash it.	*Dā chak khazāné ta yausa aw māt yé kra.*
Bring small change for three rupees.	*Da dréo rūpō māt gud rāwra.*
Do you know where my head clerk lives ?	*Tā ta mālūma dah chi zamā lōi bābū charta ōsee ?*
How many men were absent from roll call ?	*La géntrai na sōmra sari ghair hāzér woo?*
Why did he go without permission ?	*Walé bé ijāzata lār?*
He said this in my presence "Hide yourself in that thick grass."	*Haghuh dā khabara zamā puh makh ké karé dah, puh hagha ganro wākho ké zān pat kra.*
Where have you been for such a long time ?	*Dōmra dér sat charta wé ?*

Put an anna stamp on this envelope.

Pa dé lifāfa bāndé da ané tikas wō lagawa.

When will you fulfil your promise?

Kala ba khpala wāda pūra kawé ?

We attacked them with our bayonets, but soon returned.

Mūng puh khpalo san-ginūnō bāndé war bāndé hamla wo kra kho zar rā wo jār-watoo.

Tell the subedar to be back before sunset.

Subédār sāhib ta wo wāya chi luh nwar préwātuh na awàl rāshee.

Put picquets on the hills on all sides, for the camp must be protected.

Puh tōlō tarafo bāndé puh ghrūno pikatūna wo lagawa, zaka chi parāw sātal pakār dĭ.

It appears to me that the enemy has retired.

Malūmégee chi dush-man māt shaway day.

We halted there for three days.

Mūng dréo vrazō da pāra halia muqām wo kar.

Here is the list of 11 bad characters living in your village.

Dā da yawolaso bad-māshānō ferest day chi stā puh kali ké osee.

For each I require a security of Rs. 500/.

Da har yau da pāra da pinzo pinzo sawo zamānat ghwāram.

Does the climate of this country suit you ?

Da dé mulk ābō hawā dar bāndé rāsta (muafiqa) dah kuh na?

How many men have been killed in this riot ?

Pa dé balwa ké sōmra sari wajhalay shawi di ?

Do they bring horses from Afghanistan ?	*Haghui luh Afghānistān na asūna. rāwalee?*
Still the merchants make much profit.	*Biā hum saudāgar déra gata kawee.*
I came out of the post and went to pray.	*Zuh luh saukaï na rā wo watam aw mānzuh la lāram.*
Why do travellers not go that way now ?	*Walé musāfar hagha khwā ta os nuh shi tlay ?*
Because all roads are dangerous.	*Zaka chi tōlé lāré khatarnāké dī.*
How much did you pay for this horse ?	*Dā as dé puh so akhistay day?*
The elders of the tribe tried to make a money settlement but failed.	*Da qām spin giro puh rūpō bāndé da faisalé kōshash wo kar kho wo nuh sho,*
I am a cultivator and live in Yusafzai. I cultivate 10 jaribs of land.	*Zuh chalékār yam aw puh yūsufzo ké osam. lās jariba zmaka karam.*
Why did he come with a rope round his neck?	*Walé rasaï puh ghāra rāghlo ?*
My village was raided.	*Zamā puh kali dāra préwata.*
They carried off Harnam Singh's son.	*Da Harnām Singh zōi yé bōtlō.*
How can I give false evidence ?	*Sanga da darōghō shahdi war kawalay sham?*
All the sepoys want to see you.	*Tōl spāyān dé lidal ghwāree.*

Why are the people of the city not allowed to come into the cantt?

Walé da khār khalqō ta da chaunrai da rātlo ijāzat nishta ?

The flood has carried away all the bridges on the Kabul river.

Sélāb da kābul puh sind bāndé tōl pulūna woree di.

When I was in the Tirah expedition I was well acquainted with the General.

Chi zuh da Tirah puh lām bāndé wam, no jarnail sara khuh wāqif wam.

Owing to the heavy rain in Swat, the Kabul river is in flood.

Puh Swāt ké da zorā-war bārān puh sabab Da Kabal puh sind ké sélāb rāghalay day.

Where there is no river or canals the women grind their corn with hand-mills.

Charta chi sindūna yā nehrūna nuh wi no halta khuzé puh me-chanō oruh kawee.

I have a large family, I therefore have to take to service.

Zamūng lōi tabar day zaka naukari kawoo.

Who wrote the letter and sent it back to Delhi ?

Chā chitai wolikala aw Dehli ta yé biarta wo légala ?

Why did the Adjutant call you to the office What did he tell you ?

Walé Ajitan sāhib daftar ta wo balalé suh yé dar ta wo wayal ?

Mind, my dog will bite you.

Paham kawa zamā spay ba dé wo chīchi.

He said he would come himself if he wanted to see me.

Hagha wō wé chi kuh zuh dé winam, nō pakhpala ba darsham.

VOCABULARY XLII.

جاسوس	*jāsūs*	Spy.
مخبر	*mukhbér*	Informer.
پټ کول	*pat kawal*	To hide.
خور یا ناله	*khwar* or *nāla*	Ravine.
اګرچه	*agarchi*	Although.
دَ شولو پټی	*da shōlo patay*	Rice field.
توی	*tōi*	Stream.
دَ غر خوا	*da ghar khwā*	Hill side.
دز کول	*daz kawal*	To fire.
لګیدل	*lagédal*	To be hit.
مقام کول	*muqām kawal*	To halt.
لږ وخت دَ پاره	*lag wakht da pāra*	For a short while.
نړول	*narawal*	To knock down (or building).
ذکر کول	*zikar kawal*	To mention.
تازه	*tāza*	Fresh.
درک	*darak*	Trace clue.
چاپ	*chāp*	Foot print.
ظاهره	*zāhéra*	Evidently.
ګډه	*gada*	Sheep.
تالاش کول	*talāsh kawal*	To look for.
دزی وشوی	*dazé wo shwé*	Shots were fired.
کمر	*kamar*	Cliff, neck (in hill.)
هم پد هغه وخت	*hum puh hagha wakht*	At the same moment.

غائب کیدل	*ghāib kédal*	} To go out of sight.
پناه کیدل	*panāh kédal*	
روان کیدل	*rawān kédal*	To start, set out.
نور پریواتۀ	*nwar préwatūh*	Sunset.
وریسی کول	*warisé kawal*	} To remove.
یو خواته کول	*yau khwā ta kawal*	
تګی	*tagi*	Trap.
(ته) پۀ پسوني کښی کینا ستل	*ta puh psūni ké kénāstal*	} To ambush.
(ته) لارنیول	*ta lār niwal*	

Exercise 41.

While the force was encamped on a hill near Kaneguram an informer came and told the Political Officer that the Shabi Khels had all their cattle hidden in a nulla about seven miles away to the north. For this he received a handsome reward. Although it was the middle of the day and very hot we started at once for the place. On the way we passed some rice fields which were irrigated from a small stream flowing down the hill side. Near these fields was a tower from which a shot was fired at us as we approached. No one was hit, and the man who fired the shot fled before we could get up to the tower and escaped among the hills

We halted there for a short while and knocked the tower down. Then we went on, and about three o'clock reached the place mentioned by the informer. There were fresh traces of cattle on every side. but evidently their owners had taken them away for we could not find so much as a single sheep. While we were looking about some shots were fired from a neck between two hills, and at the same moment the informer, whom we had brought with us, fled. Many shots were fired after him, but he was soon out of sight. So we started back to camp and going by a different route reached it just before sunset. It was said afterwards that the informer was himself a Shabi Khel, and that he had taken care to have the cattle removed before the troops started, and that the whole thing was a trap. If we had returned by the same route as we went, the tribesmen, who had collected and made an ambush on the road while we were looking for the cattle, would have given us a very bad time.

VOCABULARY XLIII.

لۀ دن تاریخ نه *uh nan tarikh na*   From this date.

كنزل كول *kanzal kawal*   To abuse.

كمزورى *kamzōray*   Weak.

مضبوط	*mazbūt*	Strong.
خان	*zān*	Self.
قوت	*quat*	Strength.
مغرور	*maghrūr*	Proud.
پۀ حيرانتيا سره	*puh hairāntiā sara*	With astonishment.
دليل	*dalil*	Reason.
ليونیَ	*lēwanay*	Mad.
اول	*awal*	First.
وړومبیَ	*vrūmbay*	First.
څنګه چه	*sunga chi*	As.
هم دغَسی	*hum dagha sé*	The same way.
خبره دا ده	*khabara dā dah*	The true fact i٠.
بی ګناه	*bé gunah*	Innocent.
بی هيڅ	*bé hissa*	For nothing.

EXERCISE 42.

يوه ورځ يوی ښڅی خپل ځنښتن ته رو چه لۀ نن تاريخ نه پس
بيا م نۀ شی وهلیَ ۔ او نۀ راته کنزل کولیَ شی ۔ ځنښتن ورته ويل
دا خبره د پۀ ځۀ خيال و کړۀ ۔ زۀ درته کمزوری ښکاره شوم او کۀ خپل
خان درته مضبوط ښکاره شو او نۀ د خپل پلار پۀ قوت مغرورۀ شوی
چه بيا د نۀ شم وهلیَ ۔ دی ورته و چه بس ما درتۀ و ويل چه
بيا م نۀ شی وهلیَ ۔ سړی بيا ورند پۀ حيرانتيا سره تپوس و کړو چه
دا خبره تۀ پۀ کوم دليل سره کوی ۔ ليونۍ خو نۀ ئی چه لوفۍ ئی
څنګه چه ۔ ما لۀ خما ښڅد وی هم دغَسی اوس ئی او څنګه چه
زۀ وړومبیَ سنا ځنښتن و م هم دغَسی اوس هم يم ۔ نو څنګه د نۀ

شم وهلیَ ۔ هنطمی ورته یٔ جواب کښی و ویل چه خبره دا دَه چه هر
خڅ چه تَه وائی هغَه به مَنم ۔ نو چه تولی خبری د مَنم نو تۀ لیونیَ
خو نه ئی چۀ بیڼناه به م وهی ۔ یا بی هیڅ به رانه کښزل کوی ۔
سوی و خُندل نر روان شو ۔

YOCABULARY XLIV.

دوَ جمعی کیږی	*dwa jumé kégee*	A fortnight ago.
دَ شپږ رو اوؤ بجو پٔ منځ کښی	*da shpagō owo bajō puh mianz ké*	Between 6 and 7 o'clock.
اواز	*awāz*	Voice, noise.
کړ پهَار	*krapahār*	Footsteps, sound of feet.
پٔ تراټ	*puh trāt*	Galloping.
خلاص راتلل یا پٔ پوره چال راتلل	*khlās rātlal* or *puh pūra chāl rātlal*	To come on at full speed.
سور	*sōr*	Rider.
ظاهره	*zāhéra*	Evidently.
قابو	*qabū*	Control.
آس یٔ لۀ قابو نه و تلیَ وُه	*as yé luh qabū na watalay woh*	He lost control of his horse.
راڼکل	*rākhkal*	To tug.
سورلی	*swarli*	Riding, passenger
رکاب	*rekāb*	Stirrup.
واږی	*wāgé*	Reins.
ګز	*gaz*	Yard.

قدم	*qadam*	Pace.
رغزیدل	*rgharédal*	To roll.
اوږه	*oga*	Shoulder.
بازیګره	*bāzīgara*	Somersault.
بازیګره اړول	*bāzīgara arawal*	To turn a somersault.
څنډل	*sandal*	To brush.
ګرد	*gard*	Dust (flying).
خاوره	*khāwra*	Earth (lying on the ground).
خټه	*khata*	Mud.
جامی	*jāmé*	Clothes.
لۀ ښۀ نصیب	*luh khuh nasiba*	Fortunately.
لۀ بد نصیب	*luh bada nasiba*	Unfortunately.
نرم	*naram*	Soft.
بوس	*būs*	Straw, bussa.
خسانری	*khasanray*	A straw.
دز	*daz*	A shot (of gun).
دنګل	*dangal*	To bolt.
یاغی کیدل	*yāghi kédal*	To bolt, to run away out of control.
خپل ځان خوزول	*khpal zān khwazawal*	Shake oneself.
یو خوا بل خوا زنګیدو را زنګیدو	*yau khwā bal khwā zangédo rā zangédo*	Swinging from side to side.

EXERCISE 43.

About a fortnight ago when I was walking across the maidan in the early morning between six and seven, I heard the voice of foot steps behind me. Looking round, I saw a horse galloping towards me at full speed. The rider had evidently lost control of his horse, and was leaning back, tugging at the reins and swinging from side to side. His feet were out of the stirrups, and I expected every moment to see him fall. Sure enough he had not gone more than fifty yards or so after passing me when he rolled off and fell on his shoulder, turning a complete somersault. I ran up thinking he might have broken his neck but before I reached him, he was up, and shaking himself began to brush the dust off his clothes Luckily for him he had fallen in a soft place where there was plenty of loose straw and no stones. He told me his horse had taken fright at the firing of a gun and bolted with him.

VOCABULARY XLV.

جولا	*jōla*	A weaver.
اودل	*odal*	To weave.
لوم	*owam*	I weave (Present.)
پهورئ یا پټکی	*pagrai* or *patkay*	Turban.

حُجوه	*hūjra*	Guest house.
ميلمه	*melma*	Guest.
عالِم	*ālam*	A learned man.
ادب	*adab*	Respect.
(سره) جوړ تازه کول	*(sara) jōr tāza kawal*	To welcome.
مجلس	*majlas*	Assembly, gathering.
دَ عزت کول	*da-izat kawal*	To respect.
څنګ په څنګ	*sang puh sang*	Side by side, close.
هيڅ ئى نه ويل	*hiss yé nuh wayal*	Saying nothing.
دَ يقين کيدل	*da-yaqin kédal*	To believe.
چپ چاپ	*chap ehāp*	Silent.
آخر	*ākhér*	At last.
په آخر کښى	*puh ākhér ké*	In the end.
دَ مياشتى په آخر کښى	*da miāshté puh ākhir ké*	In the end of month.
دَ مياشتى په شروع کښى	*da miāshté puh shurū ké*	In the beginning of month.
روژه	*rōjha*	Fast, fasting.
ماتول	*mātawal*	To break.
نور پريواته	*nwar préwātuh*	Sunset, West.
ساعت	*sāat*	Moment.
ناګهانه	*nāgahāna*	By chance.
بيا به څه چل کيږى؟	*biā ba suh chal kégee ?*	What will happen then?

خر	*khar*	An ass, donkey.
كتهٔ	*kata*	Pack saddle.
زين	*zin*	Saddle.

EXERCISE 44.

یو جولا نی جامی واغوستی سپینه پڼهي ئی پۀ سر کپه او
دیو قاضی حجری له ورغی ۔ قاضی صاحب چه دا میلمه ولید نو
خیال ئی وکړ چه څوک دَلویي کور سړی دی او عالم هم معلومیږي
نو ډیر پۀ ادب ورته ورته پاڅید او ډیر جوړ تازه ئی ور سره وَړل هغه نور
مجلس هم دَ دۀ ډیر عزت وکړ جولا قاضی صاحب سره هڅک پۀ
هڅک کیناست هیڅ ئی نۀ ویل پۀ دی باند نور هم دَ خلقو یقین
وشۀ چه ډیر هوښیار سړی دی نو یو ساعت خو ټول مجلس سره
چپ چاپ ناست وۀ هیچا هڅ نۀ ویل آخر یو سړی لۀ قاضی صاحب
نه تپوس وکړ چه روژه پۀ هڅ وخت ماتیږي قاضی جواب ورکړ
چه لۀ نور پریواتۀ نه لرو ساعت پس دَ روژی ماتولو وخت وی ناگها نه
جولا پۀ کښ ویل قاضی صلحب کۀ نور ترنیمی شپی پوری پری
نۀ وځي نو بیا به هڅ چل کیږي پۀ دی باند ټولو وخندل او وئی
ویل چه خر هم هغه دی کته ور باند بله دۀ—

VOCABULARY XLVI.

دَ عربو یو ټولی	*da arabō yau tōlay*	A band of Arabs.
ټولی یا داره	*tōlay* or *dāra*	Party, raid.
بندَول	*bandawal*	To block.
دَ وطن خلق	*da watan khalq*	Inhabitants.
ظلم	*zulum*	Tyranny.
بي خبرٔ	*bé khabara*	Unwittingly.

(ته) وسله کيښودل	*(ta) wasla kékhōdal*	Surrender.
وسله	*wasla*	Weapon.
مغلوب يا لاند	*maghlūb or lāndé*	Overpowered.
مورچه	*mōrcha*	Strong hold.
دَ استوږنی	*da astōgné*	
ځائی	*zāi*	Fixed residence.
دَ بادشاه مشير يا صلاح کار	*da bādshāh mashir or salāh kār*	Counsellor of the king.
۶صلحت کول	*maslahat kawal*	To consult.
سره	*sara*	Together.
لری کول يا	*laré kawal or*	
وريسی کول	*warisé kawal*	To remove.
خپګان	*khapgān*	Grievances.
راج	*rāj*	State.
طاقتور	*tāqatwar*	Powerful.
لاند کیدل	*lāndé kédal*	To be subdued.
جاسوس	*jāsūs*	Spy.
۶خبر	*mukhbér*	Informer.
موقعی تد ڼتل	*muqé ta katal*	To watch opportunity.
خالي	*khāli*	Evacuated.
خپل ځان پټ کول	*khpal zān pat kawal*	Conceal oneself.
لوټ	*lut*	Plunder, loot (noun)
موقع ۶ وَندل	*moqa mundal*	To get a chance.

پسونی *psūnay*   An ambush.

شوکمار *shūkmār*   A Robber.

شوکه کول *shūka kawal*   To rob.

مړ کول یا وژل *mar kawal* or *wajhal*   To put to death.

پایه تخت *pāya takht*   Capital.

EXERCISE 45.

A band of Arabs had collected among the mountains and were in the habit of stopping and looting caravans, as they crossed the pass. The inhabitants of the country around were also in great distress because of the tyranny of these bandits, while the Sultan's troops seemed powerless to deal with them, because of the strength of the position they had taken up in the mountains. The Sultan's counsellors were very anxious to deal effectively with the band which was daily becoming more powerful as it was attracting to its banner all the bad characters of the region. They accordingly sent spies to report on the movements of the robbers. Soon after, news came in from a spy that the band had left their strong hold to raid a tribe some distance away. The counsellors seized this opportunity to despatch a regiment of troops to intercept the robbers on their return with the plunder. The operation was completely successful as the thieves fell unwittingly into the ambush. Many of them were killed and the remainder surrendered to the Sultan's troops and were brought into the capital for trial. The Sultan sentenced most of them to death.

VOCABULARY XLVII.

راکوز کیدل	*rā kūz kédal*	To come down.
خپل خپلوان	*khpal khpalwān*	Relations.
علاج	*ilaj*	Cure, remedy (noun).
دا ښۀ چل نۀ دى	*dā khuh chal nuh day*	This is not a good plan.
سترګى دۀ پټى کړى	*stargé dé paté kree*	He should shut his eyes.
خوږ.ر کیدل	*khūg kedal*	To be hurt.
رسول	*rasawal*	To cause to arrive.
مشر	*mashar*	Elder.
پۀ قهر شۀ	*puh qahar shuh*	Became enraged.
ژوندى	*jhwanday*	Alive.
خیل	*khayal*	To show, direct.
رسۍ	*rasai*	Rope.
سر	*sar*	The end, head.
پاس	*pas*	Up.
را اچول	*rā achawal*	To throw towards me or us.
ملا	*mla*	Waist.
کلک	*klak*	Hard, tight.
پۀ زور سرا	*puh zōr sàra*	With force.

را ګذار کول	*rā guzār kawal*	To throw down.
سره دَ رابريوتو	*sara da rāpréwato*	Immediately on falling.
کمبخت !	*kam bakhta !*	O you unlucky one !
دَخپل لاسَ	*da khpala lāsa*	Intentionally.
اجل	*ajal*	Fixed day for death.
ګنره	*ganra*	Otherwise.
ځان کندن يا	*zān kandan* or	
ځنکدن	*zankadan*	The point of death.
برج	*braj*	Tower.

EXERCISE 45.

يو جولا پۀ ونه کښې ختلئَ وه اوبيا نۀ شو راکوزيدئَ نو خپل
خپلوانوئي راجمع شول پۀ علاجئي نۀ پوهيدل چه خنۀ ئي راکوز کړو
چا به ويل راڅيي چه داونه ږبي کړو نو چه ونه را پريوزي نو پخپله به
تر راکوزشي بل به ويل نه داهنۀ چل نۀ دئ دئ دَ ونئ پۀ پريوتو
کښې به سږيَ مړ شي چا به ويل سترګي د پتي بوي او راتپ
د کوي پوه به هم نۀ شي او پۀ زمکه به وداردبرې بل ويل نه داهم هنۀ
چل نۀ دئ سږيَ به خوږر شي چا به ويل راڅيي چه يو پۀ بل
وداردبرو او بل پۀ بل نو پۀ دى شان بد ځان وز وزسوو او راکوز به ئي
کړو نورو ويل دا هم هنۀ خبره نۀ دَ چا به ويل راڅيي چه دَ ونئ خواته
يو برج جوړ کړو چه برج ور ورسي نو پۀ بدئي راکوز کړو بل ويل
تر برج تر جوړ ولو به سږيَ دَ لوبرى او تندى مړشي پۀ دوبي کښې
يو مشر ورۀ چه هغه راغئ نو ورته ډير پۀ قهر شو او ويلدئي چه پۀ
داسى اسان چل باند هم نۀ پو هيدرئي ؟ ورشئ يو لويه رسي

راو ورې چه رسيدلی راوره نو درسئ يو سرلی جولا ته پاس ورګذار کړ
ورته ئی ووبل چه ملا پوزی ئی کلک وتوه چه هغه درسئ سر
ملا پوری وتپلو نو دی مشر جولا د رسئ بل سر په زور سره هکته
راهکلو لاندئی راکذار کړ سړیَ سره د را پریوتو مړشو دی نورو جولا
کانو ورته و کم بخت دا دهفه ولړل دخیل لس د سړیَ ووزلو دا ورته
په جواب کښ وو چه اجل ئی وو هکه مړشو کنو ما ډیر خلق په
دی چل سره لۀ کړهي نه راویستلي دی—

VOCABULARY XLVII.

يو ځائی کیدل	*yau zāi kédal*	To join.
تحريک ياشور وشر	*tahrik* or	
	shōr-o-shar	Movement.
ظاهره	*zāhéra*	Outwardly.
څما لۀ ویری	*zamā luh*	
	veyaré	Through fear of me
پټ	*pat*	Secretly.
په جار	*puh jār*	Openly, publicly
اورول	*aurawal*	To announce.
اعتبار یا وعده	*itébār* or *wada*	Assurance.
دَ قام مشران	*da qam*	The elders of the
	masharān	tribe.
په-باند یا	*puh-bandé* or	Through, by means
په ذریعه دَ	*puh zaria da*	of.
سرحد	*sarhad*	Border.
هله ګله	*hala gula*	Disturbances.
فساد	*fasād*	Mischief.,

انگریزي سرکار	*angrézi sarkār*	British Government.
لرى کول یا رفع	*laré kawal* or	
کول	*rafa kawal*	To dispel.
رفع کیدل	*rafa kédal*	To be dispelled.
دَ پاره دَ دى	*da pāra da dé*	In order to
رعیت	*rait*	Subject.
دَ دشمنئ په نیت	*da dushmanai puh niat*	With hostile inten-tion.
نیت	*niat*	Intention.
په زړه زور تیرول	*puh zruh zōr térawal* or	
یا برداشت کول یا	*bardāsht kawal* or	
صبر کول	*sabar kawal*	To tolerate.
گمراه	*gumrāh*	Mis-guided.
بى وجى یا بى	*bé waje* or	
هیڅ	*bé hissa*	Unprovoked.
یقین	*yaqin*	Belief.
ساتل	*sātal*	To keep, watch.
منع کول	*mana kawal*	To prevent.

EXERCISE 47.

You have said my tribesmen can never join in such a movement openly for fear of me. If any one has gone, he must have gone secretly. What I now ask you, in accordance with those assurances of friendship, which you have so readily made, is that you will publicly announce

to the tribesmen throngh your local officers that,
if they cross the borders and join in disturbances
against the British Government, they will incur
your displeasure. (Lit: You will be annoyed from
them). The belief is entertained by many mis-
guided persons that they will not incur your
disapproval by acting in a hostile manner
against Government and this belief can be
dispelled if your officers will keep watch along
the river and at other places in order to prevent
your subjects from crossing the Frontier with
hostile intentions, whether secretly or openly.
I ask you therefore, to issue orders to this effect.
By so doing you may put an end to these
disturbances, which were wholly unprovoked
and cannot be tolerated.

VOCABULARY XLIX.

امزَرَیْ یا زمرَیْ	*amzaray* or *zmaray*	Tiger.
(ته) دصیحت کول	*(ta) nasihat kawal*	To advise.
کورَه	*gōra*	Look here.
ځناور	*zanāwar*	Animal.
خبردار	*khabardār*	Beware, be careful.
جهږه خلاصول	*jagara khlāsawal*	To settle dispute.
إنصاف	*insāf*	Justice.
خدائى پاک	*khudāi pak*	Pure God.

طاقت	*tāqat*	Power, strength.
مناسب دى	*munāseb di*	It is befitting.
عاجز	*ājaz*	Poor, needy.
غور	*ghōr*	Justice, care.
په خه شان سره	*puh khuh shān sara*	Satisfactorily.
بيزو	*bīzō*	Monkey.
شكل	*shakal*	Appearance.
اوږد	*ūgad*	Long.
له لرى نه	*luh laré na*	From a distance.
اوږى	*lūgay*	Smoke.
د سرى په غوږو دير بد لږى	*da sarı puh ghwagō dér bad lagee*	One can not bear to hear it.
په بنده سرپه كول	*puh bāndé sarpa kawal*	To spare.
كه د لاس د كيږى	*kuh da lāsā dé kégee*	If possible.
په بنده لاس بكيدل	*puh-bāndé lās bar kédal*	To get the better of.
منصف	*munséf*	Just (Adjective.)
لږ دير	*lag der*	Some what.
ملاويدل	*melāwédal*	To resemble.

EXERCISE 48.

يو امزرى ذيل څوى ته نصيحت كوۀ ويل ئى كوره ته به پس
له ماند په دى ځنګل کښى د ټولو ځناورو بادشاه ئى او بادشاه نوم
د خدايي دى خبردار چه په چا بيځناه ظلم ونۀ کړى ډير خلق به
در له د جګړو ځلاصولو دپاره راځي ولى تۀ په انصاف سره هره جګړه

فیصله کوۀ چا له چه خدای پاک طاقت ور کړی نو مناسب دي چه
دَ خوارو عاجزو غو. په هغه شان سره کوی مهر یاد لره په دی خذهل
کښ یو څناور دی چه په دوهؤ نبو کرهی شکل نی دَ بیزو سره
لر. ډیر ملاویدرهِ خلق ورته سړی وائی اکثر ورسخه یو تور اوبرد لرهی
وی هر کله چه مؤنر. خلق روبینی نو دا لرهی راته نیغ ونسی
دَ دی لرهی نه لربزی راوڼی او دَ دی لوبری یو داسی ناکار او
نااشنا واز وشی چه دسړی په غو.زو ډیر بد لربی او دَ دی اواز
په اوربدو سمدستی -پری زخمی شی په زمکه راپربوڅی او مرشی
نو څما خبره واؤره چه په دی څناور هیڅری صر په ونۀ کړی کۀ گنهگار
وی کۀ بیگناه خو چه وې وینی او کۀ دَ لاسِ د کیدرهِ نو وژنهئِ
انصاف ور سره مۀ کوه بچی ورته و با با نوزه په هڅ بادشاه شوم چه
انصاف ورسره نۀ کوم امزری ورته ویل بچیﹼ په هر څناور کښ
انصاف شته ولی په دۀ کښ خوبالکل نشته او دام هم اوربدلی دی
چه په خپلو ورونړوئی لاس برشی نو هم ورباند صر په نۀ کوی نو څکه
څما نصیحت واوره چه بی انصاف دشمن لۀ څان اول وژل
پکار دی —

VOCABULARY L.

بله ورځ	*bala vraz*	The following day.
جامی اغوستل	*jamé aghustal*	To dress.
زر زر	*zar zar*	Hastily
دَ کبانو ښکار	*da kabānō khkār*	Fishing
ایله ایله رڼا	*ila ila ranra*	Hardly light.
ترڅوني	*taraghune*	Dusk.
واقعه	*waqea*	Mishap, adventure.

دوغل	dōghal	Pit.
ګرب	grab	Hole.
ټوپۍ	tōpai	Cap, hat.
لرزېدل	larzédal	To shake or shaking, to tremble.
لرزان	larzān	Shaking, trembling.
د-وار خطا کېدل	da-wār khatā kédal	To be dismayed.
وار خطا	wār khatā	Alarmed, dismayed.
اوتر	autar	Alarmed, frightened
هډوکی	hadūkay	Bone.
کر کر په خندا کېدل	kar kar puh khanda kédal	To burst out laughing.
مقام	muqām	Halting place.
پراؤ	parāw	Camp.
ربر	rabar	Adventure.
جست په وخت یا په هغه وخت	jukht puh wakht or puh khuh wakht	Just in time.
ښه شروع	kha shurū	Satisfactory beginning.
بچ کېدل	bach kédal	To be saved.

EXERCISE 49.

The following day my friend and I were up in good time and after dressing hastily mounted our ponies which were in readiness at the door, and started for a twelve miles ride to the river where we were going to fish. It was nearly 3 o'clock when we started. Soon after starting I had a little mishap which might have put an end to my sport for that and many days. In the uncertain light my pony put his foot into a hole and came down with me, throwing me over his head. Luckily my topi saved me and 1 got up with nothing worse than a shaking. My friend at first was a little alarmed, but when he found there was no bone broken, he burst into a hearty laugh in which I joined. We reached our halting place without any further adventure and just in time to get the best of the early morning. A few minutes afterwards I landed my first mashir, a small one it is true, but a satisfactory beginning.

VOCABULARY LI.

تازه	*tāza*	Fresh.
مړی	*maray*	Dead body.
مړی به وشو	*maray ba wosho*	One would die.
قبر	*qabar*	Grave.
ادیره	*adira*	Graveyard.
سپرؤدل	*sparōdal*	To untie, open.
کفن	*kafan*	Shroud.
را ټول کول	*rā tōl kawal*	To collect, to undress.
کپړه	*kapra*	Cloth.
گذاره کول	*guzāra kawal*	To live on
گذران کول	*guzrān kawal*	

تنگ کیدل	*tang kédal*	To be oppressed.
پۀ لاس ورتلل	*puh lās wartlal*	To come to hand, to find.
گنړه	*ganra*	Otherwise.
اسمان	*asmān*	Sky.
ستورى	*stōray*	Star.
مرض	*maraz*	Illness.
زیاتیدل	*ziātédal*	To increase.
دارو	*dārū*	Medicine.
دَـدمه کیدل	*da-dama kédal*	To recover from illness.
وصیت کول	*wasiyat kawal*	To make a will.
وران کار	*vran kar*	Evil deed.
قیامت	*qayāmat*	The day of judgement
نیکی	*néki*	Goodness.
وجۀ	*waja*	Reason.
دعا کول	*duā kawal*	To pray for.
نیک کارونه	*nék kārūna*	Good deeds.
نتیجه	*natija*	Result.
عمل	*amal*	Act.
بخښل	*bakhal*	To forgive.
کسب	*kasab*	Occupation.
پۀ غلا	*puh ghla*	Secretly.
اولنى	*awalanay*	The first one, the former.
جوړ	*jōr*	Accordingly.
وروستنى	*vrustonay*	The last one, the latter.

خدای دٔ یٔی وبخښي	*khudāi dé yé wo bakhee*	May God forgive him !
حیادار	*hayādār*	Modest.
شرمول	*sharmawal*	To put to shame.
دَ وروستني پهٔ نیور پسې شول	*da vrūstoni puh niwo pasé shwal*	They were after arresting the latter.
(تهٔ) دَ اسمان ستوري ښيل	*(ta) da asmān stōri khayal*	To punish severely, (lit. to show the stars of the sky).

EXERCISE 50.

یو سړی وو چهٔ تٔزهٔ مړی بهٔ وشو نو دَ شپی بهٔ ورغیٔ قبر
بهٔ ئی دَ دهٔ وسپرو دلو دَ مړی نه بهٔ ئی کفن رأٰنؤٰل کٔر کور تهٔ بهٔ ئی
راوړ دا دَ کفن کپړه بهٔ ئی پهٔ یو بل خرڅوله او پهٔ دی بهٔ ئی مګذران
کاوهٔ خلق ور نه ډیر تنګ شؤ مګر پهٔ لس نهٔ ورتلو ګنړه دَ اسمان
ستوري بهٔ ئی ور تهٔ ښیٰٔلي وړ یوه ورځ ناجوړ شو مرض ئی ورځ
پهٔ ورځ زیاتیده پهٔ هیڅ دارو ئی دمه نهٔ کیده نو پوه شو چه اوسم
آخٔر وخت دی نو خپل څوي یی راوغوښتلو ورتهٔئی وصیت کاوهٔ ویل ئی
چه ګوره بچیٰٔ ماډیر وران وران کارونه کړي دی خدایٔ خبر چه
پهٔ قیامت کښ بهٔ څما څهٔ حال وی تهٔ خپل مؤنژه اوس کوه
اوبد کارونه مهٔ کوه داسی کار کوه چه خلق درنه خوشحال شي-او
ستا دنیٰٔکٔي پهٔ وجه هم دعا کوي چه کفن کښ (*kakh*) مړ
شو نو څوي ئی پهٔ زړهٔ کښ وو چه کهٔ زهٔ ډیر نیک کارونه کوم خو
نتیجه بهٔ ئی هم ماته رسیٰٔږي پلار تهٔ بهٔ م څهٔ فائده ونه رسیٰٔ څکه
چه هر سړی بهٔ پهٔ خپل عمل څلا صیٰٔږي جوړ ماله داسی کار کول
پکاردی چه ور باند م پلار تهٔ خلق دعا کوي او خدایٔ ئی وبخښي

نو هاک هم دپلار کسب شروع کړ چه دوی به وشو نو ډ شپی به
ورغی قبر به ئی دَ دۀ ومهپرود کفن به ئی تر راټول کړ او بیا به ئی
ورنه پوزه او غوږونه نه هم پری ژلَ خاقو چه دَ کَ, ولید نو ډیر څیه
شو ویل ئی اولنی کپن کښی (kakh) د څدایي وبخښی ډیر
هَ حیادار سوی ۀ کفن به ئی یوړو ولی دوی څو به ئی نه
شرمولو نو و رَبی کپن کښی (kakh) ته به ئی دعا کوله او دَ ورستنی
پۀ نیولو پسی شول—

MISCELLANEOUS COLLOQUIAL SENTENCES V.

When did you hear this news ?

Dā khabara dé kala aurédalé dah ?

It is only a rumour that the Amir of Afghanistan is coming to Peshawar.

Dā khāli yau awāza dah chi da Afghanistān Amir Pékhawar ta rāzee.

The whole of our Regt. deserted from the field of battle.

Da jang luh maidān na zamūng tōla paltan wo takhtédah.

50 of them have been taken prisoners.

Panzōs qaid shwal.

We know nothing of the others. They may have gone towards the enemy.

Da nōrō puh bāb ké hiss khabar nuh yū dushman ta ba takhtédali wi.

Wire the Police and inform the Deputy Commissioner.

Pulas ta tār war kra aw dipty comishnar khabar kra.

They all will be tried by Court Martial.

Pa kot marshal bāndé ba da dui faisala kégee.

Sign this agreement, write your name here.	Da dé iqrār nāma bāndé daskhat wō kra, dalta khpal nūm wo lika.
Do you plead guilty or not guilty ?	Tuh gunahgār yé kuh bégunāh ?
Do you want to produce witnesses in your defence ?	Tuh khpalé safāi da pāra gawāhān pésh kawal ghwāré ?
Is this your signature ?	Dā stā daskhat day?
Why don't you complain to Govt. against him ?	Walé war bāndé sarkār ta shikāyat nuh kawé.
I have seen it with my own eyes.	Mā puh khpalo stargō lidalay day.
What enmity is there between you and him?	Stā aw da haghuh puh mianz ké suh dushmani dah ?
Can he sing and dance?	Hagha sandaré wayalay shi aw gadéday shi ?
Tell the truth and nothing but the truth.	Rikhtiā rikhtiā khabara kawa.
This village is of very bad repute.	Dā kalay dér bad nām day.
The Regt. will head the list.	Paltan awal lambar ba shi.
You will get two months furlough after the grand parade.	Da lōi parait na pas dar ta da dwao miāshto razā ba milāo shee.
It is a very disgraceful thing.	Da déra da sharam khabara dah.

First take a good aim and then shoot.

Awal khuh zéray wo lagawa aw biā yé wola.

Challenge them first and then shoot.

Awal war bāndé awāz wo kra aw biā yé wola.

We stood our ground for the whole day.

Tōla vraz mūnga muqābila wo kra.

The ascent is difficult on that side, one cannot climb that way.

Puh haghe taraf cha-rāi grāna dah aw saray war bāndé kha-talay nuh shee.

It is all descent from Cherat right down to Pabbi.

Luh chirāt na ain tar pabō pōré utrāi dah.

My double barrelled gun has been stolen. I suspect my servant.

Zamā dwa naliz tōpak puh ghlā talay day puh khpal naukar bāndé zamā gumān day.

We surrounded the fort and blocked all the approaches to it.

Mūnga kalā géra kra aw tōlé lāré mo war ta bandé kré.

I am very glad to see you, Sahib.

Sahiba ? Zuh stā puh lidalō dér khushāl yam.

You only recently came to Peshawar so I thought I should come to pay my respects to you.

Tuh ōs ōs Pékhawar ta rāghalay yé no fikar mé wo kar chi pakār di chi zuh stā salām wo kram.

I am feeling very cold.

Zama déra yakhni kégee.

It is a pity that you did not tell me this before.	*Dā da afsōs khabara dah chi dā hāl tā mā ta awal wo nuh wayalo.*
Owing to the Mohmand expedition, no harvesters can be found as they all work as labourers.	*Dā Mohmando da lām puh sabab laugari mūndal grān kār day, zaka chi tōl mazdūri kawee.*
I cannot drive a tonga as I have never tried.	*Zuh tānga nuh sham chalawalay zaka chi hicharé mé kōshash nuh day karay.*
He is a great miser and will pay up with great difficulty.	*Hagha dér shūm day aw puh déra mushkela sara ba pésé war kree.*
This will be settled later on when the sahib comes back from tour.	*Vrosto ba dā faisala shee kala chi sāhib luh dauré na biarta rāshee.*
Where were you born ?	*Tuh puh kum zāi ké paida shway wé ?*
How long has your Regt been in this Station ?	*Stā paltan pa dé chāwnrai ké kala rāsé dah ?*
Do you own any land ? what revenue do you pay to the Govt ?	*Stā suh zmaka shta ? sōmra mālia sarkār ta war kawé ?*
Wake me just at 7 if I am still asleep.	*Jukht puh owuh bajé mé wikh kra kuh puh hagha wakht zuh ūduh yam.*
Bring my breakfast while I am in bed.	*Kala chi zuh puh kat ké yam, no zamā hāzéri rāwra.*

Take the horse for exercise and saddle it at 5 p. m.

Ass rōl da para bōza aw puh pinzuh bajé mazdigar yé zin kra.

Do not be late.

Nawakhta kawa ma.

Why did not you bring me some hot water as I told you?

Chi dar ta mé wo wayal no walé dé suh garmé obuh ra nuh wré?

All the towels in the house are dirty.

Puh kōr ké tōl taulyāgān khiran di.

Bring any one you like.

Sōk chi dé khwakh wi hagha rāwala.

Wind this watch as it will stop.

Dé garai la kunji war kra zaka chi banda ba shi.

Pump the cycle up I think it is punctured.

Bāisekal la bād war kra, zamā puh kheyāl ké panchar day.

Tighten the screws of the wheel.

Da pāyé dibrai sakhté kra.

Take the measurement of my foot.

Zamā da khpé nap wākhla.

The leather must be soft.

Pakār di chi sarman narma wi.

This room is full of mosquitoes, flit the whole room.

Da kamra da māshō na daka dah puh tōla kamra ké da māsko tél charqāo kra.

I shall dismiss you if you don't prove it.

Kuh da khabara sābéta nuh kré, no zuh ba dé nūm kat kram.

Is there any fishing obtainable here now?

Oss dalta suh da kabanō khkar mūndalay shi kuh na.

When the water is clear the fiishermen will come with their nets from Lalpura. — *Kala chi obuh ranré shee no machi mārān ba luh lāl pūré na sara da jālūno rāshee.*

The sky is very clear today. — *Nan asmān bilkul* or *tak shin day.*

It is getting cooler day by day. — *Vraz puh vraz yakhni kégee.*

It is cloudy and cold today, it is drizzling. — *Nan woriaz dah aw yakhni dah, sāskay dāy.*

The rain has stopped now, let us go to the city. — *Oss bārān watār day, rāza chi khahar ta lārshoo.*

Why did your pony put its foot into the hole? — *Walé stā da ass khpa puh grubi ké lāra.*

Because it was dark and he could see nothing. — *Zaka chi tyāruh wah aw hiss yé lidalay nuh shwal.*

The tiger made a will in favour of his son. — *Zmari khpal zōi ta wasiat wo kro.*

Tell your local officer to keep a watch along the river and other places so that the tribesmen may not join the disturbance. — *Da khpal qām masharāno ta waya chi da sind ghāré aw nor zāyūno ta khyāl kawee chi da qām khalq puh dé jagara ké shāmel nuh shi.*

A weaver had climbed up the tree and could not get down. — *Jōla puh wana ké khatalay woh aw biā ra kūzédalay nuh sho.*

How did the people bring him down? — *Khalqo sanga ra kūz kar?*

They had made a permanent residence on the top of the hill.	*Hagho da ghar puh sar bāndé khpal dà osédo zāi jōr karày woh.*

VOCABULARY LII.

و رودی غونډۍ	*warūké ghundai*	Low ridge.
غونډۍ	*ghundai*	Hillock.
لو رہ ژوره	*lwarā jhawara*	Low undulation.
ختل	*khatal*	Ascend.
کوزیدل	*kūzédal*	To descer.d.
تنګۀ تنګۍ	*tanga tangai*	Narrow defile.
قریب قریب	*qarib qarib*	Practically.
حد-برید	*had, brid*	Limit.
درہ	*dara*	Valley.
معمولی	*māmūli*	Precarious kind.
بیا هم	*biā hum*	Even then.
عین تر-پورې	*ain tar-pōré*	Right down till.
لائق	*lāiéq*	Fit, worthy, capable.
اباد	*abād*	Cultivated or populated.
ابادی	*abādi*	Cultivation or population.
کلپ	*kalp*	Steep.
اوبۀ خور	*obuh khwar*	Irrigation.
تل	*tal*	Bed (of the river or well.)
تلی	*talay*	Palm of hand, Sole of foot.

پټ	pat	Stealthily.
ګنر ځنګل	ganr zangal	Dense Jungle
لوخه	lūkha	Reeds.
لوی لوی واخه	lōi lōi wākhuh	High grass.
املي	imli	Tamarind.
ترا وس پوری	tar osa pōré	Still.
غريب خلق	gharib khalq	Miserable inhabitant.
ژور	jhawar	Deep.
پلن	plan	Broad.
اوبه ترزنګون زنګون پوری دی	obuh tar zangūn zangūn pōré di	The water is knee deep.
ګرزيدل	garzédal	To walk, to turn.
وران	vrān	Ruined.
زنګون يا ګوډه	zangūn or gōda	}Knee.

EXERCISE 51.

The road now leads over the low ridge on the left, and going over some low undulations, descends to the river through a narrow defile between low hills. This pass is practically the limit of the cultivation of the Mashhad valley; for though there is a little bcyond, it is of the most precarious kind. The villagers exist in constant fear from Turkoman raiders; yet under a strong government the whole valley of this river right down to Akdarhand, is capable of being kept in the highest state of cultivation, as there is abundance of water in the river, of which banks are low enough to admit of its being distributed for irrigation. The road now goes along the bed of the river, which is covered with a dense jungle of tamarind and high grass and one mile and a half further on passes the old Fort of Nazarian, where there are still a few miserable inhabitants. It then crosses the river which is here only two and a half feet deep and thirty feet broad, then turns to the left and ascends the right bank to a ruined fort. It then passes over an undulation and descends again to the bed of the river at Inayatabad.

VOCABULARY LIII.

قارغه	*qārghuh*	Crow.
پۀ امان	*puh amān*	Peacefully.
سلامتی	*salāmati*	Safety.
سلامت	*salmat*	Safe.
فارسی خوان	*farsi khwān*	Persian (man.)
پای	*pai*	Foot ⎫ Persian.
دست	*dast*	Hand ⎭
یا دست مرد	*ya dasté mard*	Either make use of
یا پای مرد	*ya pai mard*	your hands or feet. (you should fight otherwise run away to save yourself.)

مقابله کول	*muqābéla kawal*	To withstand.
دا بهتره ده	*dā behtara dah*	It is better.
خود	*khud*	Certainly.
تښتیدل	*takhtédal*	To flee.
تښتته	*tékhta*	Flight.
ادمیان	*admian*	Men.
بزدل	*buzdil*	Coward.
بزدلي	*buzdili*	Cowardice.
دین	*din*	Religion.
مذهب	*mazhab*	Religion.
روا یا حلال	*rawā,* or *halāl*	Lawful.
خصوصاً	*khusūsan*	Especially.
هر کله	*har kala*	When ever.
تیت کیدل	*tit kédal*	To bend down
لوڼه یا	*lūta* or	}Clod of earth.
غونډه	*ghunda*	
اوچتول	*ūchatawal*	To pick up, lift up.
لستوڼری	*lastōnray*	Sleeve.
لۀ لری نه	*luh laré na*	From a distance.
لۀ ورایه	*luh vrāyā*	From a distance.
سیل کول	*sail kawal*	To fly about.
خواه مخواه	*khwāh makhwāh*	Some how or other.

EXERCISE 52.

یو قارغۀ خپل څوي ته نصیحت کاوۀ ویل ئی چه ویره لۀ هرچیز
نه ښه ده هر څوک چه ویریږي نو مدام به پۀ امان او سلامت وي

فارسی خوان وائي یا دست مړد یا پایي مړد او څموږو دَ خلقو
خو دَ مقابلۍ طاقت خود نشته نو دا بهتره ده چه دشمن ته میدان
پریږدوؤ او وتښتوؤ ترنه او فرض کړه چه مؤږو مقابله هم وکړؤ نو خوا
مخواه به مو یا لاس مات شي یا ښپه نو پۀ جنګ کښ څۀ خیر دیَ؟
نو بچۍ څما نصیحت واوره هر یو څناور چه درته نیغ شي نو تښته تر
دی تینه تي ته آدمیان بزدلي وائي ؟مر څموږو پۀ مذهب کښ
روا ده خصوصاً لۀ سپو نه ډیر ویریدل پکار دی هر کله چه دیَ زمکی
ته ټیټ شي نو سمدستی تر الوتۀ څکه چه دا لۀ زمکی نه کانړی یا
لوټه را اوچتوي بچي ورته پۀ جواب کښ وو چه با با ؟ کۀ دغه
سپي پۀ لستوڼي کښ پټ ؟ ان دَ څان سره کانړی راوړی وي نو زۀ
به یې څۀ وکړم دابه ښۀ وي چه سپي لۀ لری نه و وینم نو به تر والوتۀ
پلار ورته و شاباش ؟ تۀ لۀ ماته هوښیار ئي ورځه سیل کوه هر چرته
چه څی سلامت به ئی ——

VOCABULARY LIV.

ټټو	*tatu*	Pony.
روان کیدل	*rawān kédal*	To set out.
نوار خاتۀ	*nwar khātuh*	Day break.
اوبۀ ډکول	*obuh dŭkawal*	To draw water.
ګیره	*gira*	Beard, whiskers.
بریت	*brét*	Moustache.
ګنړل	*ganral*	To consider.
اوتر	*autar*	Alarmed.
پس لۀ هغۀ	*pas luh hagha*	Afterwards.
پیری	*péray*	Genie.
خاپیري	*khāpérai*	Fairy.

EXERCISE 53.

I arrived with the Regiment I was attached to all safe at Agra where I bought a pony for eleven rupees and in company with four or five other sepoys, who had got leave also, I set out for my village. I reached my home early one morning before it was light and waited outside till day break. When my mother came out to draw (fill) water, I called to her, but she did not recognise me in the least, for during the four or five years I had been absent, I had grown from a boy into a man. I had also whiskers and a moustache and considered myself a handsome sepoy. My mother seemed so alarmed when I spoke to her, that I also became frightened, but afterwards my father told me that my uncle had written home to say that I had been killed so my mother thought at first that I was a genie.

VOCABULARY LV.

اعتبار	*itébar*	Trust.
محتاج	*muhtaj*	Needy.
شتهٔ من	*shtuh man*	Rich.
دا يوه عامه خبره ده	*dā yawa āma khabara dah*	This is a common thing.
پردی	*praday*	Stranger.

خلق ور ته نۀ شي کتی	*khalq war ta nuh shi katay*	The ·people cannot bear to see him.
شرميدل	*sharmédal*	To be ashamed.
حاکم	*hākam*	Ruler.
سپک کول	*spak kawal*	To insult.
برباد کول یا تالا کول نړول	*barbād kawal* or *tālā kawal* or *narawal*	To ruin.
کۀ داسی نۀ شي کیدی	*kuh dāsé nuh shi kéday*	If this is impossible.
کوهی	*kūhay*	Well (of water.)
ور گذار کول	*war gūzār kawal*	To throw down.
گذار	*gūzar*	A blow.
خیر	*khér*	Well.
دـپۀ سر	*da puh sar*	Against.
مخبر	*mukhber*	Informer.
سرۀ زر	*sruh zar*	Gold.
سپین زر	*spin zar*	Silver.
زیر	*ziar*	Brass.
تانبه	*tānba*	Copper.
مور	*mōr*	Rich, replete.
مارۀ	*māruh*	Rich, replete (Plural.)
جور	*jōr*	Accordingly.
اندر پایه	*andrapāya*	Ladder.
گټ	*gut*	Corner.
پهره	*péhra*	Sentry go.

سنتری اودرول	*sentri ōdrawal*	To post a sentry.
پۀ ډاګ کښ	*puh dāg ké*	
اچول	*achawal*	To post (a letter).
پۀ باند لاس پوری	*puh bāndé lās*	
کول	*pōré kawal*	To start. commence.
کالي	*kāli*	Ornaments.
نغدی روپئ	*naghdé rupai*	Cash.
پنډ	*pand*	Parcel, bundle.
مالګه	*mālga*	Salt
اوچت پاڅیدل	*ūchat pāsédal*	Get up straight.
نمک حلال	*namak halāl*	Loyal.
نمک حرام	*namak harām*	Disloyal.
نمک	*namak*	Salt (Urdu.)
او ریدل	*aurédal*	To cross over.

EXERCISE 54.

دَ خلیلو پۀ علاقه کښ پۀ یو کالي کښ یو دولتمند زمیندار وو چه
خلقو ورباند دَ ډیر لوی دولت اعتبار کاوۀ ډیر ښه سړی وۀ دَ خدای
پۀ نامد به یې غریبانو او محتاجانو له ډیر ښۀ ورکول مګر دغه یوه
ګناه ئی وه چه شتۀ من وۀ نو ورځ پۀ ورځ به ئی پۀ کلي کښ
دشمنان زیاتیدل او دا یوه عامه خبره ده چه دَ پښتنو پۀ وطن کښ
څوک دولتمند شي او خدای پاک ورله ـعزت ورکړي نو دَ ډیلو پردو
بدي شي او ورته نۀ شي کتی او دَ هر یو دَاخوښدوی چد دی
څوار شوی بد نام شوی وشرمیدی نو یاخوړی دَ علاقی پۀ حاکمانو
سره لو ببدوی ئی او کۀ دانۀ شی ـیدی نو پټیله ورته ښۀ
نباخۀ دوهی وکنی پۀ کښ ئی ورکُداء کُوی خیر دَ دی دولتمند

زمیندار پۀ سر ییری مخبریي غیر علاقی ته لاړی چه کۀ دا ره
پروکوئي نو پۀ سرو سپینو به ماړه شي جو ړ یوه شپه دَ پنقۀ ریشتو
اپریدو یوه داره چه ورسره دَ کلي بدمعاشان هم یو ځائی شول پۀ
نیمه شپه پۀ کلي راننوته اندر پاتي یی وتولی او سم دَ دی زمیندار پۀ
کور ورواوریدل اول خوئی دَ کور تول سري او ځوکیدار وتولو او بیا ئی
دَ کور ... یو خواته وشولی او پهره ئی پر ودروله چه شور ونۀ کوي
او بیا ئی پۀ لوت لاس پوری کړ تول کلي جامی او نغدی روپئی ئی
راجمع کړلی پنیوونه ئی تر وتول چه روانیدل نویر په کیس ور چه داده
روتني راځنی چه ویي خورۀ جو ړ تول راجمع شول روتني ئی
وخوره پدی کیس یو مشرۀ اوچت پاڅید ویل ئی راځئ چه
ځوړ چه دَ دی کور نمک مو وخو پر نو غلا ئی نۀ کوۀ آخر موژر کیس خو
هم ځۀ پیتو شته لارل پنیوونه ئی پۀ ځائي پرینبودل—

VOCABULARY LVI.

میدان	*maidān*	Open ground, plain
خوشی	*khushay*	Deserted, useless.
خالی	*khāli*	Empty.
کوچ	*kōch*	March.
شهه	*shaga*	Sand.
ځاڅکی	*sāskay*	A drop.
موسمی باران	*mōsami bārān*	Periodical rain.
تلاو	*talāw*	Tank.
اوچ	*och*	Dry.
سفر	*safar*	Journey.
زری	*zaray*	Guide.
زیری	*zéray*	Good news.

پاؤ باندې يو ميل *paw bande yau mil* — 1¼ mile.

تالاش *talash* — Search.

كنودل *kanòdai* — To dig.

مشک *mashk* — Mussak.

دَ مخ کښې ضرورت *da makh ke zarurat* — Future necessity.

EXERCISE 55.

After leaving this place we proceeded twenty three miles and encamped near a well on a piece of open ground in the jungle. Many deserted (empty) villages were met with on the march and the road was, for the most part, over heavy sand, (there was much sand on many parts of the road) without a drop of water near. Periodical rains had failed in this part of the country, the tanks and wells had mostly dried up, which rendered the heat and length of our journey that day all the more distressing. Luckily the guide whom we had brought with us and who had frequently travelled along this road, informed us that at about a mile and quarter distant were a few huts, the inhabitants of which were supplied with water from a spring. We set out immediately in search of it and our great joy found it was not dried up (When we found that it was not dried up we were very much pleased) and

on digging up a little in the sand an abundance
of water flowed out, from which we drank our-
selves and watered our horses and camels and
made the bhisties fill their mussacks for future
necessities.

VOCABULARY LVII

ملاقات	mulāqāt	Interview, visit.
لنډ	land	Short.
لنډه خلاصول	landa khlāsawal	To cut short.
خبره داده	khabara dā dah	The true fact is.
عام	ām	Common.
ګوته	guta	Finger.
بر خلاف	barkhélāf	Against.
بر ناحقه	barnāhaqa	Without any cause or reason.
نو څۀ چل وشي	no suh chal woshee	Then what happens.
لخته	lakhta	Stick, cane, power.

EXERCISE 56.

يو زميندار دَ ډيټی کمشنر صاحب ملاقات دَ پاره تللی وۀ چه وئی
غوښتو نو پۀ ملاقات کښې ترې نه صاحب پښتنه وکړه چه ماته دَ پښتنو ټول
حال روايه چه داخنله خلق دی دی سړی ورته و چه صاحب
دَ پښتنو قصی خو ډيری او لوئی لوئی دی نو لنډه ئی خلاصه کړم او
کۀ دا اوږدی قصی درته راشروع کړم صاحب ورته و لنډه ئی وايه څکه
چه ماته دومره وخت چرته دی چه داسی لوئی لوئی قصی واورم

دهٔ ورنه و صاحبَ ؟ خبره دَ اده چه پهٔ پښتنو کښن يو سرسیَ لهٔ
عامو خلقو نه يوه گوته اوچت شي نو خلق ئی خوا مخواه برخلاف شي
او چه دوه گوتی اوچت شي نو خلق ئی بر ناحقه دشمنان شي
او چه دری گوتی اؤچت شي نو بيا يی وژنی نهٔ نی پريږدی په
دی باند صاحب ږدر وخندل او تپوس ئی تر وکړو چه کهٔ خلوو گوتی
او چت شي نو بيا خهٔ چل وشی زمیندار و بيا سلامت شي دا
خاورمه گوته ستاسو لهَته دَه چه چاله ئی پهٔ لس ورکړئی نو طاقت ئی
پيدا شي او خپل خان پر بچولیَ شي—

VOCABULARY LVIII.

پهٔ باند بحث	*puh bāndé*	
کول	*bahas kawal*	
	or	To discuss.
خبره ، اترِي کول	*khabaré ataré kawal*	
فيصله کول	*faisala kawal*	To decide, to settle.
ټُکره	*tukra*	Piece.
دَ حق شفعی	*da haq shufé*	To claim a right ?
دعوی کول	*dawa kawal*	of pre-emption.
جګړه	*jagara*	Quarrel.
شريعت	*shariāt*	Mohammedan Law.
کهٔ داسی نهٔ کوی	*kuh dāsé nuh kawi*	If they refuse to do so.
پهٔ باند لښکر کول	*puh-bāndé lakhkar kawal*	To raise an army against.
پهٔ باند پهٔ زور کول	*puh-bāndé puh zōr kawal*	To compel.
قبضه	*qabza*	Possession.

پښتو *pukhtu*	Pathan honour.
عرضی *arzi*	Petition.
پۀ پښتو کښ دا *puh pukhtu ké*	
کار, نۀ دی پکار *dā kār nuh day pakār*	The Pathan honour forbids this.
لو کول *law kawal*	To harvest.
څۀ خاص کار *suh khās kār*	Particular business.
کۀ دی کښ ورته *kuh dé ké war*	Should it be made
څۀ خیر وی *ta suh khér wi*	worth their while.

EXERCISE 57.

The matter was discussed at a full Jirga of all tribes. It will be remembered that the Mondo Khel purchased and forcibly took possession of a piece of land over which the Takhli Khel claimed a right of pre-emption. It was decided that the Mondo Khel should be offered an opportunity of deciding the dispute according to the Mohammadan Law and that if they refused to do so the united tribes should raise an army to compel them. The Mondo Khel said that if they had known that there would have been all this trouble, they would never have taken the land but as they have actually got possession, Pathan honour forbade them withdrawing then. They accordingly sent an application to three tribes asking for their assistance. Had it been worth their while, these tribes would certainly have joined in, as they had finished cutting

their crops and at that time had no particular
business of their own to attend to.

VOCABULARY LIX.

لت	*lat*	Slothful.
ناراستي	*narāsti*	Laziness.
خوزيدل	*khwazédal*	To move, (intransitive.)
نور	*nwar*	Sunshine.
لاروی	*lāraway*	Traveller.
لۇ کوټي	*lukūti*	Little.
مونږ سوري ته کوي	*mūng sōri tā krai*	Take us into the shade
بعضی	*bazé*	Some.
ساده	*sāda*	Simple.
خوار	*khwār*	Poor, helpless.
راکوزيدل	*ra kūzédal*	To come down, dismount.
خدای دِ و بخښه	*khudāi dé wo bakha*	May God forgive you !
ثواب	*sawāb*	Reward from God.
ثواب به دِ وشي	*sawāb ba dé wo shee*	You will get reward from God.
بينت	*baint*	Cane, stick.
بی غيرتَ	*bé ghairata*	Oh, you shameless one !
دومره نۀ شرميږی	*dōmra nuh sharmégé*	Have you not so much shame ?
روغ موټ	*rōgh mōt*	Safe and sound.

بچوُ	bachū	My son! (in a sarcastic manner.)
ازار	āzār	Curse.
بيره	béra	A wild plum.
غلیَ	ghálay	Silent.
خان د كوُنې كر	zān dé kūnr kar	You pretended to be deaf.
حد	had	Limit.
دۀ لۀ حدَ وريستۀ	duh luh hada wo wista	He has gone beyond the limit.
كم بخت	kam bakht	Unlucky.
كوړى شه	kuré sha	Get out you beast. (driving away a dog)
لۀ دۀ نه بۀ څوک څۀ خيروړى	la duh na ba sōk suh khér vree	What good is he to people?
حكومتكول	hukūmat kawal	To rule.

EXERCISE 58.

پۀ يو ځائ كښې دَ يوى ونى لاند درى لۀان پرانۀ ۇو ـ ناراستى
ئى دى حد ته رسيدلى وۀ ـ چه دَ ځاىَ نۀ خوزيدل ـ چه نور بۀ
پر راغىَ نو دَ لارى لۇۇ تۀ بۀ ئى وو چه لوكوُنى خو مۇنْ،رسوزى تۀ
كوى ـ بعضى بۀ چه سادۀ خلق ۇو نو دوىَ بۀ ئى سوزى تۀ كړل
يقين بۀ ئى وشو چه خواړان بۀ ناجوړ وى ـ ھغه لۀ ځاىَ نۀ شى
خوزبدىَ ـ او چا بۀ،ور پورى و خندل تر بۀ تير شو يو ـ ورځ وربانډ
يو سور راغىَ ـ چه دَ دولى خوا تۀ را ليزدى شو نو يو ورته اواز وۇ ـ
چه خوانَ لوكوُنى دَ دى اسَ را كۇز شه او لبرى اوبۀ راكړه ـ خدای
د، ريغښنه ـ ثواب بۀ د، وشى ـ سور چه د، خبره واوريده نو ورته ډير

پۀ قهر شو ورغیٰ او یو څو بینتونه ئی پر واچول او وئی ویل چه بی
غیرتَ دومره نۀ شرمیدری چه ما دَ اسَ را کوزَ وی او تۀ پخپله روغ
موټ ئی دَ ځای نۀ پا څی چه اوبۀ وسکی ۔ هغه بل ور باند
اواز وکړ ویل یی بچوَ څنګه؟ څما ازار روهای کۀ نه ۔ هغه بله ورځ
م درته واز وکړ چه لوکوټی راشه دا بیره راته پۀ څولۀ کښی واچوه
نو څنګه د ځان غلیٰ کړ ۔ هغه دریم دی سورته اواز وکړ ویل ئی
صاحب یو څوئی نورهم روهه دَ ناراستۍ څو هم یو حد وی ۔ دۀ لۀ
حدَ رویسته ۔ هغه بله ورځ یو سپی راغیٰ څما مغ ئی څټولو ۔
دی کم بخت ورته دَ ناراستۍ نه دومره نۀ ویل چه کوری شه ۔ لۀ
دۀ نه به څوک څۀ خیر و ری ۔ سور چه دَ دی بل لپه دا خبره
واوریده نو اول خو حیران شۀ او بیائی ډیر وخندل ۔ او وئی ویل
چه کۀ دا حال وی نو څنګه به دَ هندوستان خلق پۀ خپل ملک
بنډ حکومت وکړی ۔

VOCABULARY LX.

خاندان	*khānadān*	Family.
ملا	*mula*	Priest.
بهادری	*bahādari*	Adventure, bravery.
تکړه ژوندون	*takra jhwandūn*	Active life.
هغه به لار نیوله	*haghuh ba lār niwala*	He took to the road.
مشهور	*mashhūr*	Famous.
داسی چل وشو	*dasé chal wo sho*	It so happened.
فرض یا کار	*farz* or *kār*	Duty.
پسی کیدل	*pasé kédal*	To hunt down.

نیول	*nıwal*	To capture.
مفرور	*mafrūr*	Outlaw.
انعام	*inām*	Prize or reward.
نوی اودریدلی	*nawé odrédalé*	Newly raised (regt.)
د گائی پلقن	*da gāid paltan*	The Guides Regt.
کوشش کول	*kōshash kawal*	To try.
تنبؤ یا خیمه	*tanbū* or *khéma*	Tent.
خیال	*kheyāl*	Thought.
خیال کول	*kheyāl kawal*	To think.
لار	*lār*	Path, road.
خور	*khwar*	Nullah, ravine.
دره	*dara*	Valley.
غاښَی	*ghākhay*	Pass (on the top of the hill).
دا خاص دَ گائیی دَ پاره لائق دیَ	*dā khās da gāid da pāra lāieq day*	He is just the man for the Guides.
چټی یا خط	*chitai* or *khat*	Letter, note.
راغوښتل	*rāghukhtal*	To invite.
پرؤ	*parāw*	Camp.
معامله	*māmela*	Matter, affair.
په دی معامله کښین خبری اتری کول	*pa dé māmela ké khabaré ataré kawal*	} To talk this over.
دَ په سر روپئی (یا پیسی) منل یا ورکول	*da-puh sar rupai (or pesé) manal or warkawal*	} To put a price on someone's head.

دَ خبره منل	*da khabara manal*	To accept invitation.
رسوُخ،اعتبار	*rusūkh* or *itébār*	Reputation.
عزت	*izzat*	Honour.
سرکار	*sarkār*	British govt
لرل	*laral*	To possess, have.
ګوره.	*gōra*	Look here !
ز وړند کول	*zwarand kawal*	To hang.
دَ خاقو دَ وړاند	*da khalqo da vrāndé*	Publicly.

EXERCISE 59.

Delawar Khan was a Khatak of good family. He was brought up as a priest, but his love of adventure let him to a more active life. He took to the road and in time he became the most famous robber in the whole of Yusafzai. It happened that one of Sir Harry Lumsden's duties was to hunt down and capture Delawar Khan, who was now an outlaw with a price of two thousand rupees on his head. Many a time did Lumsden and his newly raised 'Corps of Guides' try, but they could not capture Delawar. One day sitting in his tent Sir Harry Lumsden thought that this man must know every path, nullah and pass in the District. He is just the man for the Guides. I will send him a note. A

letter was therefore sent to Delawar Khan invit-
ing him to come into the Camp to talk this
matter over. One day Delawar Khan in answer
to this letter, came up to Lumsden. This man,
with a price on his head, accepted the invitation.
It says much for the reputation for honour which
the British possessed in borderland. Lumsden
said to him, " Look here, Delawar, you are
a fine fellow, but one day I will catch you
and hang you publicly on a tree".

VOCABULARY LXI.

د پﮧ‑ستركو كوتى	*da-puh stargo*	To blame (lit. to
منډل	*gōtè mandal*	push fingers into some one's eyes).
شار	*shar*	Barren (land), un-couth, uneducated (person).
وينځه	*winza*	Slave girl.
بى بى	*bi bi*	Wife, mistress.
چاودل	*chawdal*	To split or burst (Intrans).
چاودی	*chawday*	Burst (past part.)
مولی	*maula*	God.
شادولا	*shadaula*	Saint (lit. small headed).
پﮧ زور كلی نﮧ	*puh zōr kali*	It cannot be done
كيږی	*nuh kégi*	by force.

پۀ سبق کېنول	*puh sabaq kénawal*	To send to school.
مندرسه	*mandrasa*	School.
کېنول	*kénawal*	To make to sit.
نۀ دَ دین شو او نۀ دَسادین شو	*nuh da din sho aw nuh da sādin shō*	He became useless for this world and the next.
زکه پکه	*zaka paka*	The last brass farthing.
باج کول یا داؤکول	*bāj kawal* or *dāw kawal*	To spend uselessly.
تل ټوکره	*tal tŭkra*	Land.
صبر	*sabar*	Patience.
(تۀ) خولۀ چینځکول	*(ta) khula chingawal*	To ask for help (lit to grin).
پۀ بانډ زړه کول	*puh-bandé zruh kawal*	To want to ask but hardly daring to.
(سره) لاس کول	*(sara) lās kawal*	To give a helping hand to.
دَ فکر پۀ ټال زنګیدل	*da fikar puh tal zangédal*	To be undecided.
زنګل یا زنګیدل	*zangal* or *zangédal*	To swing, (intrans.)
تش لاس	*tash lās*	Empty handedness
کۀ رشتیا رابانډ وائی	*kuh rishtia rā bandé wāyé*	If I tell you the truth.
کته	*kata*	Pack saddle.
تبخی	*tabakhay*	Chapati cooking pan (Urdu Tawā.)
کتوری	*katŏray*	Copper cup (Urdu Katŏra)

کندول	*kandōl*	Earthen cup.
خلی	*salay*	Heap, grave-mound.
نقل	*naqal*	Copy.
ننگ	*nang*	Modesty.
پخوا	*pakhwā*	Formerly.
گدوری	*gadūray*	Lamb.
پریوتل	*prėwatal*	To fall.
(ته) لس ورکول	*(ta) lās war kawal*	To shake hands with, help.
خان خپل خان	*zāna khpala zāna*	Every one for himself.
گنره	*ganra*	Otherwise.
هیندکی	*hindkay*	Indian (i. e. non-Pathan.)
یادول	*yādawal*	To mention, to talk about.
قل ته کول	*tal ta kawal*	To defeat.
اغزی	*aghzay*	Thorn.
موټی	*mūtay*	Fist.
تینګول	*tingawal*	To hold firmly.
که خبره په خوی	*kuh khabara pūh zŏi wāchawė*	If you talk about the son...
د پوزی سرئی غوند شو	*da pōzé sar yé ghund sho*	He grew up (lit. the tip of his nose became round.)
ته خوک او زۀ	*tuh sōk aw zuh sōk*	What do I care for you !

پﮥ باند تﺎﻧﺮﻩ ﮐﯧﺪﻝ	*puh bānde* *tānra kédal*	To be quartered on some one (exceeding laws of hospitality.)

EXERCISE 60.
(IDIOMATIC)

سﺮﯤ ﻫﺮ سﺮﯤ راﺧﻠﻲ او ﺧﻤﺎ ﭘﮥ سﺘﺮﮔﻮ ﮐﻮﺗﻲ ﻣﻨﺪﯤ ﭼﮥ ﺧﺎﻣﺲ در
ﻧﮥ ﺷﺎم ﺷﻮً دَ وﯦﻨﻜﻲ مﺎﺕ سﺮ وﯦﻨﻲ او دَ ﺑﻲ ﺑﻲ ﭼﺎودﯦﯤ زړﮤ ﺧﻮك
ﻧﮥ وﯦﻨﻲ با با ؟ ﭘﮥ زور ﺧﻮ ﮐﻠﻲ ﻧﮥ ﮐﯧﺪﺭﯤ دَ جﻤﺎﻋﺖ ﭘﮥ سﺒﻘﯧﻢ ﮐﯧﻨﻮﻝ
دَﻣﻨﺪﺭسﻲ ﭘﮥ سﺒﻘﯧﻢ ﮐﯧﻨﻮﻝ ﭼﮥ ﻧﮥ ﮐﻮﯤ ﻣﻮﻟﻮﻱ ﻧﻮ ﺧﮥ ﺑﮥ وﮐړﻱ ﺷﺎدوﻻ ﻣﺸﻬﻮﺭﻩ
ﺧﺒﺮﻩ دَﻩ ﭼﮥ ﻧﮥ ﺧﻲ وابﮥ دﺧﻠﻢ ﭼﮥ ﻧﮥ ﺧﻮﺭﯤ ﺧﮥ ﺑﮥ دﮐړم ﻧﮥ دَ دﯦﻦ ﺷﻮً
او ﻧﮥ دَ سﺎدﯦﻦ ﺷﻮً ﺧﻤﺎ ﺧﻮ ﭼﮥ ﺧﮥ زﮐﮥ ﭘﮑﻪوَﻩ ﻫﻐﮥ م وﺭبﺎﻧﺪ بﺎﺝ ﮐﮥ اوس
دَﺧﻠﻘﻮ زړﻩ دﯤ ﭼﮥ دا ﻗﻞ ﻗﻮﮐﺮﮤ م ﮐﻪ دام ﻫﻢ وﺭبﺎﻧﺪ داﯤ ﮐﻮﯤ وﻟﻲ
زﻩ ﺧﮥ وﮐﺮم ﮐﮥ ﮐﻮﺷﺖ ﮐﺮان ﻧﻮ ﺻﺒﺮ ارزان آﺧﺮ زﮤ ﺧﻮ ﻫﻢ ﭘﺨﺘﻮًﻥ ﯾﻢ
ﭘﺨﺘﻮﻧﮥ راﮐﻨﺲ ﭼﺎﻧﮥ ﺧﻮ ﺧﻮﻟﮥ ﻧﮥ ﺷﻢ ﭼﯧﻨﻪﻮﻟﯤ او ﮐﮥ ﭘﮥ ﭼﺎ بﺎﻧﺪ زړﮤ
وﻫﻢ ﮐﻮم ﻧﻮ ﭼﮥ وﯦﻲ ﻏﻮاﺭم ﭘﮥ دﯤ ﺧﻮﻟﻲ ﻧﻮ ﺧﻮﺭم بﺪﯦﻲ ﭘﮥ ﮐﻮﻣﮥ ﺧﻮﻟﻲ
آﺧﺮ ﮐﮥ ﺧﻮك ﭼﺎسﺮﻩ ﺧﮥ ﻻﺱ وﮐﺮﻱ ﻧﻮ ﺧﻮﺭاﮐﻲ ﺧﻮ ﯾﻲ ﻧﮥ ﺷﻲ ﻗﻮﻟﮥ ورﺥ
دَ ﻓﮑﺮ ﭘﮥ ﻗﻞ زاﻧﮑﻢ ﭼﮥ ﺗﺸﮥ ﻻﺱ ﺗﮥﻢ دﺷﻤﻦﯤ او ﮐﮥ رﺷﺘﯿﺎ رابﺎﻧﺪ
وﯤ ﻧﻮ ﺧﻤﺎ ﺧﻮ ﻫﻢ دﻏﮥ دَﮐﻨﻲ او دَ ﺗﺒﻐﻲ ﺧﺒﺮﻩ دَﻩ اوس ﺧﻮداﺳﻲ
وﺧﺖ راﻏﻠﯤ دﯤ ﭼﮥ ﮐﮥ ﮐﻪﻮﺭﯤ ورﮐﻮﯤ ﻧﻮ ﮐﻨﻮﻝ ﺑﮥ ﭘﺮﻫﻮك دﺭ ﻧﮥ ﮐﻮﯤ
ﭘﮥ ﭘﺨﺘﻨﻮ ﻻﺭﻝ ﻛﻠﻲ جوﺭ ﺷﻮﻝ او ﻧﻘﻠﻮً ﻧﮥ ﯤ ﭘﺎﺗﻲ ﺷﻮﻝ ﻧﻦ ﺧﻮ
ﭘﺨﺘﻮ دَ ﭘﺨﺘﺎﻧﮥ ﻻﺮﻩ او ﻧﻨﮓ او ﻏﻞ ﻻﭘﺮﭘﺨﻮا بﮥ ﭘﺨﺘﻮﻥ ﭘﮥ ﭘﺨﺘﻮن سﺮ
اﯦﯧﻨﻮ او اوس ﭼﮥ ﺧﻤﻮًﻧﺮﻯ ﻣﻔﺮور ﯾﺎﻏﺴﺘﺎن ﺗﮥ ورﺷﻲ ﻧﻮ دَ سﻠﻮ روﭘﻮ
ﮐﻪﻮﺭﯤ ﺷﻲ ﭘﺨﻮا بﮥ ﭼﮥ ﺧﻮك ﭘﺮﯦﻮﺗﻮ ﻧﻮ ﭼﺎ ﺧﻮ بﮥ ﻻﺱ وﺭﮐﺮ اوس
ﺧﻮ ﺧﺎن ﺧﭙﻞ ﺧﺎن ﮐﮥ وﯤ دﺭ بﺴﺨﮥ ﺧﻮ ﺧﻮﺭﻩ ﮐﻨﺮﻩ ﻣﺮﻩ ﺧﻠﻘﻮ بﮥ
ﻫﻨﺪﮐﯿﺎن ﯾﺎدوﻝ اوسﻨﻲ ﻫﻐﻮﻱ ﻗﻞ ﺗﮥ ﮐﻮﯤ دﯤ او ﮐﮥ رﺷﺘﯿﺎ درﺗﮥ

ووايم نو د دى زمانى خامن څۀ دى که دا د دشمن سترگه کښې
اغزى نه وى نو چاله څۀ کوى بس چه د مرقبى د ټبذهؤلوشى
نو ښى در نه چرګ څو يو مارغۀ دى چه چا وئيوۀ دهغۀ دى کمور
زړۀ پۀ څوى او دکٌوى زړۀ پۀ اوچ ديوال پۀ دنيا کښې هم يو
پلار دى چه زړه ئى غوارى چۀ څوى رانه اوچت شوى او که خبره
په څوى واچوى نو دٌليدو نه ئى پۀ نۀ ليدو خوشحال وى تر هغه
دٌکٌوى وى چه لا ئى چرګورى بانګ نه وى ويلى څو چه دپوزى
سرئى غونډ شى نو بس تۀ څوک او زۀ څوک داخو لا پرېرٌده چه
ورارۀ م هم راغلى دى پۀ ما تانو دى--

Section 13.

The student is advised to learn the following idiomatic sentences carefully before going up for his Examination :—

1. Since I came to this place.	*Kala rāsé chī zuh dé zāi ta rāghalay yam.*
2. Until this is satisfactorily settled, the tribal allowances as well as your own are stopped.	*Tar sō põré chi da dé puh khuh shān sara faisala wō nuh shee, da qām mājéb aw stā khpal dwāra ba band wee.*
3. The ducks are swimming in the water.	*Hilai puh ōbō ké garzı.*
4. Tell the syce to cut some grass for the horse.	*Sāis ta wo wāya chi da ass da pāra suh wākhuh wo kree.*

5. We were cutting wood when they attacked us and carried off all our cattle.

Mūng largee wahal chi rā bāndé yé hamla wō kra aw tōl zamūng māl yé bōtlo.

6. I have nothing to do with him.

Zamā war sara hiss gharaz nishta.

7. I owe him five rupees.

Da haghuh rā bāndé pinzuh rūpai dee.

8. Yesterday you said he owes you some money.

Parūn khō tā wo wé chi zama puh haghuh bāndé suh rupai dee.

9. Yes, he owes me five rupees.

Ho zamā war bāndé pinzuh rūpai dee.

10. I can't help it, I will have to send you back to your own country.

Pa dé ké zuh gram nuh yam, zuh ba tā khwā makhwā khpal watan ta biārtā légam.

11. I will try my best to keep you as my own orderly but I do not know whether the colonel will be willing to allow this.

Sōmrā chi mé da wasa kégee, dōmra kōshash ba wo kram chi tā da zān ardali kram, magar zuh khabar nuh yam chī karnail sāhib ba pa dé rāzee shi kuh na.

12. I tried my best to send him to my own regt. but the Colonel did not agree.

Sōmra chi da wasa mé kédalo, dōmrā kōshash mé wō kar chi zuh yé khpalé paltané ta wo légam, magar karnail sāhib wo na manala.

13. This man says you have beaten him, what have you to say for yourself?

Dā saray wāyee chi zuh dé wahalay yam, puh dé ké stā suh jawāb day?

14. How far is it to the Mess ? — *Miskōt sōmra laré day?*

15. What is that firing? — *Hagha dazé da suh dee?*

16. What is that noise ? — *Dagha shōr da suh day ?*

17. I will write a letter when I have eaten food. — *Chi rōtai wo khuram nō chitai ba wō likam.*

18. When I had arrived in Kohat I met an old man. — *Kala chi zuh Kohāt ta wo rasédalam nō yau sṗin giray ṗuh makha rāghlo.*

19. I saw him before he saw me. — *Hagha lā zuh lidalay nuh wam, chi mā hagha wōlid.*

20. If he had killed me he would have been as sorry as I should have been if I had killed him. — *Kuh zuh yé wajhalay way, nō haghuh ba dōmra afsōs karay woh, laka chi da haghuh ṗuh wajhalo (or marg) mā ba karay woh.*

21. I wish I had gone to Kabul. — *Armān day chi zuh Kobāl ta talay way.*

22. I wish I had been married. — *Armān day chi mā wāduh karay way.*

23. I wish I had come before four. — *Armān day chi zuh luh salōrō bajo na awal rāghalay way.*

24. He not only beat me with a stick but if you had not come he would have certainly killed me. — *Zuh yé nuh seraf ṗuh largee bāndé wo wahalam, balké kuh tuh rāghalay nuh way no zuh ba yé wajhalay wam.*

25. What do you do with your pay ? *Tuh khpál talab suh kawé ?*

26. Let alone English I can not speak my own language well. *Angrézi kho prégda chi zuh khpala jhaba hum kha nuh sham wayalay.*

27. See if my book is on the table. *Gōra chi zamā kitāb puh méz bāndé kho nishta.*

28. See if the sahib is coming. *Gōra chi sāhib kho nuh rāzee.*

29. The doctor advised him to drink two seers of milk every day. *Daktar war ta wo wé chi da vrazé dwā séra pai ska.*

30. Come to my house every day and bring me some flowers. *Mudām zamā kōr ta rāza aw rā la suh gulūna rāwra.*

31. Every kind of shooting can be had in this country. *Pa dé watan ké har rang khkār mundalay shee.*

32. My only brother committed a serious crime and became an outlaw. *Zamā khāli yau vrōr woh aw haghuh hum yau sakht juram wō kar aw mafrūr sho.*

33. This is the very man whom I wanted to see. *Dā hum hagha saray day chi mā wayal zuh ba yé gōram.*

34. We started on the very moment and reached Kabul the same day. *Hum puh hagha sāat mūng rąwān shoo aw Kābal ta amrōza wo rasédoo.*

35. The thanadar laughed at the old woman *Thānra dār būdai pōré wo khandal aw yé wo*

and said "This is the way with you people".

wayal chi dā stāso da khalqō lār dah.

36. Why did you laugh at him ?

Walé dé war pōré wo khandal ?

37. The dog began to bark but no one stirred.

Spay puh ghapa sho magar hésōk wo nuh khwazéd.

38. The sahib is about to come. Just wait he will be here in a moment if you want to see him.

Sāhib rātlūnkay day (or) puh rātlo ké day puh yaw sāat ké ba rāshee kuh yé gōré.

39. I suppose you consider yourself wiser than I am.

Zamā khyal day chi tuh khpal zān luh mā na hukhyār ganré.

40. A little more than three years later this city was again attacked by Aurangzéb.

Luh dréo kalō na lag suh ziāt pas, puh dé khahar bāndé Aurangzéb biā hamla wo kra.

41. He himself did not stay there any longer but left his Sardars to complete the work.

Pakhṭala kho dér halta paté nuh sho magar khṭal sardārān yé da kār pūra kawalo da pāra halta prékhōdal.

42. Take either this or that.

Ya da wākhla ya hagha wākhla.

43. I will take neither.

Zuh yau hum nuh akhlam.

44. Give them five annas each.

War ta pinzuh pinzuh ané war kra.

45. I must have seen this man but I cannot remember now.

Dā saray ba mé lidalay wi, kho os rā ta yād nuh di.

46. Remind me when I go to the Office.

Chi daftar ta lārsham no rā ta yud kra.

47. I threw a stone at him.

Mā hagha puh kānri wo wishtalo.

48. When did you meet him ?

Kala puh makha daraghay ?

49. I met an old man whom a little boy was leading by the hand.

Yau spin giray puh makha rāghlo chi yau warūki halak luh lās na biwalo.

50. I was just missed otherwise my sight would have been destroyed for ever.

Zuh ila bach shwam ganra da ūmar da pāra ba me nazar barbād shaway woh.

51. The old man who had only one eye was telling stories to the boys in the Hujra.

Spin girai chi puh yawa starga kānray woh, halakāno ta puh hūjra ké qésé yé wayalé.

52. The old man's evidence should be accepted as he said he had read the marriage service.

Da spin giri gawāhi dé manzūra shi chi wāyee chi mā yé nikāh taralay day.

53. On the further side of the plain a river had to be crossed twice.

Da mairé puh bala khwā luh yau sind na dwa zala poréwatal woo.

54. He has to go to the office.

Hagha khwā makhwāh daftar ta ba zee.

55. My dog got a thorn stuck in his foot, went lame and would not work.

Zamā da spi puh khpa ké aghzay māt sho. gud sho aw kār yé nuh sho kawalay.

56. I shall pay him out when he comes back.

Chi biarta rāshee no ba war sara poh sham.

57. He was very disconcerted when the stolen property was found in his pocket.

Chi da ghlā māl yé luh jéb na barāmad sho, no dér kacha sho.

58. Needless to say he himself was convinced of his bad habit.

Puh dé ké shak nishta chi hagha pakhpala hum puh khpal bad ādat qāil woh.

59. I had many misfires but even then I shot 125 head of game.

Dér zala mé tōpak ghal sho, kho biā hum mé pinzuh da pāsa shpag shalé marghān wo wishtal.

60. I would have shot many more, but my cartridges were beginning to get wet and would not go off.

Nōr dér ba mé hum wishtali wōo khō kārtūsūna mé puh laundédo rāghlal aw nuh khlāsédal.

61. I have caught cold.

Zuh yakhnai wahalay yam.

62. Who has caught fever?

Sōk tabé niwalay day?

63. The villagers have small pox.

Puh kali wālo bāndé nanakai khatali di.

64. My servant has plague.

Zamā puh naukar bāndé tāūn lagédalay day.

65. After I came back from the office I had to go to the city.

Luh daftar rātlo na pas zuh khwā makhwah khahar ta lāram.

66. After I finish my work I will have to go to the cantt.

Chi kār khlās kram nŏ khwā makhwāh ba chawnrai ta zam.

67. Don't fire unless you are fired at.

Kuh dar bāndé daz wo nuh shi no tuh daz muh kawa.

68. Don't fire unless it is absolutely necessary.

Kuh bilkul zarūrat pékh nuh shi no daz muh kawa.

69. Don't allow him to go unless he has a proper pass.

Kuh war sakha barābar pāss nuh wi no tlo ta yé muh prégda (or muh yé prégda chi lārshee).

70. If I were or had been there I would not have let you do this work.

Kuh zuh halta way, no mā ba tuh dé kār kawalo ta prekhay nuh wé.

71. If he is there I shall certainly produce him before the Magistrate.

Kuh hagha halta wi no zarūr ba yé zuh majestarait ta pésh kram.

72. He abused me vilely but I said nothing.

Rā ta yé dér (or bad bad) kanzal wo kral, kho mā hiss wo nuh wayal.

73. The tribe gave 10 hostages and deposited 15 Snider rifles as security.

Qām las tana yargha-mal war kralo aw pinzalas kuniz topak yé da zamānat pa taur war kral.

74. Formerly this land had no means of irrigation except rain fall.

Puh khwā zamāna ké dā zamaka bārāni (or lalma) wah.

75. Wait here until I come back from the city.

Tar sō p̄ōré chi zuh luh khahar na biarta rā nuh sham dalé isār sha.

76. I sold my horse to him for 50 rupees.

Mā khp̄al ass puh haghuh bāndé puh p̄anzōs rūpai khars kar.

77. Never mind I will engage a barrister and prosecute him in the law court.

Hess bāk nishta yau wakil ba wōnisam aw war bāndé ba puh adālat ké dawa wo kram.

78. I have engaged a mali, who really knows his job.

Yau māli mé sātalay day chi waqi p̄uh khp̄al kār khuh p̄ōhégee.

79. Challenge him first and then shoot.

Awal war bāndé awāz wo kra aw biā yé wola.

80. Will you call out to my servant?

Lūkūti zamā naukar ta khō awāz wo kra?

81. My village was raided on the 15th of last month.

Da téré miāshté p̄uh p̄inzalasam tārikh zamā p̄uh kali bāndé dāra p̄réwata.

82. If the stolen property is not found the tribes will be heavily fined.

Kuh da ghlā māl wo nuh mūndalay shi no pa qām bāndé ba lōi jurum p̄réwozi.

83. Button your coat.

Da kōt batanūna dé wāchawa.

84. Tie on your putties.

Patai dé wo tara (or tāw kra)

85. Put on your turban.

Patkay dé p̄uh sar kra or wo waha.

86. Put on your shoes. — *Panré dé puh khpo kra:*

87. If you like to start so early you will have to put on your gloves. — *Kuh dāsé wākhtī rāwānégé nō khwā makhwāh ba dastāné puh lās kawé.*

88. Do not be angry with me. — *Luh mā na muh khapa kéga.*

89. I am sorry I did not notice you until you passed on. — *Zuh afsōs kawam chi tar hagha wakhta mé wo nuh lidé chi tér shwé.*

90. Open your mouth, you must take this medicine at once, otherwise the fever will recur. — *Khuluh wāza kra, dā dārū dar la samdasti skal pakār di, kuh nuh wi nō taba ba darbāndé biā rāshee.*

91. Shut your mouth after drinking medicine. — *Luh dāro skalo na pas khuluh dé piché kra.*

92. Open your eyes and look towards me. — *Stargé wō gharawa aw zamā taraf ta wo gōra.*

93. Shut your eyes and don't open them till I speak to you. — *Stargé paté kra aw muh yé gharawa tar sō pōré chi zuh dar sara khabaré wo nuh kram.*

94. Open your book and start from where we had got up to. — *Kitāb dé wo ghwarawa aw tar kuma zāia pōré chi mō lawastay day, luh hagha zāi na shūrū kra.*

95. Listen to me. — *Ghwag kégda,*
96. Do you hear ? — *Ghwag dé day ?*
97. I know what you mean. — *Sta puh matlab zuh pōhégam.*

98. I asked him what village he came from.

Ma war na tapōs wo kar chi da kum kali yé.

99. I have nothing to do with him.

Zamā war sara hiss gharaz nishta.

100. Can not you write with a pencil ?

Tuh puh pensan nuh shé likalay ?

101. I cannot give him any more.

War ta nōr nuh sham warkawalay.

102. In spite of all his good evidence the magistrate had to punish him.

Sara da haghuh da khé gawāhai majestarait war ta khwā makhwāh sazā war kra.

103. I will let you off if you tell me the whole truth.

Kuh tōla khabara rā ta rishtiā rishtiā wō kré no pré ba dé gdam.

104. Let us go to that large village and arrange for grass for our horses.

Rāza chi hagha lōi kali ta lār shōo aw da khpalo asūno da wākho da pāra bandūbast wo kroo.

105. Sahib, I have suffered much injustice.

Sāhiba puh mā bāndé déra be insāfi shawé dah.

106. He must come himself and bring all the books with him.

Pakār di chi pakhpala rāshee aw tōl kitābūna da zān sara rāwree.

107. After three days we found out that the ropes of the tents were missing.

Dré vrazé pas mūng khabar shoo chi da tambwānō rasaı vraké di.

108. Put it.

Ké yé gda.

109. Give it to me

Rā yé kra.

110. He has two sons, one takes after his mother and the other takes after his father.

Dwa zāman yé di, yau mōr ta talay day aw bal plār ta tzlay day.

111. I would rather sit in the veranda than out in the field.

Da bahar pati na kho zamā khwakha dah chi puh baranda hé kénam.

112. He lives next door to me.

Hagha rā sara déwāl puh déwāl osee.

113. Next door but one there lives a gambler.

Puh drem kōr ké yau jawārgar osee.

114. Last year the Malik's wife eloped with a Peshawari barber.

Parosakal da malak khaza yau pekhawri nāi sara lāra or matiza shwa.

115. I saw him passing by my door.

Mā hagha wo lidalo chi zamā puh dar-wāza térédo.

116. You ought to have gone yesterday.

Tā la parūn tlal pakār woo (or) *pakar woo chi tuh parūn talay way.*

117. I must write to the General about the deficiency of rations.

Da rasan da kami pa bāb ké pakār di chi zuh jarnail sāhib ta wo likam.

118. Wind the watch otherwise it will stop.

Garai la kunji war kra ganra wo ba drégi.

119. May God make you the king of this country !

Khudāi dé da dé mulk bādshāh kra !

120. This made me think that my regt.

Pa dé khābara mé fikar wo kar chi bala

would move on the next day.

vraz ba paltan mé rawānégee.

121. Wind your turban round my gun.

Patkay dé zamā luh tōpak na tāw kra.

122. I saw him coming.

Hagha mé wo lido chi rātlo.

123. I shot him dead with a revolver.

Hagha ṇé puh tamā-cha wo wishto au mar mé kro.

124. A scorpion stung my toe.

Yau laram da khpé puh gōta wo chichalam.

125. He fired at me and hit my finger.

Rā bāndé yé daz wo kar aw puh gōta yé wo wishtam.

126. Have my watch repaired.

Garai mé puh chā muramata kra.

127. Come on this day week.

Puh nananai vraz rāsha.

128. Learn your yesterday's lesson.

Parūnay sabaq dé yād kra.

129. Take care not to come by this road again.

Paham kawa chi biā pa dé lār rā nuh shé.

130. He may come.

Gundé hagha rāshee.

www.ingramcontent.com/pod-product-compliance
Lightning Source LLC
Jackson TN
JSHW011353130125
77033JS00023B/664